NEW TAX GUIDE

for Writers, Artists, Performers, and Other Creative People

NEW TAX GUIDE

for Writers, Artists, Performers, and Other Creative People

Fifth Edition

Peter Jason Riley, CPA

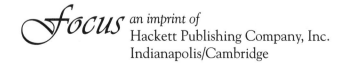

focus an imprint of
Hackett Publishing Company, Inc.
Indianapolis/Cambridge

A Focus book

Focus an imprint of
   Hackett Publishing Company

19 18 17 16   1 2 3 4 5 6 7

For further information, please address
   Hackett Publishing Company, Inc.
   P.O. Box 44937
   Indianapolis, Indiana 46244-0937

   www.hackettpublishing.com

Cover design by Elizabeth L. Wilson
Composition by Aptara, Inc.

Library of Congress Cataloging-in-Publication Data

Names: Riley, Peter Jason, author.
Title: New tax guide : for writers, artists, performers, and other creative
   people / Peter Jason Riley, CPA.
Description: Fifth Edition. | Indianapolis : Focus, an imprint of Hackett
   Publishing Company, Inc., [2016]
Identifiers: LCCN 2016022462 | ISBN 9781585108336 (pbk.)
Subjects: LCSH: Artists—Taxation—Law and legislation—United States. |
   Entertainers—Taxation—Law and legislation—United States. | Theatrical
   producers and directors—Taxation—Law and legislation—United States. |
   Musicians—Taxation—Law and legislation—United States. |
   Authors—Taxation—Law and legislation—United States.
Classification: LCC KF6369.85 .R55 2016 | DDC 343.7305/20247—dc23
LC record available at https://lccn.loc.gov/2016022462

∞

Contents

Dedication

Thanks to:

- ✓ My lovely, wise, and extraordinary visual artist Ruth Riley who puts up with my endless discussions and ruminations on taxes and who patiently proofreads my work.
- ✓ My brother Mark T. Riley for editing and proofreading early versions of this book and offering suggestions.
- ✓ Thomas F. Ryan, editor-in-chief of the (sadly missed) journal *The Undertoad* and author of the wonderful *Following Atticus* (from HarperCollins) for offering me a regular outlet for my writing years ago. Without you, Tom, this book would never have happened.
- ✓ My bro' Rick Coleman, who opened my eyes to the deep joys of the great R&B music of New Orleans and the great Fats Domino.
- ✓ My first employers when I entered the accounting profession many years ago, Peter Mandragouras, CPA, and Jim Powers, CPA. They always showed me that caring about the client is the very heart of our business.
- ✓ "Dr. Ike" Padnos, who honors me by allowing me to be a part of the amazing Ponderosa Stomp festival in New Orleans and the Ponderosa Stomp foundation where I have met so many amazing musicians.

Introduction

I thank you for reading this book and want to tell you how I came to write it. This volume is a follow-up to the now long-out-of-print *New Tax Guide for Performers, Writers, Directors, Designers, and Other Show Biz Folk*, written by R. Brendan Hanlon. I originally discovered Mr. Hanlon's book quite by accident while browsing in the Bleecker Street Bookstore, many years ago during a trip to New York City. As an amateur guitar player and CPA, I had a strong interest in all the arts and wondered why there seemed to be no books that specifically addressed the unique tax situations that folks in the arts encounter. I was very excited when I saw the book, and rushed to tell my wife that this was the book I had long been looking for. I purchased Mr. Hanlon's subsequent revisions and, as a testament to the book's value, I would often have clients bring the book into their appointments with me.

I periodically thought of contacting Mr. Hanlon, but sadly, never did. When I heard about his death many years ago, my first thought was that I hoped this valuable book did not pass away with him. I contacted Proscenium Publishers and offered to pick up authorship. Although the book you hold is entirely rewritten and extensively revised, I would like it to serve the same purpose as Mr. Hanlon's did: to be an easy-to-read guide for the arts practitioner, to provide an understanding of unique tax situations and thereby make the tax preparation process less onerous, and most importantly, to save you tax dollars!

While this book is not primarily intended to be a detailed "how to prepare your income tax return" book (for this I recommend *J.K. Lasser's®️ Your Income Tax*), this edition has 2015 sample tax returns that will help the reader better understand what the finished product might look like. I still feel strongly that the actual preparation of income tax returns for folks in the arts is best left to professionals because of the inherent complications. I think that good tax preparers and advisors should be able to save you more money than they charge by helping you with tax planning. My goal is to give you an overall understanding of the unique aspects of taxation for people in the arts. By reading this book and using my deduction checklists (found on artstaxinfo.com), I want to help you do a better job of collecting data throughout the year so you can be better prepared to present that information to your income tax advisor. I will use a lot of real-life examples to illustrate the many situations an artist may encounter. By understanding your specific situation, you will be better prepared to choose an appropriate income tax advisor. Keep in mind that no matter how good your tax advisor is, *you* are the one who has to develop a basic understanding of your taxable income and what is deductible, so you can save the proper receipts and documentation for your tax return.

I am going to focus mainly on your professional income and deductions and will not really discuss other income you may have, such as interest, dividends, capital gains, pensions, rents, and other deductions, such as mortgage interest or charitable contributions.

The website for this book—artstaxinfo.com—will always be updated with the latest information, including tax tips, a glossary, FAQs, and our "Taxes QuikGuide," which will give you all the current tax rates, mileage deductions, exemptions, deadlines, and tax-law changes.

Our cast of characters throughout the book will be four artist friends whose professional lives will illustrate what the heck we are talking about:

1. **Ima Starr**—Actor, model, and writer. Ima (our only holdover from Mr. Hanlon's book) is very busy as both actor and model. She is also a part-time singer and has even written a book. She is a member of Actors' Equity Association and the Screen Actors Guild (SAG).

2. **Sonny Phunky**—Musician. Sonny is a freelance bass player and songwriter, and does some teaching on the side. He works both as an employee and a contract player, and is a member of a limited liability company (LLC).

3. **Liz Brushstroke**—Artist and college professor. Liz is a tenured college professor, but she also has an active life as an independent visual artist and is represented by galleries in New York City and Dublin.

4. **Guy Focal**—Writer. Guy has a full-time job as a magazine staff writer, but also has earnings writing freelance book reviews and articles for other publications. He has published several children's books as well.

In each of the chapters that focus primarily on our characters (Chapters 4 through 7), we will feature completed tax returns. You will be able to visit our website, artstaxinfo.com, and download annually updated returns to accompany the illustrations. As you read the chapters centered on each of the above characters, you will be able to follow along by reviewing a finished 1040 tax return.

The main thing that most folks worry about when they prepare their income taxes is the dreaded audit! Luckily, because of the Freedom of Information Act, the Internal Revenue Service (IRS) is required to actually publish its internal audit guidelines. These Market Segment Specialization Program (MSSP) guides give us direct insight into what the IRS agent will be looking for during an audit (the actual MSSP guides are available for download on our website, artstaxinfo.com). We will be discussing audits in Chapter 7. We are pleased to note that this book is now a reference resource for Internal Revenue Service auditors in the Boston office!

Finally, I intend the book to be approached in the following fashion:

The book begins with three primary chapters everybody should read:

1. Income
2. Crowdfunding for Creative People
3. What Can I Deduct?

Next, choose the chapter that best describes your primary activity (keeping in mind that situations presented in all the chapters might be helpful):

4. For Actors, Directors, Dancers, and Other Performers
5. For Musicians and Singers
6. For Visual Artists
7. For Writers

Finally, everyone should read the last six chapters:

8. Setting Up a Business Entity
9. The Audit Process, Record Keeping, and Your Taxpayer Rights
10. Other States, Other Taxes, Other Countries, and the "Tax Home"
11. Choosing a Tax Advisor
12. Tax Planning
13. In Closing

Remember to visit and include www.artstaxinfo.com in your Web browser favorites to keep up with the latest information. The official website of this book, www.artstaxinfo.com, allows you to print and download various checklists, worksheets, and links to websites listed in Appendix A and gives you important updates on all the latest tax changes that affect creative professionals.

Disclaimer

Information

The information provided in this book is only intended to be a general summary of information to the reader. It is not intended to take the place of either the written law or regulations. Tax law changes frequently and tax strategies must be individually designed for specific persons or companies. Before using any of the information supplied in this book, please consult your professional tax advisor.

Listings of External Websites

Websites outside Peter Jason Riley, CPA; Riley & Associates, PC; and www .artstaxinfo.com are listed for the convenience of the reader. Such use does not constitute an official endorsement or approval by Peter Jason Riley, CPA or Riley & Associates of any website, product, or service.

IRS Circular 230 Disclosure

To ensure compliance with requirements imposed by the IRS, Peter Jason Riley, CPA and Riley & Associates, PC informs you that any U.S. federal tax advice contained within this book is not intended or written to be used, and cannot be used, for the purpose of (i) avoiding penalties under the Internal Revenue Code or (ii) promoting, marketing, or recommending to another party any transaction or matter addressed herein.

1

Income

I will address the types of income a person involved in the arts might earn and introduce the most important point in the book: the difference between employment income and self-employment/contract income. In these days of multidisciplinary artists, it is common for folks to have income and expenses from both employment and self-employment. According to this differentiation, income and expenses will appear in different places on the income tax return. But first things first: *what is income?*

In essence, income is practically everything of value you receive in exchange for your products or services as a performer, visual artist, or writer (hereafter referred to as "artist"). You can be "paid" in cash, services, or property; you can even have barter income. Taxable income may or may not be reported on a tax form such as a 1099-MISC, W-2, or K-1 at year-end. Most of you will be familiar with the first two tax forms, but perhaps not with the K-1. The Form K-1 is a means of transferring income from a partnership to a partner, a limited liability company (LLC) to a member, or an S-type corporation to the stockholder. In other words, if the artist is a member of an LLC, then he or she will get a K-1, which will show their share of income from the business. This amount will be reported as income on their personal income tax return. For information on K-1 forms, LLCs, and S-type corporations, see Chapter 8.

As well as the obvious form of cash payments for services directly performed or artwork delivered, your income may come in the form of "free" merchandise that a company gives you in exchange for a product endorsement. Actors often receive free or discounted products in exchange for the use of their name in advertisements. Musicians receive free merchandise for endorsing a particular instrument, brand of strings, or other supplies. The types of activities and/or products for which an artist may receive income include:

✓ Book publishing
✓ Recording
✓ Acting

✓ Product endorsements (including samples of the products endorsed)

- ✓ Personal appearances
- ✓ Sales of artwork
- ✓ Digital-image licensing and sales
- ✓ Music downloads
- ✓ Ringtones
- ✓ Performance art
- ✓ Modeling
- ✓ Voice-overs
- ✓ Touring
- ✓ Dance performances
- ✓ Choreography
- ✓ Lecturing
- ✓ Teaching
- ✓ Master classes
- ✓ Instructional videos
- ✓ Commissions
- ✓ Studio and artwork rentals
- ✓ Stipends

- ✓ Website design fees
- ✓ Website content
- ✓ Crowdfunding such as Kickstarter and Indie-GoGo (see Chapter 2)
- ✓ Publication of articles
- ✓ Sales or rental of photographs
- ✓ Sales of CD or DVDs
- ✓ Sales and licensing of videos
- ✓ Fees collected for streaming web content such as instructional videos
- ✓ Directing
- ✓ Production
- ✓ Consulting
- ✓ Television and radio appearances

While not exhaustive, the list gives a sense of the many activities that produce taxable income for the artist. These types of professional income will be added to your other income, whether *unearned income* (such as interest, dividends, capital gains, rental income, alimony, prizes, unemployment income) or other *earned income* that is unrelated to your professional life (for instance, the musician who moonlights as a music store clerk or the actor who works as a waiter). These types of *unearned income* and unrelated *earned income* are handled on your income tax return in exactly the same fashion as they would be on anybody else's income tax return. It is with your professional income that things diverge.

What Type of Income Is It, and Why? Employee Wages versus Contract Income

It is important to understand the difference between being paid as an employee who receives a Form W-2 and receiving income for self-employment or as a contractor, which is typically reported on a Form 1099-MISC (this is sometimes referred to as "freelance" income). When you are paid as an employee on a W-2, the employer withholds federal, state, and local (if applicable) income tax, as well as The Federal Insurance Contributions Act (FICA) taxes—Social Security and Medicare. If you are hired and paid as a contract worker, you will receive a Form 1099-MISC at year-end and generally no taxes will have been withheld. Understanding this distinction is critical because it determines how and where your income will be reported and where your professional expenses will be deducted. It is significant because if you have a substantial amount of contract income, you can end the year with a large amount of income for which no taxes have been paid (withheld)—yet!

So who and what decides how your income is going to be treated? Generally the payer/employer will decide whether you are a contractor or employee. He or she will use the Internal Revenue Service (IRS) rules cited below to arrive at the handling of your situation. In many cases the decision is fairly obvious. The key to whether someone is an employee or a contractor rests largely on how much independence the worker has or, conversely, how much control the person hiring the artist has over how the artist performs his or her duties (please note that state rules can vary from federal rules in the treatment and definition of contractors versus employees; some states are issuing more stringent regulations regarding this relationship). IRS publication 15-A discusses the three-part test that establishes the distinction between an employee and an independent contractor—these are called the "Common-Law Rules":

> In any employee-independent contractor determination, all information that provides evidence of the degree of control and the degree of independence must be considered.
>
> Facts that provide evidence of the degree of control and independence fall into three categories: behavioral control, financial control, and the type of relationship of the parties as shown below.
>
> 1. **Behavioral control.** Facts that show whether the business has a right to direct and control how the worker does the task for which the worker is hired include the type and degree of instructions the business gives the worker. An employee is generally subject to the business' instructions about when, where, and how to work. All of the following are examples of types of instructions about how to do work:
>
>   - When and where to do the work
>
>   - What tools or equipment to use
>
>   - What workers to hire or to assist with the work

- Where to purchase supplies and services

- What work must be performed by a specified individual

- What order or sequence to follow

The amount of instruction needed varies among different jobs. Even if no instructions are given, sufficient behavioral control may exist if the employer has the right to control how the work results are achieved. A business may lack the knowledge to instruct some highly specialized professionals; in other cases, the task may require little or no instruction. The key consideration is whether the business has retained the right to control the details of a worker's performance or instead has given up that right.

- Training the business gives the worker. An employee may be trained to perform services in a particular manner. Independent contractors ordinarily use their own methods.

2. **Financial control.** Facts that show whether the business has a right to control the business aspects of the worker's job include:

- The extent to which the worker has unreimbursed business expenses. Independent contractors are more likely to have unreimbursed expenses than are employees. Fixed ongoing costs that are incurred regardless of whether work is currently being performed are especially important. However, employees may also incur unreimbursed expenses in connection with the services they perform for their business.

- The extent of the worker's investment. An independent contractor often has a significant investment in the facilities he or she uses in performing services for someone else. However, a significant investment is not necessary for independent contractor status.

- The extent to which the worker makes services available to the relevant market. An independent contractor is generally free to seek out business opportunities. Independent contractors often advertise, maintain a visible business location, and are available to work in the relevant market.

- How the business pays the worker. An employee is generally guaranteed a regular wage amount for an hourly, weekly, or other period of time. This usually indicates that a worker is an employee, even when the wage or salary is supplemented by a commission. An independent contractor is usually paid by a flat fee for the job. However, it is common in some professions, such as law, to pay independent contractors hourly.

- The extent to which the worker can realize a profit or loss. An independent contractor can make a profit or loss.

3. **Type of relationship.** Facts that show the parties' type of relationship include:

- Written contracts describing the relationship the parties intended to create.

- Whether the business provides the worker with employee-type benefits, such as insurance, a pension plan, vacation pay, or sick pay.

- The permanency of the relationship. If you engage a worker with the expectation that the relationship will continue indefinitely, rather than for a specific project or period, this is generally considered evidence that your intent was to create an employer-employee relationship.

- The extent to which services performed by the worker are a key aspect of the regular business of the company. If a worker provides services that are a key aspect of your regular business activity, it is more likely that you will have the right to direct and control his or her activities. For example, if a law firm hires an attorney, it is likely that it will present the attorney's work as its own and would have the right to control or direct that work. This would indicate an employer-employee relationship.

So let's look at some examples of how these IRS rules might play out in your life.

Example One: Actor Ima Starr recently appeared in a production of *Love Letters* at the Goodwrench Theatre in Philadelphia, where she was obviously under the direct control of the production company and the theatre. She also did some modeling and a product endorsement, for which she received contractor income. At year-end she will receive a W-2 for her work at the Goodwrench Theatre, but for her modeling work she may receive either a W-2 or a 1099-MISC form, depending on how the agency treats the situation.

Example Two: Our good friend, musician Sonny Phunky, signed to play bass on a national tour with a famous rock band. He was considered to be an employee and received a W-2 from the band's production company at year-end. In the same year he gave private lessons, did some occasional studio work, played club dates, toured, and did other things that were considered contractor income. Sonny will not necessarily receive 1099s for all this income; for example, his private students would not issue him a 1099.

Example Three: Next is our painter, Liz Brushstroke. Liz is a tenured professor of art at a local college for whom she is an employee. Liz sells her independently produced artwork through prominent New York City and Dublin art galleries. Sales of her artwork generate self-employment income for Liz, as she is clearly not under the control of the gallery owner in any way. At year-end she will receive her W-2 from the college. She may or may not receive a tax form from the gallery, as her income was derived from the sale of tangible property.

Example Four: Finally, we will visit our writer friend, Guy Focal. In his regular job, Guy is a staff writer for *Swamp Life Living*, a Louisiana magazine that celebrates living life on the swamp. As a staff writer, Guy reports daily to the magazine offices in New Orleans, uses equipment owned by the magazine, is not reimbursed by the magazine for his expenses, and is given assignments and deadlines for articles and features to write. This is clearly an employment situation. In his spare time, Guy writes and publishes children's books and does freelance book reviews and articles for other publications. Any royalties from his children's book sales will be self-employment income, as will income from his freelance writing (though it could be employment income). Both of these activities are clearly independently produced. At the end of the year, Guy will receive a W-2 from Swamp Life Magazine Inc., a 1099-MISC from the publisher (or agent) of his children's books for his royalties income, and 1099-MISC forms from the various magazines that published his reviews and articles.

Why are we spending so much time on this esoteric IRS stuff, and how does this relate to your activities as an artist? In a single year, an artist will often have both employment (W-2) *and* contractor/freelance (1099-MISC) income. As we will soon see, the type of income you receive will guide how and where the income is reported on your income tax return and, more importantly, how and where the expenses are deducted.

The Mysteries of the W-2 Revealed

W-2s are sometimes issued on the completion of a particular job, but are supposed to be received no later than January 31 of the following year. Keep in mind that it is up to you to let your various employers know your correct address. I recommend that artists keep a diary of their employers during the year, as the number of W-2s due can add up and it is easy to forget one. Start a checklist at the beginning of the year (why not download one from www .artstaxinfo.com?) so you can use it as a guide at year-end. As you do this, be sure to retain copies of all pay stubs. Note not only the name of the employer, but also the name of the payroll company, because the W-2 may be issued in the payroll company's name. You may also receive unexpected W-2s for residual work in prior years (an issue for actors and musicians). I advise clients who move often to obtain a central, stable mailing address for W-2s and other tax forms, such as a manager's, business agent's, or accountant's address. Some artists use a family address or a post office or private mailbox that can be instructed to forward mail to their current address.

The following is a key to the 21 boxes found on the 2016 W-2 form:

Box 1	Federal taxable wages and tips—This is where federal taxable wages are reported; other taxable fringe benefits may be reported here.
Box 2	Federal income tax withheld—This is the amount of federal income taxes withheld from your income.
Boxes 3, 4, & 7	Social Security wages and withholdings—Social Security taxes are withheld at a rate of 6.2%, capped at the first $118,500 in 2016 (adjusted annually—www.ssa.gov).
Boxes 5 & 6	Medicare wages and tax withholdings—Medicare taxes are withheld at a rate of 1.45% with no cap.
Box 8	Allocated tips—If you worked in a restaurant with at least ten employees, your employer will report your share of 8% of gross receipts unless you reported tips at least equal to that share.
Box 9	Advance earned income payments—If you filed Form W-5 asking for part of the credit to be added to your wages, it will be included here.
Box 10	Dependent care benefits—Advances from your employer for dependent care benefits under a qualifying plan.
Box 11	Nonqualified plan distributions—Distributions for nonqualified deferred compensation plans.
Box 12 (A-D)	Catch-all box for such things as retirement plans, life insurance, moving expenses, travel allowance reimbursements, etc. Coding printed on back of your W-2 indicates exactly what the items in this box pertain to.
Box 13	Checkboxes to inform the IRS of pension plan availability and other information.
Box 14	Miscellaneous payments—Where employers can choose to put other items they wish to report to the employee.
Boxes 15–20	State and local tax information—These boxes will show your state and local taxable income as well as state and local taxes withheld (if applicable).

The taxable income amounts totaled from all your W-2s in the year will be reported on Line 7 of your 1040.

Now let's look at the W-2 live and in person:

Our resident actor, Ima Starr, receives a W-2 from her acting work in *Love Letters* at the well-known Goodwrench Dinner Theatre in Philadelphia. Even though Ima resides in New York City, the fact that she is performing in Philadelphia means she is subject not only to Pennsylvania state tax, but also to a Philadelphia municipal tax. This will mean that Ima will have to file both nonresident Pennsylvania *and* Philadelphia income tax returns at year-end (see W-2 boxes 16–19). Note that in Box 15 "Pension Plan" is checked, which indicates to the IRS that Ima has a retirement plan available to her; in this case it is her Actors' Equity Association (AEA) union plan. This fact will limit her ability to take an IRA deduction.

a Employee's social security number			1 Wages, tips, other compensation	2 Federal income tax withheld
111 LL-5555	OMB NO. 1545-0008		6905	1779

b Employer identification number (EIN)	3 Social security wages	4 Social security tax withheld
22-1500020	6905	431.56

c Employer's name, address, and ZIP code	5 Medicare wages and tips	6 Medicare tax withheld
GOODWRENCH DINNER THEATRE INC.	6905	96.67

Form **W-2** Wage and Tax Statement   **2015**

15 State	Employer's state ID number	16 State wages, tips, etc.	17 State income tax	18 Local wages, tips, etc.	19 Local income tax	20 Locality name
PA	22-1500020	6905	181.90	6905	368.96	PHILA

Copy C — For EMPLOYEE'S RECORDS (See *Notice to Employee* on the back of Copy B.)

Department of the Treasury—Internal Revenue Service

Safe, accurate, FAST! Use *e-file*

Plate One

Our bass player, musician Sonny Phunky, has been hired to play on a national tour with the Butterball Kings rock band. In this case, Sonny was considered an employee and the Butterball Kings, Inc., production company was his employer. Prior to their tour, the group rehearsed in New York City for 3 weeks. Sonny is not a New York City resident, so he was given a $316-a-day per diem by the production company to cover his living expenses (a total of $6,636). This is indicated in Box 12A with a code "L." Sonny rehearsed with the Butterball Kings for 3 weeks (21 days) in New York City. The IRS per diem in Manhattan for July of 2016 was $316 per day (lodging of $242 and meals of $74). Therefore, Sonny's per diem was the same as the IRS-approved rate (www.gsa.gov) and the number had no impact on his taxable income. You will also note that Sonny, even though he is a resident of Rockridge, Maine, will be paying New York state taxes on this income earned in New York and will need to file a New York nonresident income tax return.

What if Sonny was paid *less* than the Internal Revenue Service's approved rate? Then he would be able to take the shortfall as an employee deduction on Form 2106 (Employee Business Expenses). For example, let's say in the above example Sonny had only been paid $300 a day (a more likely scenario!). Then, the additional $16 per day would become a deduction on Form 2106. He would report a total expense for travel and meals of $6,636 (reported separately on Form 2106), then show the per-diem payment of $6,300, for a net of $336.

If Sonny had been paid *more* than the Internal Revenue Service's approved rate? The extra amount would have been added to his W-2 income in Box 1 of his W-2 and taxed.

While we are reviewing what the W-2 (and the IRS) tells us, it is interesting to note what the W-2 does *not* tell us. It does not indicate when the money

a Employee's social security number		This information is being furnished to the Internal Revenue Service. If you are required to file a tax return, a negligence penalty or other sanction may be imposed on you if this income is taxable and you fail to report it.	
	OMB No. 1545-0008		
b Employer identification number (EIN) 22-0000000		1 Wages, tips, other compensation 30000	2 Federal income tax withheld 3462
c Employer's name, address, and ZIP code THE BUTTERBALL KINGS LLC		3 Social security wages 30000	4 Social security tax withheld 1860
GRAND STREET		5 Medicare wages and tips 30000	6 Medicare tax withheld 435
NEW YORK, NEW YORK 10019		7 Social security tips	8 Allocated tips
d Control number		9	10 Dependent care benefits
e Employee's first name and initial Last name Suff. SONNY PHUNKY		11 Nonqualified plans	12a See instructions for box 12 L 6636
RR1		13 Statutory employee Retirement plan Third-party sick pay	12b
ROCKRIDGE, ME 03905		14 Other	12c
			12d
f Employee's address and ZIP code			

15 State Employer's state ID number	16 State wages, tips, etc.	17 State income tax	18 Local wages, tips, etc.	19 Local income tax	20 Locality name
ME 22-0000000	30000	2171			

Form **W-2** Wage and Tax Statement **2015** Department of the Treasury—Internal Revenue Service

Copy C — For EMPLOYEE'S RECORDS (See *Notice to Employee* on the back of Copy B.) Safe, accurate, FAST! Use *e-file*

Plate Two

was earned, how long the artist worked, or the weekly gross. Often, because the issuer will be a generic payroll service or production company, it does not indicate for whom the artist was working. Although the Social Security income ceiling in 2016 is $118,500 (adjusted annually—www.ssa.gov), if the artist works for a number of different employers and earns more than that amount, he or she might overpay into Social Security. This amount of over-payment will be refunded when he or she files a 1040 at year-end.

As an employee, you control the amount of federal income taxes with-held by filling out the federal Form W-4 with the employer. This is something that your tax advisor can help you with. By calculating the total amount of expected annual income, you can arrive at a reasonable estimation of what your withholdings should be.

In Search of Form 1099

While there are a multitude of different 1099 forms (including the common ones issued for interest and dividend income), the artist is mainly concerned with the 1099-MISC. The 1099-MISC is fairly straightforward, with thirteen self-explanatory boxes. The IRS requires payers to issue a Form 1099-MISC for each person to whom they pay at least $10 in gross royalty payments or $600 for services in the course of a calendar year. If you receive a Form 1099-MISC for your services as an artist, you are generally considered self-employed, especially if these services constitute a substantial part of your income for the year. You may even be issuing a Form 1099-MISC *yourself,* if you have paid anyone in excess of $600 for personal services or compensa-tion. Let's look at a few examples of 1099 forms that the artist might receive.

Our author Guy Focal may receive a 1099 from his children's book pub-lisher that looks like Plate Three.

Guy will report this income on the federal form Schedule C, not on the often misused Schedule E. While there is a line on federal Schedule E for royalties (and it is not uncommon to see royalties for writers reported on that line), Schedule E royalties are gas, oil, and mining royalties. Royalty income for authors is always considered self-employment income for tax pur-poses. The amount reported as royalties on the 1099-MISC will generally be reported gross by the agent or publisher, before commissions, foreign taxes, and other expenses. The income listed on the 1099 will be reported as income on Guy's Schedule C on Line 1, and the agent commissions and other charges will be reported as expenses on Schedule C.

For some miscellaneous studio work that looked like this, our friend and bass player Sonny got a 1099-MISC (see Plate Four).

Plate Three form:

CORRECTED (if checked)		
PAYER'S name, street address, city or town, state or province, country, ZIP or foreign postal code, and telephone no. Kids are Great Publishers Inc. Delancy Street New York, NY 10019	**1 Rents** $ **2 Royalties** $ 5141	OMB No. 1545-0115 20**16** Form **1099-MISC**	**Miscellaneous Income**
	3 Other income $	**4 Federal income tax withheld** $	**Copy B** **For Recipient**
PAYER'S federal identification number RECIPIENT'S identification number 04-0000000 444-55-6666	**5 Fishing boat proceeds** $	**6 Medical and health care payments** $	
RECIPIENT'S name Guy Focal	**7 Nonemployee compensation**	**8 Substitute payments in lieu of dividends or interest**	This is important tax information and is being furnished to the Internal Revenue
Street address (including apt. no.) Camp Place	$	$	Service. If you are required to file a return, a negligence penalty or other
	9 Payer made direct sales of $5,000 or more of consumer products to a buyer (recipient) for resale ▶ ☐	**10 Crop insurance proceeds** $	
City or town, state or province, country, and ZIP or foreign postal code New Orleans, LA 23000	**11**	**12**	sanction may be imposed on you if this income is taxable and the IRS
Account number (see instructions) FATCA filing requirement ☐	**13 Excess golden parachute payments** $	**14 Gross proceeds paid to an attorney** $	determines that it has not been reported.
15a Section 409A deferrals **15b Section 409A income** $ $	**16 State tax withheld** $ $	**17 State/Payer's state no.**	**18 State income** $ $

Form **1099-MISC**   (keep for your records)   www.irs.gov/form1099misc   Department of the Treasury - Internal Revenue Service

Plate Three

Sonny's studio work will be shown in Box 7 as nonemployee compensation and will be reported on Schedule C.

Plate Four form:

CORRECTED (if checked)		
PAYER'S name, street address, city or town, state or province, country, ZIP or foreign postal code, and telephone no. Hogs Breath Recording Studio LLC South Michigan Chicago, IL 22331	**1 Rents** $ **2 Royalties** $	OMB No. 1545-0115 20**16** Form **1099-MISC**	**Miscellaneous Income**
	3 Other income $	**4 Federal income tax withheld** $	**Copy B** **For Recipient**
PAYER'S federal identification number RECIPIENT'S identification number 30-4552222 222-33-4444	**5 Fishing boat proceeds** $	**6 Medical and health care payments** $	
RECIPIENT'S name Sonny Phunky	**7 Nonemployee compensation**	**8 Substitute payments in lieu of dividends or interest**	This is important tax information and is being furnished to the Internal Revenue
Street address (including apt. no.) RR 1	$ 2150	$	Service. If you are required to file a return, a negligence penalty or other
	9 Payer made direct sales of $5,000 or more of consumer products to a buyer (recipient) for resale ▶ ☐	**10 Crop insurance proceeds** $	
City or town, state or province, country, and ZIP or foreign postal code Rockridge, ME 03905	**11**	**12**	sanction may be imposed on you if this income is taxable and the IRS
Account number (see instructions) FATCA filing requirement ☐	**13 Excess golden parachute payments** $	**14 Gross proceeds paid to an attorney** $	determines that it has not been reported.
15a Section 409A deferrals **15b Section 409A income** $ $	**16 State tax withheld** $ $	**17 State/Payer's state no.**	**18 State income** $ $

Form **1099-MISC**   (keep for your records)   www.irs.gov/form1099misc   Department of the Treasury - Internal Revenue Service

Plate Four

☐ CORRECTED (if checked)				
PAYER'S name, street address, city or town, state or province, country, ZIP or foreign postal code, and telephone no.	1 Rents $	OMB No. 1545-0115		Miscellaneous Income
Muddy Mudskippers BBQ Inc. Main Street Philadelphia, PA 19999	2 Royalties $	2016 Form 1099-MISC		
	3 Other income $ 1000	4 Federal income tax withheld $		Copy B For Recipient
PAYER'S federal identification number RECIPIENT'S identification number	5 Fishing boat proceeds	6 Medical and health care payments		
22-3232320 111-22-3333	$	$		This is important tax information and is being furnished to the Internal Revenue Service. If you are required to file a return, a negligence penalty or other sanction may be imposed on you if this income is taxable and the IRS determines that it has not been reported.
RECIPIENT'S name Ima Starr	7 Nonemployee compensation	8 Substitute payments in lieu of dividends or interest		
Street address (including apt. no.) 5th Ave Apt #9	$	$		
	9 Payer made direct sales of $5,000 or more of consumer products to a buyer (recipient) for resale ▶ ☐	10 Crop insurance proceeds $		
City or town, state or province, country, and ZIP or foreign postal code New York, NY 10019	11	12		
Account number (see instructions) FATCA filing requirement ☐	13 Excess golden parachute payments $	14 Gross proceeds paid to an attorney $		
15a Section 409A deferrals 15b Section 409A income $ $	16 State tax withheld $ ---- $	17 State/Payer's state no.	18 State income $ $

Form **1099-MISC**   (keep for your records)   www.irs.gov/form1099misc   Department of the Treasury - Internal Revenue Service

Plate Five

Ima Starr won a prize when she entered a contest while in Philadelphia. She won a historic, fully restored Yugo automobile that was worth $1,000. Her 1099-MISC will reflect this in Box 3 and look like Plate Five.

I cite this example because Box 3, "Other," is often used as a real catch-all box when the issuer does not know where to put a particular item. It is not uncommon to find products given in product endorsement situations put in here. In the case of Ms. Starr's Yugo, because she did not give any services in exchange, the value of the car is not considered self-employment income. If she had done a product endorsement (for example, if she had done a commercial for the car restoration company), the value of the auto would be reported as self-employment income because the product would have been given in exchange for services, namely the endorsement.

Another point to bear in mind is that, as an artist, the IRS treats you as a "cash-basis taxpayer." Cash basis means that, generally speaking, your income is the value of what you *receive* during the calendar year. So income reported on the 1099 is not necessarily income for the recipient in the same year. For example, our musician Sonny did some studio work at the end of the year. The studio wanted the deduction on that year's tax return so they issued and mailed the $925 check on December 31 and correctly put the payment on the 1099-MISC they issued to Sonny for that year (after all, they had in fact paid it that year). Sonny did not receive the check until January 4 of the following year; consequently he does not have to consider that payment as income in the same year as the 1099 would indicate. In these cases the artist can show the income not received as an adjustment to the 1099 and add the income to his or her return in the subsequent year.

The Joys of Being Self-Employed

So what does it mean to be self-employed and have self-employment income? Understand that when you receive a substantial part of your income reported on Form 1099, you are considered self-employed. It is critical to understand how self-employment income is taxed. Self-employment income is subject to *two separate taxes* on your federal tax return: income tax and self-employment tax. Self-employment income is reported on federal Schedule C, and self-employment tax is calculated on federal Form SE (for self-employment). The following diagram indicates how self-employment income is taxed on the 1040:

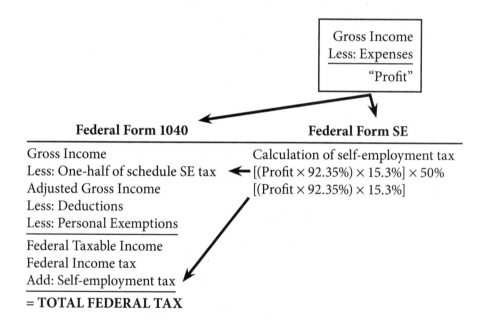

Gross Income
Less: Expenses
"Profit"

Federal Form 1040   **Federal Form SE**

Gross Income   Calculation of self-employment tax
Less: One-half of schedule SE tax   ← [(Profit × 92.35%) × 15.3%] × 50%
Adjusted Gross Income   [(Profit × 92.35%) × 15.3%]
Less: Deductions
Less: Personal Exemptions

Federal Taxable Income
Federal Income tax
Add: Self-employment tax

= **TOTAL FEDERAL TAX**

We can see from this diagram that income from self-employment is subject to two levels of taxation:
  ✓ The first is the 15.3% self-employment tax. This tax has two elements: 2.9% is Medicare tax and 12.4% is Social Security taxes that the IRS collects on behalf of the Social Security Administration.

Medicare tax is calculated on all the self-employment income. Social Security tax is applied only on the first $118,500 of income in 2016 (adjusted annually—www.ssa.gov). Remember that your personal exemptions and deductions for your home mortgage interest, real estate tax, and state taxes, etc., do not affect the calculation of this tax. The one caveat to this is if you are taking a deduction on the home office then there will be a percentage of home mortgage interest and real estate taxes that will impact the calculation of self-employment tax.

✓ The second level is the federal income tax.

Estimated Taxes

Because self-employment income will not generally be subject to withholding tax it is *very easy* to get into trouble and end up owing unexpected amounts of money on April 15th. Therefore, as a self-employed artist you will probably be required to pay estimated taxes quarterly. If a substantial amount of your income is going to be in the form of self-employment income, I say, get thee to a good tax advisor! Your tax advisor will help you estimate what your potential federal and state tax liability might be for the year. Keep in mind that your taxable income is your gross income *minus* your expenses and deductions. Estimated taxes are paid quarterly on April 15th, June 15th, and September 15th of the current year and January 15th of the following year on federal Form 1040-ES. To make a reasonable estimate of your potential tax liability you have to be able to determine what your income-related expenses are going to be. This is where the record keeping becomes vital (more on that later)!

So What's All the Hubbub, Bub?

The hubbub is that you must understand the mix of your W-2 and 1099 income to properly organize and be prepared to do your income taxes. Very few folks in the arts these days are involved purely in one activity; for many artists it is a multidiscipline *thang*!

Our own Ima Starr is a member of the Actors' Equity Association and received multiple W-2 forms this year (as is common with AEA members). These W-2s will be added up and put on Line 7 of her 1040 income tax form. Her expenses associated with these activities will be found on Form 2106—Employee Business Expense (more on that later). Ima is also the sultry lounge singer in the group The Blue Jazzbos. She published a book about her life in show business last year. That means she has three streams of self-employment income: one for music, one for writing, and one for modeling (her acting is employment income). She must, to the best of her abilities, allocate her business expenses among these various activities, as they will need to be entered on various forms on her personal income tax return. She might even have to pay estimated income taxes on her self-employment income, especially if the movie rights for her book are optioned!

In the world of the arts, actors play in rock bands, musicians write books or teach, dancers perform and teach dance, visual artists teach and design websites, writers lecture and teach, etc. These various activities require you to compartmentalize your income and expenses to a certain degree, without driving yourself insane! Next we will look at the other side of our equation: expenses and deductions.

2

Crowdfunding for Creative People

"Rewards-based" crowdfunding is fast becoming a primary funding source for creative individuals. Project runners who have a fan base and a flair for the interactive nature of social media are going to be able to utilize crowdfunding as a major pillar of their professional cash flow.

In the early days of crowdfunding, folks often saw this outlet as a one-time shot. They felt that this was a well you could not go back to multiple times. As crowdfunding has matured, we are seeing artists use this model regularly for projects. They are finding that as long as the fan base is happy with the artist's work, they are more than willing to keep supporting new crowdfunded projects. As we move forward, you are going to see creative people using crowdfunding as the major financial arm of their creative business.

To Be or Not to Be Income, That Is the Question . . .

The first hurdle with crowdfunding is deciding whether all that cash is taxable income. While there is no definitive guidance from taxing authorities regarding crowdfunded income, there are principles that can be applied in deciding the taxation of crowdfunding income. A majority of rewards-based crowdfunding project receipts will be considered income because there is an exchange for a product or an implied exchange for services. The backer is supporting the project because he or she wants to read the book; hear the music; or see the performance, movie, or play. The musician will be giving away signed copies of the CD; the filmmaker will be giving away signed DVDs, film posters, or invites to premieres; the author will be giving autographed special-edition books; the performer might offer a Skype master class; the writer might offer to read a draft. Receiving that special reward and seeing a project to fruition is the primary motivation of the project backer.

Some professionals argue that there can be the component of a gift in the crowdfunding model. I think they base this (partially) on the example that exists with 501c3 nonprofit organizations. For example, when you give a $100 to PBS and receive a "premium" back (say, a $15 umbrella), only $85 will be considered a tax-deductible charitable contribution. Some have argued that this same paradigm exists in the crowdfunding world: if the value of the reward being given is diminutive compared to what the backer is paying, the amount over and above the fair market value of the reward might be considered a gift by the project runner. I think this is erroneous reasoning because, of course, the project runner is generally not a nonprofit organization and, again, even if the value of the reward is diminutive or even $0, the backer is still expecting the project runner to do something in return for their backing the project: producing the recording, film, book, play, etc. Under the IRS code, a tax-free gift is by its very nature a transaction made out of "detached and disinterested generosity." That is clearly not the core foundation of rewards-based crowdfunding.

The other argument that is sometimes made is that the project backer is making what is called a "nonshareholder" contribution to the project runner. This approach has even less promise than the argument for gifting. Very few rewards-based crowdfunding projects are run by corporations, and even if the project runner were incorporated, it is unlikely that the project backer would meet the five IRS requirements for the nonshareholder contribution.

My feeling as a tax professional is that any project that offers a backer some sort of reward is going to be considered fully taxable income by the Internal Revenue Service, regardless of the value of the reward.

In Art, Timing Is Everything . . .

One important consideration when starting your crowdfunded project is timing. You always want to match income and expenses in the same tax year. One of the worst mistakes a project runner can make is to collect funds late in the calendar year while not expending the cash until the next year. In that case, the project runner (as a cash-basis taxpayer) ends up with all the taxable income in one year and all the expenses in another tax year—the worst of all the possible outcomes.

Expenses and Deductions and Other Issues

Once we decide that our rewards-based crowdfunding project is a legit trade or business, either by way of being part of an ongoing creative enterprise or in and of itself, then all we have to do is organize our related expenses for the project. Typically, the project runner is looking to cover a distinct group of expenses: the costs of recording a record, editing a film, or publishing a book, for example. Clearly our filmmaker who raises $30,000 to edit and finish a movie will deduct those costs against the income from the rewards-based crowdfunding project. And one must not forget the costs of the backer rewards! Many a project runner has greatly underestimated the cost and energy required to fulfill the rewards that were offered to backers, and all those costs are also deductible against the project income. These include the costs of companies that are springing up to handle fulfillment for project runners.

As you can discern from this brief discussion of expenses, the entire subject of whether crowdfunding income is taxable is pretty academic for the majority of creative crowdfunding project runners. While I am sure it has happened, I have never personally seen any project runner make a "profit" on their crowdfunding campaign. Most project runners who collect more money from backers than they requested simply expand the project to utilize and expend the additional dollars.

Crowdfunding platforms are only required to issue a 1099-K for projects that gross more than $20,000 in income and have two hundred or more transactions in a calendar year. For projects that gross less, there will be no third-party reporting to Internal Revenue Service. The income will be reported gross on Schedule C as income and the commission taken by the crowdfunding site will be listed as an expense.

As rewards-based crowdfunding becomes a key pillar in the income stream of more and more creative individuals, a lot of this information will become second nature; until that time, however, this subject will cause difficulties for some creative artists.

3

What Can I Deduct?

In this chapter I will take a bird's-eye view of expenses and deductions. We will see how the IRS interprets the general deductibility of the more common expenses that all artists have, such as automobile use, travel, meals, entertainment, and the controversial home office. I will also look at the qualified performing artist (QPA) provision, start-up costs, and the also controversial "hobby loss" rules. Following chapters will deal more specifically with the deductible expenses in the various disciplines, but for now let's get an overview.

The heart of saving money on your tax return is making sure you do not miss any deductions or expenses. As we have said, the artist has to be concerned about the type of income the deduction is associated with. This is the core of where the deduction goes on the tax return, i.e., does this expense relate to W-2 employment earnings or 1099 self-employment income?

Let's look at what the IRS says regarding expense deductions in general in its Publication 583:

> You can deduct business expenses on your income tax return. These are the current operating costs of running your business. To be deductible, a business expense must be both ordinary and necessary. An ordinary expense is one that is common and accepted in your field of business, trade, or profession. A necessary expense is one that is helpful and appropriate for your business, trade, or profession. An expense does not have to be indispensable to be considered necessary

And from Publication 334:

> You cannot deduct expenses that are lavish or extravagant under the circumstances.

So we can see the IRS has only three fairly simple criteria for deductible business expenses:

1. Must be incurred in connection with your trade, business, or profession.
2. Must be ordinary and necessary.
3. Must *not* be lavish or extravagant.

As I mentioned in the first chapter, as an artist you are treated as what the IRS calls a "cash-basis taxpayer." This means that, generally speaking, your expenses and deductions are anything you expend money or value on during the calendar year. If you pay for a tax-deductible expense via check, cash, barter, or charge card (even if you don't pay off the credit card until the following year), the expense will qualify as a deduction in the current year. This all seems straightforward but, as the saying goes, "the devil is in the details."

First, let's tackle the matter of whether the deduction is related to employment (W-2) income or self-employment (Form 1099 or K-1) income. While the types of expenses that are deductible will usually not change between employment and self-employment, the manner in which the deduction is taken and its effect on your tax return can be critical. Important point: the deductibility of specific items can be largely identical for employees and for the self-employed; it is basically a mechanical matter as to how they are treated during the preparation of the income tax return. Put another way, the "employee" artist might (and indeed, will often) have the exact same group of deductions as the "self-employed" artist. The following chart illustrates the flow of income and deductions:

Employment	Self-employment
Income from W-2 Form	Income from Form 1099-MISC/K-1
↓	↓
Expenses found on Form 2106, Employee Business Expenses	Expenses found on Schedule C, Form 2106 or 2106 type form

So what is the key difference between these two methods? An employee's Form 2106 will usually become an itemized deduction on Schedule A of the 1040 and be subject to a 2% floor (except for the QPA). In other words, if your adjusted gross income is $100,000, you will *automatically* lose $2,000 ($100,000 × 2%) of your professional expenses. In addition, if the artist does not have any other itemized deductions, such as home mortgage interest, real estate taxes, or state tax payments, then the value of the employee business expenses can be reduced even further. On the other hand, deductions against self-employment income are written off dollar for dollar directly against the self-employment income on the Schedule C.

The exception to this is the Form K-1. If the artist is a member of an LLC (taxed as a partnership) or a partner in a partnership, they will be able to take allowable business deductions directly against the K-1 income through the use of a type of 2106 substitute form on Schedule E (we will see an example of this in Sonny Phunky's 1040 in Chapter 5; note that this type of deduction is not available on an S corporation).

Let's see how this plays out with our four artists:

Ima Starr is a member of Actors' Equity, so the bulk of her annual income is reported on the W-2 forms she received. That means that all of her acting expenses will be reported on Form 2106 as employee business expenses. For self-employment, Ima sings in a jazz group, did some modeling, and even wrote a book. She and her accountant will be allocating expenses associated with those activities to her Schedule C. These expenses might include auto usage, publications, music equipment purchase, digital and streaming music, and home office. It is not always easy to figure out this "allocation" I mention. What if all of Ima Starr's incomes were earned only in New York City (NYC) where she lives? That is, all the acting jobs, music gigs, modeling assignments, etc., are in NYC.

How does one allocate expenses in a situation like that? The answer is: very carefully and systematically! In cases where a clear-cut differentiation is impossible, try for a methodical and consistent approach. This might be done by allocating the expenses according to income received, days worked, or some other formula (an income-based allocation is what the Internal Revenue Service discusses in its audit guidelines). In other words, first assign the expenses you can clearly and directly associate with each type of income, then allocate general expenses via a formula. It is clear that Ima's Actors' Equity dues would be an expense on Form 2106 against her employment income. The sound system and music downloads she purchased for her singing career would be deducted against her self-employment income. For her home office or her new MacBook Pro notebook or iPad it can be argued that they benefit all her activities equally, so these expenses might be allocated according to an income-based formula (the formula the IRS prefers). If 25% of her gross earnings were from her self-employment activities, she may choose to assign 25% of her home office and technology expenses to her Schedule C. While this gross income method is not perfect, it is logical, defensible, and easy to explain in an IRS audit situation!

Now for our bass player, Sonny Phunky. Let's deal with just four of Sonny's expense line items for the year: the purchase of a new bass guitar, music supplies, auto mileage, and travel and meals. When Sonny arrives at his accountant's office he will have his W-2 from Butterball Kings, Inc., for his tour (Plate Two). He will also have 1099-MISC forms for some of his studio work and gigs. And he will have some unreported (to Internal Revenue Service) income from privately teaching the bass guitar to his students. So how will Sonny and his accountant differentiate the expenses for these items on the tax return? It turns out that the Butterball Kings specifically requested that he play a chartreuse-colored bass to match their other stage equipment, which forced Sonny to purchase a new custom-painted bass guitar for the tour. This would be grounds for Sonny's accountant to write off (*depreciate*—more on this later) the new bass against his W-2 by using Form 2106. In regard to the music supplies, Sonny and his accountant may choose to take all the expenses purchased during his time with the Butterball Kings as a deduction against the W-2, because that was his primary professional activity in that time frame. They would probably use the same approach for auto mileage. Sonny's use of his car to drive from Maine to NYC and for transportation in and around New York while he was in the city for rehearsals could all be used as a deduction against the W-2 on Form 2106.

For his living expenses while in NYC, Sonny may not have any deductions. You will remember that the Butterball Kings' W-2 indicated to the IRS (Box 13-Code L) that Sonny was given a per diem allowance to cover them. If this allowance did cover all his meals and lodging, then Sonny would have no write-off for these expenses. In his case, Sonny's allowance, while more than the Internal Revenue Service prescribed per diem, was less than he actually paid to be in NYC, so he was able to avail himself of additional write-offs on his Form 2106 for the amount over and above the allowance.

Sonny's expenses for the rest of the year for music supplies, travel, mileage to the studio and gigs, etc., would become a deduction on his Schedule C against his self-employment income and against the K-1 he is receiving. We can see from this example that Sonny will have many of the same expense line items on both his 2106 and his Schedule C forms when we review his 1040 tax return in Chapter 5.

Let's look at our visual artist, Liz. As a college professor, she may have no deductions at all because the college would probably be supplying all her teaching materials. But Liz would indeed have expenses for her work as an independent artist. Her expenses for framing, art supplies, home studio, mileage to visit the gallery in NYC, and travel to the gallery in Dublin would all be deductions on her Schedule C form.

Finally, our writer, Guy. The magazine Guy works for will probably be supplying all his materials and equipment, as well as reimbursing him for his auto use on the job, so the only deduction he had against his W-2 (found on Form 2106) was a trip to NYC (*Swamp Life Living* magazine does not reimburse this type of travel). Guy would indeed have expenses for his work as an independent writer, which might include the use of a home office, purchase of books, travel, and home computer. These expenses would appear on Schedule C as deductions against his royalties and other freelance writing income.

It's time to delve into some of the larger expense line items that typically affect all artists.

The Automobile

The use of a car for business is the most common expense an artist has and is often the single largest deduction. The IRS has two basic methods for writing off the business use of your automobile. It allows you to use either the annually adjusted IRS standard mileage rate or the actual expense of operating your car. The IRS sums it up in the following language in Publication 334:

> For local transportation or overnight travel by car or truck, you generally can use one of the following methods to figure your expenses:
>
> **Standard Mileage Rate.**
>
> Standard mileage rate. You may be able to use the standard mileage rate to figure the deductible costs of operating your car, van, pickup, or panel truck for business purposes. For 2016, the standard mileage rate is 54 cents a mile for business travel [this is adjusted annually—see the Taxes QuikGuide on www.artstaxinfo.com for the latest rate].
>
> Caution: If you choose to use the standard mileage rate for a year, you cannot deduct your actual expenses for that year except for business-related parking fees and tolls.
>
> Choosing the standard mileage rate. If you want to use the standard mileage rate for a car or truck you own, you must choose to use it in the first year the car is available for use in your business. In later years, you can choose to use either the standard mileage rate or actual expenses. If you want to use the standard mileage rate for a car you lease, you must choose to use it for the entire lease period.
>
> Standard mileage rate not allowed. You cannot use the standard mileage rate if you:
>
> 1. Use the car for hire [such as Uber or a taxi],
>
> 2. Operate two or more cars at the same time,
>
> 3. Claimed a depreciation deduction using ACRS or MACRS in an earlier year,
>
> 4. Claimed a section 179 deduction on the car,
>
> 5. Claimed actual car expenses after 1997 for a car you leased, or
>
> 6. Are a rural mail carrier who received a qualified reimbursement.

Parking fees and tolls. In addition to using the standard mileage rate, you can deduct any business-related parking fees and tolls. [Parking fees you pay to park your car at your place of work are nondeductible commuting expenses.]

Actual Expenses

Actual expenses. If you do not choose to use the standard mileage rate, you may be able to deduct your actual car or truck expenses.

TIP: If you qualify to use both methods, figure your deduction both ways to see which gives you a larger deduction.

Actual car expenses include the costs of the following items:

Depreciation	Lease payments	Registration fees
Garage rent	Licenses	Repairs
Gas	Oil	Tires
Insurance	Parking fees	Tolls

If you use your vehicle for both business and personal purposes, you must divide your expenses between business and personal use. You can divide based on the miles driven for each purpose.

For an example of how to divide expenses related to vehicle use, imagine you are a musician and you drove your van for a total of 20,000 miles during the year. 16,000 miles were for going to gigs, including delivering equipment, and 4,000 miles were for personal use. You can claim only 80% (16,000/20,000) of the cost of operating your van as a business expense.

The easiest method for most folks is to use the generous IRS standard mileage allowance. This option does not require retention of receipts of any kind. All you need to have is a record in your diary or appointment book of business miles driven.

As a rule, personal miles (going to the grocery store, the dentist, out to dinner, etc.) and commuting mileage are not deductible. If you have a legitimate office at home it tends to make all business miles deductible; after all there can be no commute if you work at home. Otherwise, your commute would normally be the first and last trip every day. To illustrate, if our visual artist Liz left her college job at noon, drove to pick up some art supplies, stopped by to speak to a gallery owner, then drove back to school to check in before going home, all her miles from the time she left school until she arrived back to school would be deductible business miles; the balance would be non-deductible commuting miles.

By keeping an accurate appointment book you should have all the info you need to estimate your business miles.

The Home Office/Studio

If you use a room (or rooms) in your home exclusively as your office *and* you have no other office space available to you, you will most likely qualify for the home office or home studio deduction. To qualify as a deductible home office the space must generally be:

1. The principal place of business

2. The place where the taxpayer meets with clients, customers, or colleagues

The room can be used as an office; a storage area for equipment, manuscripts, and supplies; for recordkeeping for the business; marketing, etc. For the actor, dancer, filmmaker, and musician it can be a space for keeping business records, preparing correspondence, performing promotional activities, rehearsing, and storing library/manuscripts. For the writer and visual artists, the home office is where you write, paint, or sculpt. It could also be a home darkroom for the photographer.

The home office is a fairly straightforward deduction to calculate on federal Form 8829. It simply utilizes a formula based on the square footage of the business portion (the home office) of your home versus the total square footage of the house or apartment and then applies that percentage to all associated costs. The costs might be rent (if you do not own your home), mortgage interest, real estate taxes, condo fees, utilities, insurance, repairs, etc. If you own your own home, you can even depreciate that portion of your house for an additional write-off.

For example:

Business use (square footage)	250
Total square footage of home	1250
Business use percentage (250/1250)	20%

Mortgage Interest	$ 7,500
Real Estate Tax	$ 2,500
Utilities	$ 1,820
Water & Sewer	$ 820
Insurance	$ 400
Repairs	$ 225
Total home expenses	$ 13,265

Potential home office deduction:
($13,265 × 20%)   **$2,653**

Other rules that come into play here include the "exclusive use" requirement. This rule states that the home office must be used only for the business—no "mixed use" is allowed. Put another way, the home office or studio cannot be a part of a larger room (such as the living room) unless the business part is partitioned off somehow. Be careful when allocating home office expenses. The Internal Revenue Service could decide that one of the activities is really a "hobby" and not a legitimate business and then the entire home office will be blown off the return. Why? Because it would no longer be "exclusive use."

If these rules sound kind of complicated, the Internal Revenue Service instituted a "Simplified Method" of deducting the home office in 2014 and it looks like this:

- Standard deduction of $5 per square foot of home used for business with a maximum 300 square feet of space (this means a maximum deduction of not more than $1,500).
- Allowable home-related itemized deductions claimed in full on Schedule A (for example, mortgage interest, real estate taxes).
- No home depreciation deduction or later recapture of depreciation for the years the simplified option is used.
- All other rules apply regarding exclusive and regular use.

You will want to discuss this with your tax professional to see if this method might benefit you. If you are doing your own taxes this is certainly an easier process, but keep in mind it will almost always yield a smaller tax deduction.

For instance, if Ima Starr's accountant felt that her book writing would not pass muster as a true business, he would do well to not allocate any home office expense to it.

If you are planning on selling your home in the near future, you are probably assuming that there will not be a tax, thanks to the $250,000 ($500,000 if a jointly owned residence) exclusion of gain on the sale of a principal residence. However, if you have a home office, or have taken home office deductions in the past, you may have an extra bit of planning to do in order to make sure you receive the full benefit of the exclusion.

The IRS rules no longer require taxpayers who claim the home office deduction to allocate the gain between business and personal use if the business occurred within the same dwelling unit as the residential use. Instead, only the amount of depreciation you deducted in the past as a home office expense will be subject to a recapture tax.

Equipment Purchases and Depreciation and Amortization of Recordings, Films, and Books

This section concerns the purchase of equipment used by the artist. It pertains to the purchase of any large assets such as computers, printers, tablets, smartphones, scanners, digital cameras, cell phones, software, musical instruments and audio equipment, cameras and photographic equipment, sculptors' welding equipment, presses or other devices used by visual artists, video cameras and equipment, and sound and audio devices. The purchase of a violin or computer is considered intrinsically different from paying the phone bill, in that when you purchase the violin or computer it will have a life beyond the year it is bought, unlike the phone service, which has no "life." Therefore, depreciation of equipment is a method of dividing the cost of the asset over its IRS-defined "useful life" and deducting it a little bit at a time, year by year, until the entire purchase price has been deducted.

In Publication 334 the IRS discusses depreciation this way:

> If property you acquire to use in your business is expected to last more than one year, you generally cannot deduct the entire cost as a business expense in the year you acquire it. You must spread the cost over more than one tax year and deduct part of it each year on Schedule C, C-EZ or Form 2106. This method of deducting the cost of business property is called depreciation.
>
> **What can be depreciated?** You can depreciate property if it meets all the following requirements:
>
> It must be used in business or held to produce income.
>
> > ✓ It must be expected to last more than one year. In other words, it must have a useful life that extends substantially beyond the year it is placed in service.
> >
> > ✓ It must be something that wears out, decays, gets used up, becomes obsolete, or loses its value from natural causes.
>
> **What cannot be depreciated?** You cannot depreciate any of the following items:
>
> > ✓ Property placed in service and disposed of in the same year.
> >
> > ✓ Inventory.
> >
> > ✓ Land.
> >
> > ✓ Repairs and replacements that do not increase the value of your property, make it more useful, or lengthen its useful life. You can deduct these amounts on Schedule C, C-EZ, or Form 2106.

Depreciation method. The method for depreciating most tangible property placed in service after 1986 is called the Modified Accelerated Cost Recovery System (MACRS). [Tangible property is property you can see or touch.] MACRS is discussed in detail in Publication 946.

Section 179 deduction. You can choose to deduct a limited amount [for 2015 and 2016, up to $500,000] of the cost of certain depreciable property in the year you buy it for use in your business. This deduction is known as the "section 179 deduction." For more information, see Publication 946. It explains what costs you can and cannot deduct, how to figure the deduction, and when to recapture the deduction.

Listed property. Listed property is any of the following.

✓ Most passenger automobiles.

✓ Most other property used for transportation.

✓ Any property of a type generally used for entertainment, recreation, or amusement.

✓ Certain computer and related peripheral equipment.

✓ Any cellular telephone (or similar telecommunications equipment).

You must follow additional rules and recordkeeping requirements when depreciating listed property. For more information about listed property, see Publication 946.

What are the typical "lives" of commonly purchased assets according to the IRS?

✓ Computer and technology assets = 5 years
✓ Automobiles and light trucks = 5 years
✓ Office furniture, fixtures, musical instruments, and machinery = 7 years
✓ Commercial real estate = 39 years

Depreciation is calculated and reported on Form 4562, and is then carried either to the Schedule C if written off against self-employment income, or the Form 2106 if deducted against W-2 employment earnings.

A common depreciation/deduction question that comes up in the arts concerns the purchase of collectables and other antiques. For the actor or director, it can be the acquisition of a film or theatre prop or poster; for the musician it can be a vintage instrument; for the visual artist it could be a piece of artwork; and for the writer it may be a signed, first edition book. While these items may be related directly to your profession, the IRS generally feels such items are personal in nature and are not deductible or subject to depreciation. That is because they are often not used directly in the artist's profession, but are decorative in nature. The other reason the IRS does not allow a deduction is because the nature of a collectable is to appreciate in value, not depreciate. The IRS has lost several court cases over a musician writing off an antique instrument. In two cases it was critical that the musician used the instrument in actual performance and recording. By doing this, one taxpayer argued that the use of the bass viol did diminish the value of the instrument due to the perspiration from the performer's hands and through oxidation of the wood. In tax court cases, the IRS can either agree with the court or not agree. In these cases, the IRS did not acquiesce to the decisions of the tax court. So you cannot rely on these court rulings as a precedent. If you do decide to depreciate an antique or collectable, be sure that you are actually using it in your job as an artist and prepare for an argument!

The creation of film, videos, books, and recordings follows a concept similar to depreciation: they are assumed to have some value beyond the year in which they are created and are written off over a period of time. In the case of film and recordings, the term used is *amortization*. The total cost of creating the film or recording is capitalized and then written off using one of two IRS-approved formulas. Unlike the purchase of a computer, the IRS does not define a predetermined life for film and recordings. The two methods are:

1. The individual-film-forecast method [the most common method]—the creator estimates the amount and timing of the income stream from sales of the film, book or recording and expenses the costs associated with the creation or acquisition over that period of time. For instance, if the recording or film cost $50,000 to produce and the income was expected to be earned over 3 years in the following formula: 65%-25%-10%, then the $50,000 would be written off $32,500-$12,500-$5,000.

2. Straight-line over the useful life—if the creator expects the film, book or recording to have a useful life of 5 years [probably the shortest life the Internal Revenue Service would generally allow], then he or she would divide the $50,000 production cost by 5 and take approximately $10K in expense each year.

An exception to the above concerns music videos. If the artist creates a music video to be used primarily for shopping the artist to record companies, then the cost of the video is immediately deductible as advertising expense, not subject to amortization.

Keep in mind that this quick outline on amortization of film costs is a very simplified overview of some very complex issues. If your artistic endeavors take you into this area be sure you seek out qualified tax professionals to help you.

Travel and Meal Expenses

After the business use of the automobile, travel can be the next most common (and thorny) issue for the artist. Before we discuss travel for the artist, let's see what the IRS says about business travel in its Publication 463, which includes an excellent chart (Table 1) of what types of items are deductible:

> Deductible travel expenses include those ordinary and necessary expenses you have when you travel away from home on business. The type of expense you can deduct depends on the facts and your circumstances.
>
> Table 1 summarizes travel expenses you may be able to deduct. You may have other deductible travel expenses that are not covered there, depending on the facts and your circumstances.
>
> **Records.** When you travel away from home on business, you should keep records of all the expenses you have and any advances you receive from your employer. You can use a log, diary, notebook, or any other written record to keep track of your expenses.
>
> **Travel expenses for another individual.** If a spouse, dependent, or other individual goes with you (or your employee) on a business trip or to a business convention, you generally cannot deduct his or her travel expenses.
>
> **Employee.** You can deduct the travel expenses you have for an accompanying individual if that individual:
>
> ✓ Is your employee,
>
> ✓ Has a bona fide business purpose for the travel, and
>
> ✓ Would otherwise be allowed to deduct the travel expenses.
>
> **Business associate.** If a business associate travels with you and meets the conditions in (2) and (3) above, you can claim the deductible travel expenses you have for that person. A business associate is someone with whom you could reasonably expect to actively conduct business. A business associate can be a current or prospective (likely to become) customer, client, supplier, employee, agent, partner, or professional advisor.
>
> **Bona fide business purpose.** For a bona fide business purpose to exist, you must prove a real business purpose for the individual's presence. Incidental services, such as typing notes or assisting in entertaining customers, are not enough to warrant a deduction.
>
> **Example:** Jerry drives to Chicago to audition for a play and takes his wife, Linda, with him. Linda is not Jerry's employee. Even if her presence serves a bona fide business purpose, her expenses are not deductible.
>
> Jerry pays $115 a day for a double room. A single room costs $90 a day. He can deduct the total cost of driving his car to and from Chicago, but only $90

a day for his hotel room. If he uses public transportation, he can deduct only his fare.

Travel expenses you can deduct

This chart summarizes expenses you can deduct when you travel away from home for business purposes.

TABLE 1:

IF you have expenses for:	THEN you can deduct the costs of:
Transportation	Travel by airplane, train, bus, or car between your home and your business destination. If you were provided with a ticket or you are riding free as a result of a frequent traveler or similar program, your cost is zero. If you travel by ship, see additional rules & limits on Luxury Water Travel & Cruise Ships.
Taxi, commuter bus, and airport limousine	Fares for these and other types of transportation that take you to or from: 1) The airport or station and your hotel, and 2) The hotel and the work location of your staff, crew, band members, customers or clients, your business meeting place, or your temporary work location.
Baggage and shipping	Sending baggage, wardrobes, sets & props, sample or display material between your regular and temporary work locations.
Car	Operating and maintaining your car when traveling away from home on business. You can deduct actual expenses or the standard mileage rate, as well as business-related tolls and parking. If you rent a car while away from home on business, you can deduct only the business-use portion of the expenses.
Lodging and meals	Lodging and meals if your business trip is overnight or long enough that you need to stop for sleep or rest to properly perform your duties. Meals include amounts spent for food, beverage, taxes, and related tips.
Cleaning	Dry cleaning and laundry.

Telephone	Business calls while on your business trip. This includes business communication by fax machine, cellular phone or other communication devices.
Tips	Tips you pay for any expenses in this chart.
Other	Other similar ordinary and necessary expenses related to your business travel. These expenses might include transportation to or from a business meal, public stenographer's fees, computer rental fees, and operating and maintaining a house trailer.

In short, deductible travel is when you are taken away from your home for a direct, clearly identifiable business purpose. Keep in mind: meals are almost always only 50% deductible.

Examples:

On Wednesday, Liz Brushstroke drives to NYC to deliver some artwork to the gallery for a new show. The opening is taking place 2 days later, on Friday. Both Liz and the gallery owner know that it will be good for business if Liz is at the opening, so she stays on in NYC through Friday and drives back on Saturday. This is primarily business. Consequently, Liz will be able to deduct almost 100% of the costs of the trip. She can use either the IRS per diem rates for meals while in NYC or keep her actual receipts (remember that meals are only 50% deductible).

Guy Focal has a chance to go to the "Printers Row Lit Fest" in Chicago to promote his new children's book. The publisher has agreed to pay for his flight to Chicago, but he will have to cover all his expenses while there personally. Guy has a good friend in Chicago who he stays with, so his lodging expenses will be zero. What deductible travel expenses will he have? He will be able to deduct all his meals, taxi fares, and other ground transportation; he has some entertainment expenses for taking his publisher out to lunch; and he purchases some other children's books at the show for research purposes, etc.

Use of the IRS Per Diem Rates

The U.S. Government publishes and continually adjusts per diem rates for meals, incidentals, and lodging worldwide (www.gsa.gov). Per diem rates for meals and incidentals work a little like the standard mileage allowance discussed earlier. If the artist decides that keeping receipts is too time consuming, he or she can choose to use these standard rates for all their meals and incidentals while traveling in a particular year. The IRS explains the standard rate in its Publication 463:

You generally can deduct a standard amount for your daily meals and incidental expenses (M&IE) while you are traveling away from home on business. In this publication, "standard meal allowance" refers to the federal rate for M&IE (which varies based on where and when you travel).

Incidental expenses. These include, but are not limited to, your costs for the following items:

1. Laundry, cleaning and pressing of clothing.

2. Fees and tips for persons who provide services, such as porters and baggage carriers.

Incidental expenses do not include taxicab fares, lodging taxes, or the costs of telegrams or telephone calls.

The standard meal allowance method is an alternative to the actual cost method. It allows you to deduct a set amount, depending on where and when you travel, instead of keeping records of your actual costs. If you use the standard meal allowance, you still must keep records to prove the time, place, and business purpose of your travel.

Caution. There is no optional standard lodging amount similar to the standard meal allowance. Your allowable lodging expense deduction is your actual cost.

Who can use the standard meal allowance? You can use the standard meal allowance whether you are an employee or self-employed, and whether or not you are reimbursed for your traveling expenses. You cannot use the standard meal allowance if you are related to your employer.

Use of the standard meal allowance for other travel. You can use the standard meal allowance to prove meal expenses you have when you travel in connection with investment and other income-producing property. You can also use it to prove meal expenses you have when you travel for qualifying educational purposes. You cannot use the standard meal allowance to prove the amount of your meals when you travel for medical or charitable purposes.

Amount of standard meal allowance. The standard meal allowance is the federal M&IE rate. For travel in 2016, the rate is $51 a day for most areas in the United States. Other locations in the United States are designated as high-cost areas, qualifying for higher standard meal allowances of up to $74 per day (visit www.gsa.gov/perdiem for the most current information).

If you travel to more than one location in one day, use the rate in effect for the area where you stop for sleep or rest.

50% limit may apply. If you are not reimbursed or if you are reimbursed under a non-accountable plan for meal expenses, you can generally deduct only 50% of the standard meal allowance. If you are reimbursed under an accountable plan and you are deducting amounts that are more than your reimbursements, you can deduct only 50% of the excess amount.

Standard meal allowance for areas outside the continental United States. The standard meal allowance rates do not apply to travel in Alaska, Hawaii, or any other locations outside the continental United States. The federal per diem rates for these locations are published monthly in the Maximum Travel Per Diem Allowances for Foreign Areas.

The general CONUS (continental United States) per diem rate for 2016 is $140 a day. This is allocated as $89 for lodging and $51 for meals and incidentals. Locations deemed to be "high cost" localities, such as New York City and Los Angeles, will have higher meals and incidental per diem rates. The U.S. Government also publishes foreign per diem rates OCONUS (outside continental United States) to be used for foreign travel. Rates vary from city to city; to get the latest per diem rates go to our website www.artstaxinfo.com for a link or visit the U.S. General Services Administration Website, www.gsa .gov/perdiem. The GSA also has a killer per diem app for your smartphone.

Artists can choose to use the meals and incidentals per diem rates for all their business travel in lieu of keeping receipts. Please note: you cannot use a per diem rate for lodging; for that you must always have receipts. If your employer reimburses you using the U.S. Government per diem rates, you may be able to deduct any amount that you spend in excess of the per diem.

A question frequently asked is whether the artist has any tax deductions if the employer covers or reimburses the artist for all expenses. The answer centers on what type of expense plan the employer operates. The IRS allows two basic plans:

1. Accountable Plan—If the employer has what is called an "accountable plan," the artist will typically not have any tax-deductible costs. In this scenario, either the artist is reimbursed using the U.S. Government per diem allowances or the artist submits all receipts and details on an expense report (or similar document) and the employer reimburses the artist directly for all the costs. Sometimes the employer may pay a hotel bill and other expenses directly. In an accountable plan, if all the costs are being covered by the employer, the artist will have not have any tax deductions. If your employer would have covered a particular expense but you forgot to submit it, can you deduct the expense? Absolutely not! Say our bassist, Sonny Phunky, notices when he is doing his tax returns that he forgot to submit a hotel bill to a band he was employed with during the year. If his contract clearly stated that all living

expenses would be covered (the IRS will review these contracts if they audit him), he will not be able to deduct the bills, even if he is past the point of getting reimbursed by the employer. This hotel bill becomes what I call a "tax orphan" that nobody gets to deduct!

2. Nonaccountable Plan—This plan allows the employer simply to give the artist a flat amount in addition to wages on the W-2 to "cover" expenses. Using this system, the artist would be able to deduct all allowable expenses incurred.

Entertainment Expenses

The issue of entertaining, like many others, takes on a different hue for the artist. While some entertaining the artist might do is clearly business related (such as meeting with his or her agent over lunch), a lot of entertaining the artist considers "business related," the IRS views with suspicion. Before looking at specific examples of business entertainment, let's see how the IRS views the subject in their Publication 463:

General rule:

You can deduct ordinary and necessary expenses to entertain a client, customer, or employee if the expenses meet the directly related test or the associated test.

Definitions:

✓ Entertainment includes any activity generally considered to provide entertainment, amusement, or recreation, and includes meals provided to a customer or client.

✓ An ordinary expense is one that is common and accepted in your field of business, trade, or profession.

✓ A necessary expense is one that is helpful and appropriate, although not necessarily indispensable, for your business.

Tests to meet the directly related test:

✓ Entertainment took place in a clear business setting, or

✓ Main purpose of entertainment was the active conduct of business, and

✓ You did engage in business with the person during the entertainment period, and

✓ You had more than a general expectation of getting income or some other specific business benefit.

Associated test

- ✓ Entertainment is associated with your trade or business, and

- ✓ Entertainment directly precedes or follows a substantial business discussion

Other rules

- ✓ You cannot deduct the cost of your meal as an entertainment expense if you are claiming the meal as a travel expense.

- ✓ You cannot deduct expenses that are lavish or extravagant under the circumstances.

- ✓ You generally can deduct only 50% of your unreimbursed entertainment expenses.

You can see the IRS takes a hard line view on business entertainment (no surprise there!). It is up to the artist to keep the kind of records necessary to support the deduction. Interestingly, although the IRS does not require a receipt if the cost of the entertainment is less than $75, they are definitely going to ask for substantiation. Your main friend here will be a detailed schedule diary (such as printouts from your computer, smartphone, or tablet) that lists who was present, what business matters were discussed, and where the event was held. Contemporaneous notes are critical and highly valued by the IRS.

Substantiating Your Deductions for Travel, Meals, and Entertainment

The area of travel, meals, and entertainment presents difficult substantiation issues for the artist. It is easy to keep records when you pay your business phone, buy a professional book or magazine, pay an agent, etc., but when you take a potential employer, buyer, agent, publisher, producer, or colleague out to lunch, how do you "account" for that? What will the IRS ask for to substantiate your travel, meals, and entertainment deductions?

You will need two types of records in case the IRS comes knocking:

1. A printed record of your activity (you may live in the digital world, rest assured the Internal Revenue Service does not). No matter what technology you use—computer, smartphone, or tablet, on the cloud or not—print out a hard copy of your schedule or safely back it up so you can. Record the details of the travel, entertainment, and meals, including time, place, who was present, and the specific business purpose.

2. Receipts and itemized bills for meals and entertainment instances under $75 don't require a receipt (an entry in your "diary" will do);

lodging, meals, and entertainment *over* $75 do. For these costs, keep all receipts and itemized bills.

Here are the exceptions (you knew they were coming!):

1. Receipts for transportation expenses of $75 or more are required only when they are readily obtainable. This is in response to our era of "ticketless" travel. In this case, if you do have a boarding pass or receipt, keep it.

2. A canceled check or credit card statement is not usually considered adequate in and of itself, though many IRS agents will accept them as corroborating evidence. If you cannot provide a bill, receipt, or voucher, you may be able use other evidence such as written statements from witnesses.

Receipts should show the following:
- ✓ Amount of expense
- ✓ Date of expense
- ✓ Where the expense occurred

In addition to the above information (which would typically be preprinted on most receipts), the artist should get into the habit of writing the "who, why, and where" directly on the receipts or in their diary/schedule book. For a meal or entertainment expense jot down:

1. *Who* was there.

2. *Why* they were there—what the business purpose was (and be as specific as possible!).

3. *Where* the event was—was it in an atmosphere conducive to business discussions?

The IRS always wants itemized receipts of such things as hotel bills in order to ferret out personal items such as phone calls, gift purchases, and movie rentals that may be lurking on the bill.

Are there excuses for *not* having adequate records?

1. Substantial Compliance: If you have made a good faith effort to comply with IRS requirements, you will not be penalized if you do not satisfy every requirement. In other words, missing one or two receipts or forgetting to make notes on a few meal receipts will not necessarily be grounds for the IRS to throw out an expense.

2. Accidental Destruction of Records: House fire, flood, mudslides, or other circumstances beyond your control cause your records

to be destroyed. In this situation you are allowed to reasonably reconstruct your deductions.

3.   Exceptional Circumstances—I doubt if anyone knows what the heck this means; the IRS certainly doesn't explain it in its regulations. The IRS states that if due to the "inherent nature of the situation" you are unable to keep receipts or records you may present alternative evidence.

Be very careful in relying on these "excuses." As Internal Revenue Service audits have become more stringent, I am not sure that these would prove very effective.

The "QPA"—Qualified Performing Artist

The concept of the QPA entered the tax code during the tax act of 1986. In that act, many, many deductions were diminished or completely abolished by moving them around on the return. One such move was Form 2106, used to deduct employee business expenses. Prior to 1986, the 2106 was a very common form, quite logically used to take employee business deductions directly on the front page of the 1040 with no need to itemize. In 1986, the 2106 was moved from the front page of the 1040 and became an itemized deduction on Schedule A. Not only that; it was now subject to a dreaded 2% floor! This means that you automatically lose part of your deductions: the amount that is equal to 2% of your adjusted gross income. Due in part to the work of Actors' Equity Association and of Stage Source (among others), a provision was installed in the code of 1986 for what is termed the "qualified performing artist," or QPA. The IRS explains the QPA this way in its Publication 529:

> If you are a qualified performing artist, you can deduct your employee business expenses as an adjustment to income rather than as a miscellaneous itemized deduction. To qualify, you must meet all three of the following requirements:
>
> 1.   You perform services in the performing arts for at least two employers during your tax year. [You are considered to have performed services in the performing arts for an employer only if that employer paid you $200 or more.]
>
> 2.   Your related performing-arts business expenses are more than 10% of your gross income from the performance of such services.
>
> 3.   Your adjusted gross income is not more than $16,000 before deducting these business expenses.
>
> If you do not meet all of the above requirements, you must deduct your expenses as a miscellaneous itemized deduction on schedule A subject to the 2% limit.

Special rules for married persons. If you are married, you must file a joint return unless you lived apart from your spouse at all times during the tax year.

If you file a joint return, you must figure requirements (1) and (2) above separately for both you and your spouse. However, requirement (3) applies to your and your spouse's combined adjusted gross income.

Where to report. If you meet all of the above requirements, you should first complete Form 2106 or Form 2106-EZ. Then you include your performing-arts related expenses from line 10 of Form 2106 or from line 6 of Form 2106-EZ on line 32 of Form 1040. Then write "QPA" and the amount of your performing-arts related expenses on the dotted line next to line 32 (Form 1040).

There has been great consternation regarding the fact that the QPA is so limited. These thresholds have never been increased since the measure was adopted in 1986! So, the QPA provision is useful to fewer and fewer folks each year, but it is still a great tax benefit for low-income performers.

The "Hobby Loss" Issue

When you begin your career in the arts, it is quite likely that your expenses will exceed your income, resulting in a loss on your tax return. When this happens in succeeding years you have the potential for the IRS to declare your career as an artist a "hobby."

How does the IRS deem an activity to be a hobby (something "not engaged in for profit" to use its terminology)? This is how it is explained in Publication 535:

> If you do not carry on your business or investment activity to make a profit, there is a limit on the deductions you can take. You cannot use a loss from the activity to offset other income. Activities you do as a hobby, or mainly for sport or recreation, come under this limit. So does an investment activity intended only to produce tax losses for the investors.
>
> The limit on not-for-profit losses applies to individuals, partnerships, estates, trusts, and S corporations. It does not apply to corporations other than S corporations.
>
> In determining whether you are carrying on an activity for profit, all the facts are taken into account. No one factor alone is decisive. Among the factors to consider are whether:
>
> 1. You carry on the activity in a businesslike manner,
>
> 2. The time and effort you put into the activity indicate you intend to make it profitable,

3. You depend on income from the activity for your livelihood,

4. Your losses are due to circumstances beyond your control (or are normal in the start-up phase of your type of business),

5. You change your methods of operation in an attempt to improve profitability,

6. You, or your advisors, have the knowledge needed to carry on the activity as a successful business,

7. You were successful in making a profit in similar activities in the past,

8. The activity makes a profit in some years, and

9. You can expect to make a future profit from the appreciation of the assets used in the activity.

Many things that one would consider a "hobby" are obvious. Examples would include the attorney who attempts to turn his stamp collecting into a business, thus creating a tax deductible loss, or the doctor who tries to write off his horse-breeding hobby as a business. Unfortunately, the IRS has established a codified "test" for deciding what constitutes a hobby. This "presumption of profit" test below is from Publication 535:

An activity is presumed carried on for profit if it produced a profit in at least 3 of the last 5 tax years, including the current year. You have a profit when the gross income from an activity is more than the deductions for it.

If a taxpayer dies before the end of the 5-year period, the period ends on the date of the taxpayer's death.

If your business or investment activity passes this 3-years-of-profit test, presume it is carried on for profit. This means it will not come under these limits. You can take all your business deductions from the activity, even for the years that you have a loss. You can rely on this presumption in every case, unless the IRS shows it is not valid.

Using the presumption later. If you are starting an activity and do not have 3 years showing a profit, you may want to take advantage of this presumption later, after you have the 5 years of experience allowed by the test.

You can choose to do this by filing Form 5213. Filing this form postpones any determination that your activity is not carried on for profit until 5 years have passed since you started the activity.

The benefit gained by making this choice is that the IRS will not immediately question whether your activity is engaged in for profit. Accordingly, it will not restrict your deductions. Rather, you will gain time to earn a profit in 3 out of the first 5 years you carry on the activity. If you show 3 years of profit at the end of this period, your deductions are not limited under these rules. If you do not have 3 years of profit, the limit can be applied retroactively to any year in the 5-year period with a loss.

Filing Form 5213 automatically extends the period of limitations on any year in the 5-year period to 2 years after the due date of the return for the last year of the period. The period is extended only for deductions of the activity and any related deductions that might be affected.

This "hobby loss" is an audit trap that you do not want to land in, as it can be very expensive. The IRS is not automatically tracking this deduction through its computer (at least not yet), and it is only likely to come up in an audit situation when the agent has the opportunity (or reason) to look at several consecutive years of returns. Are artists dead in the water if they have had three consecutive years of losses? Not necessarily. The Second Circuit Court said in a decision issued in 1995: "Code section 183 [the section where the "hobby loss" provisions live] isn't designed to punish the inept—only those who deliberately engage in unprofitable activities and with a view to sheltering income." There are numerous instances where the tax court has allowed folks to write off continual losses against the wishes of the IRS, but be prepared for a fight. Complete and detailed records of your ongoing activities can make a huge difference.

To me, the hobby loss is where you see the palpable difference between the person who opens a local hardware store and the artist. That's because success is obviously and historically far more elusive for the artist than it is for the retail store owner. When Fred opens his corner hardware store he will quickly close it if he is not making money, whereas folks in the arts will often go on for years racking up losses searching for that "big break."

Unfortunately for us, when this issue rears its head the IRS agent often views the artist and Fred's Corner Hardware store in exactly the same light. In the same way he or she examines Fred's hardware store, the IRS agent will look at your career in the arts as strictly a business proposition, so you will need to clearly prove that you have a profit motive. The heart of this matter is that you have to show that you are attempting to *make money*. It's that simple. Your records need to show clearly a concerted, consistent, ongoing, business-like effort to land the next acting job, sell the next article, publish the new book, get the gig, land the recording contract, or sell the artwork. Your career in the arts needs to have all the attributes of a business in every sense of the word.

Start-up Costs

If you are new to your profession as an artist, you may initially incur what the IRS calls "start-up costs." Start-up costs are legitimate, deductible expenses that occur before the business has actually started; for example, a writer who spends the first 2 years of a career writing his or her first book. Since no manuscripts were produced and, more importantly, no marketing of any of the author's works was undertaken, all the deductions from the first 2 years would be deemed by the IRS to be start-up costs. If you have start-up costs, the expenses are added together and then written off (*amortized*) over 5 years.

In Closing . . .

We have looked at some of the larger expense issues and have seen how the IRS views these matters by looking at their publications. Now let us move on to more specific applications. In the next four chapters we will visit our four artists-in-residence in turn and see how all this information plays out in each of their returns.

4

For Actors, Actresses, Directors, Dancers, and Other Performers

In this chapter I will look in detail at the activities of our good friend Ima Starr, the kind of income and deductions she had for the year, and how they manifest themselves in her 2016 tax return.

First, let's walk through some of the expense items for show biz folks specifically. I will also note in parentheses the type of record keeping the IRS would require:

1. Union dues, professional societies, and organizations (invoices and payment verification).

2. Professional fees for agents, attorneys, and accountants (invoices and payment verification).

3. Professional registries (both printed and cloud based) including Players Directory, The Creative Index, IMDb (Internet Movie Database), IBDb (Internet Broadway Database), RoleCall, etc. (invoices and payment verification).

4. Classes and coaching lessons (invoices and payment verification).

5. Cosmetics and dressing room supplies—this does not include street makeup or what you use going to auditions, but does include makeup for showcases. The IRS can be very aggressive on makeup, so write the name of the show the makeup was used for on the back of the receipt (sales receipts, invoices, credit card receipts, and payment verification).

6. Hair care—this must be for a specific job, not general, looking-for-work upkeep. I recommend that if a director wants you to change hairstyle or color and is not going to pay for it, ask to have a rider put into your contract stating this fact (sales receipts, invoices, credit card receipts, and payment verification).

7. Photographs, headshots, and résumés—including videos, CDs, CD-ROMs, DVDs, and digital image transfers for use on the Internet or your personal website (sales receipts, invoices, credit card receipts, and payment verification).

8. Stationery and postage (sales receipts and payment verification).

9. Theatre and film books, scripts, musical scores, sheet music, batteries, tapes, CDs, etc.—these fall under the heading of supplies and may need to be allocated between employment income and contract income (sales receipts, invoices, credit card receipts, and payment verification).

10. Telephone, Skype, cellular phone, and Internet communications—actual business calls on your home phone are deductible, but the IRS does not allow the allocation of the base monthly rate. You can deduct only the actual long distance charges. The same rule is true with your cellular or online phone service. If you utilize a call forwarding service you might have to allocate that service between business and personal. If you get a second phone line strictly for business then it can be considered 100% deductible (bills and payment verification).

11. Wardrobe—this is professional wardrobe not conventional street wear! The rule says if you can wear it on the street, you can't deduct it. Remember that if the wardrobe is deductible then the cleaning is as well. Write on the back of the bill the name of the show that the wardrobe was used in (sales receipts, invoices, credit card receipts, and payment verification).

12. Viewing theatre, films, and concerts (live, DVD, online video, as well as streaming services such as Netflix, HULU, Amazon, and, of course, cable)—I often call this expense line item "research"; others refer to it as "performance audit." Whatever you call it, make sure to allocate some of this expense to personal use. After all, you must sometimes take part in these activities for personal enjoyment; it can't be all business. I quote to clients the old Wall Street saying, "the pigs get fat and the hogs get slaughtered." This is the type of deduction that you must not get piggy with. While the IRS typically hates this deduction, it does clearly acknowledge its validity in its audit guidelines. In an audit you would need to explain specifically what the professional value was (ticket stubs, receipts, and diary entries).

13. Promotional tickets—only your ticket is deductible, not your date's. That is, unless your date is your agent, a producer, or some other professional colleague (ticket stubs, receipts, and diary entries).

14. Rehearsal hall rental (invoices and payment verification).

15. Accompanist, arranger, personal assistant, etc.—this person must have a defined business purpose. For instance, if your assistant is paying your personal bills or engaging in nonbusiness activities, it will not be deductible (bills, invoices, and payment verification).

16. Office rent—you must be able to prove you need one (bills, invoices, and payment verification).

17. Purchase of equipment—computers, tablets, smartphones, printers, cameras, video, and sound equipment, etc. (bills, invoices, and credit card receipts).

18. Repair of equipment used in your profession—computers, musical instruments, sound and video equipment, cameras, etc. (bills, credit card receipts, invoices, and payment verification).

19. Tax preparation, bookkeeping and accounting fees (bills, invoices, and payment verification).

20. Demo tapes, videos, DVDs, and commercial prints used in promotional activities (bills, invoices, and payment verification).

21. Trade advertisements (bills, invoices, payment verification, and credit card receipts).

22. Travel—hotels, airline, meals (per diem generally), Airbnb, Uber, train, bus, baggage fees, etc. (confirmation and payment verification). Very important: documentation proving the reason for the trip (bills, invoices, payment verification, and credit card receipts).

23. Internet service—for research purposes, business e-mail, and e-mail while on the road. Be sure to allocate some of the costs for personal use (bills, invoices, and credit card receipts).

24. Web hosting and cloud services (bills, invoices, payment verification, and credit card receipts).

25. Trade papers and professional magazines (bills, invoices, payment verification, and credit card receipts).

26. Backstage tips—note: you cannot give these folks gifts (payment verification and diary entry).

27. Insurance (bills, invoices, and payment verification).

28. Copyright fees (invoices and payment verification).

We already know our resident actor, Ima, has been very busy. She is a member of Actors' Equity and received multiple W-2s this year for her work in theatre and films. She was also a part-time singer in the group The Blue Jazzbos. She had even found the time to do some modeling, and she finally finished her book, a book about the struggles of an African-American, multi-disciplined female artist/performer in the modern world. Luckily, she downloaded our Excel spreadsheet for performers and writers (found on www .artstaxinfo.com), loaded it on her notebook computer at the beginning of the tax year, and carefully tracked her expenses all year!

We will now review Ima's 1040 income tax return in detail (remember, you can download the current year's version from our website, www.artstaxinfo .com).

We'll review some of Ima's employment (W-2) income. In Chapter 1 we saw her W-2 from the Goodwrench Dinner Theatre in Philadelphia for her work in *Love Letters*. We discover that the Goodwrench is barely surviving, so it could not offer her any expense reimbursements. This means that Ima can deduct virtually all her costs while staying in Philadelphia. These include meals, using the Philadelphia per diem rate of $64 (ww.gsa.gov), actual hotel accommodations, clothes cleaning, communications costs, cell phone, Internet service, and any commissions associated with that gig. She can also deduct any professional costs associated with the show: wardrobe (if unsuited for street wear), scripts, etc.

Ima also had a small W-2 for some residual income from a TV production she was in the prior year.

Ima's next gig was a great job in California: a small part in a movie starring Mel Funn. Mel's production company—Springtime for Kaminsky, Inc.—employed her. She was paid $40,000 on a W-2 for this work. Because the company paid all her transportation and living expenses she will have no deductions for those (both Actors' Equity and the Screen Actors Guild [SAG] operate "Accountable Plans" as far as expense reimbursements are concerned, which means that Ima's reimbursements will not usually appear on her W-2). To prepare for her role, Ima purchased Blu-rays of all of Mr. Funn's movies and bought a Kindle book about his life. She also bought a new Blu-ray player; together these expenses will all be deductible as research on her Form 2106 (employee business expense). The Blu-ray player could be depreciated over 5 years, or she could use the Section 179 election and write it all off this year. She might choose to allocate some of the Blu-ray player cost as personal expenses and write off only a percentage of the player. To do further research into Mr. Funn's career, Ima used her Internet service, making part of her Internet service deductible. All the expenses associated with this job will be deducted on her Form 2106.

All of Ima's W-2 forms will be aggregated and reported on Line 7 of her 1040 form.

On the strength of some of the connections Ima made in California during the above-mentioned gig, she made a second trip to California. Ima wanted to be certain the trip would be 100% deductible, so she set up appointments in advance and consulted *Variety* (a tax-deductible expense) to see what open auditions and productions would be taking place during her stay. She needed to ensure she had enough daily activity to show the IRS that the trip was primarily business. During her 6-day stay in California, Ima set up lunch appointments almost every day with various industry types who had job potential for her. She arranged in advance an appointment with folks in Mel Funn's production company regarding other potential film assignments. While in California Ima stayed with a friend at no cost to her, consequently there will be no deduction for hotel. She was able to take the $64 Los Angeles per diem rate for meals. Ima will be able to deduct her travel, taxi (or rental car), etc., as business related, and her meals with the industry types as business entertainment deductions. Ima dutifully noted the "who, what, and where" of each meal in her smartphone, which she later printed out to retain a hard copy for her permanent record. Indeed, she recorded notes in her smartphone regarding all her business activity while in LA. By doing her homework and planning her trip in advance she had made it far more likely that an IRS agent would consider the trip a legitimate business deduction.

What if Ima did not have a friend in LA to stay with; would she be able to deduct her hotel or Airbnb costs and nonentertainment meals while there? Absolutely yes! This trip will also be deducted on her Form 2106 because the expenses are related to her (potential) W-2 employment income.

As a result of this second visit to California, Ima got a part in a movie playing Katherine Stinson, a famous woman aviator. To prepare for the role she searched the Internet and located an individual who owned a plane similar to the one this famous flyer would have flown. She offered to pay the plane's owner to take her flying and help give her a feel for the plane. This individual did not charge her, but she did have to travel some distance to meet with him. Because this research was for a particular role and had a clear, well-defined purpose, all the costs associated with this trip will be fully deductible. Ima will need to have some evidence of the trip, such as a letter from the plane's owner or perhaps a photograph of her with the plane.

During the summer, Ima landed some summer stock work on Cape Cod. The theatre offers no monetary reimbursement, but provides the players a place to live while there. Ima would have expenses for meals and incidentals, but obviously not for lodging. Ima uses the IRS per diem rates for all her meals and incidentals throughout the year. The daily rate for Martha's Vineyard on Cape Cod, MA (a designated high-cost locality), is $74 a day for 2016. Of course, her mileage driving to the Cape, including the ferry, and auto use while there, would be deductible on her Form 2106.

In late summer Ima had a chance to audition for a musical being staged in London's West End. She flew to London for the audition, then decided to stay on for several weeks for a vacation. Her agent had arranged for her to meet with other theatre and film folk while there. She and her accountant decided that she had spent about 30% of her time on clearly defined, business-related activities. These activities included appointments with agents, casting directors, and other actors. She kept business cards and made notes in her schedule book regarding each meeting so that she had records backing up the business purpose. To gauge what the British theatre scene was like, she attended some performances. The IRS might balk at these theatre ticket expenses, but Ima figures it is worth a try. She kept all the ticket stubs and noted the business reason in her diary. Because the trip was outside the United States and more than 25% of the trip was personal, Ima will prorate the trip's costs, taking 30% only as a business expense. As this would be potential W-2 income, these deductions are found on her Form 2106.

Next, Ima goes on a tour singing with The Blue Jazzbos. This activity will be reported on its own Schedule C on her 1040. It was a short southern tour with no expenses reimbursed. She had considered setting up an LLC with her bandmates but it seemed too complicated for such a small tour. It was decided that she would declare all the income from the tour on her tax return and then pay her band as sidemen as a deduction. This will be her largest expense and she will need to make sure she obtains their names, addresses, and Social Security numbers, as she will need to have her accountant issue them 1099s at year-end (this expense will be found as part of Line 4 of her Schedule C).

Ima decided to purchase a new Yamaha sound system and Sennheiser microphone, as the one she had been using was no longer adequate and she was not sure if the clubs would have good sound systems.

The income from the tour will be reported on Ima's Schedule C because it is self-employment income. The depreciation for the sound system and microphone will be written off over 5 years and deducted on her Schedule C, as will all her travel expenses. To help her work up a Peggy Lee medley for the tour, Ima downloaded a new *Singles* box set by Ms. Lee; this will become another expense on her Schedule C. Ima also took a few lessons, which are tax deductible, from a noted New York singer to work on her stage presence. The leader of the Jazzbos wanted the band members to get new formal wear for the tour. As you know, for clothing to be deductible it has to be:

1.   Required to keep your job
2.   Not suitable for wear when not working

Ima bought an evening gown expressly for this tour. This is not a clear-cut deduction, but the IRS has allowed the deduction of formal wear for musicians. If Ima can deduct the clothing, she can also deduct the cleaning of the gown. The band members will also have some income from selling copies of their self-produced CD. Copies of the CD that Ima purchases to sell will become a "cost of goods sold" on her Schedule C.

Back in New York, Ima did a series of small modeling assignments. These were all paid as contract income and, other than some mileage expenses going between jobs, she did not have any direct expenses. For simplicity, and because the modeling income was relatively low, Ima's tax preparer chose to include this income on Schedule C for The Blue Jazzbos.

Because Ima is fairly well known in NYC, she had a unique opportunity to endorse a well-known local brand of pizza during the year. Lombardi's Pizzeria starred Ima in its local cable TV ad. In addition to her pay, she received free pizza for a year. At the end of the year, the pizzeria estimated that Ima had received about $550 worth of pizza. Ima declared the $550 value of the pizza as self-employment income on her modeling Schedule C.

Ima received the first $13,000 advance royalty income from her book in January. This income will be reported on a separate Schedule C. She had allocated some expenses for her home office, computer, tablet, printer, office supplies, Internet use, etc. She added the expense of a writing class she had taken at Columbia University earlier in the year while she was finishing her book. For the Columbia class, Ima has the choice of using the Lifetime Learning credit or taking the expense as a deduction on her Schedule C. Her accountant will calculate it both ways to see what yields the most tax benefit. She included some research expense, as she had purchased a Kindle and read some other famous Hollywood and theatre memoirs. In May, as she was finishing her book, she flew out to California to visit with a colleague to check on the accuracy of some incidents she had used. She was in LA for 2 days interviewing her friend. The entire cost of this trip would be deductible against her book income.

· In response to some bootleg videos showing up on YouTube, Ima decided that she wanted to set up a personal website where she could post her résumé, pictures, sound and video clips of her singing with The Blue Jazzbos, and perhaps even some video clips of her acting. The costs of setting up the website, registering her domain name, and hosting the site will all be deductible. The IRS stipulates that website development be written off (amortized) over 3 years. So all the costs of setting up and designing the site will be added up (capitalized) and expensed over 3 years.

In the fall, Ima decided to purchase some video equipment to experiment with filmmaking and allow her to shoot her own promotional videos. Because it is directly related to her career, the cost of the equipment will be deductible. She did not have the cash to purchase the equipment outright, so she charged it on her credit card and is paying a little off each month. The full cost of the equipment will be deductible in the current year and will be depreciated over 5 years.

Near the end of the year, an audition opportunity in Chicago came up. Ima arrived in Chicago on Monday evening and had her audition on Tuesday morning. She waited in town to hear back from the director on Wednesday. On Wednesday afternoon she received a callback, and met with the director again on Thursday morning. After the callback, she decided to stay on and visit with a friend for a few days; she returned to NYC on Sunday. She can clearly show that a preponderance of time was spent in directly related business activities. Therefore, 100% of her airline travel expenses to Chicago would be deductible. Her other expenses, such as hotel, meals, and incidentals, would be fully deductible through Thursday (the day the business part of the trip ended). The meals and lodging expenses while she was visiting her friend would not be deductible. These expenses would be found on her Form 2106. (FYI: if the scales tip the other way and the trip begins to be more personal than business, none of the travel expense is deductible.)

Ima is considering moving to California and calls her accountant to ask them if the move would be deductible. She finds out that she has two main criteria to meet. The first concerns distance, the second relates to time. Here are the details from IRS Publication 521:

1. Your move will meet the distance test if your new main job location is at least 50 miles farther from your former home than your old main job location was from your former home. For example, if your old job was 3 miles from your former home, your new job must be at least 53 miles from that former home.

2. If you are an employee, you must work full time for at least 39 weeks during the first 12 months after you arrive in the general area of your new job location. For this time test, count only your full-time work as

an employee; do not count any work you do as a self-employed person. You do not have to work for the same employer for the 39 weeks. You do not have to work 39 weeks in a row. However, you must work full time within the same general commuting area. Full-time employment depends on what is usual for your type of work in your area.

The moving deduction can be a difficult issue for folks in the arts such as Ima. Employment and income is often not consistent, making it hard to meet the 39-week rule. The key phrase to focus on is: *employment depends on what is usual for your type of work in your area.* Ima will have to be ready to argue that her employment and work circumstances were typical for her acting, singing, and modeling jobs. If she thinks she will have a tax-deductible move she will be saving receipts for the following costs according to the IRS Publication 521:

1. Moving your household goods and personal effects (including in-transit storage expenses), and

2. Traveling (including lodging but not meals) to your new home.

Actors, Directors, & Other Performing Artists

Continuing Education

Coaching & Lessons	
Dance Training	
Music—Arrangements	
Tapes, CDs, & Recordings	
Training	
Rents—Rehearsal Hall	
Tickets—Performance Audit/Research	
Voice Training	
Other: _____	

Promotional Expenses

Audition Tapes, Videos, & DVDs	
Business Cards	
Film & Processing	
Mailing Supplies—Envelopes, etc.	
Photos—Professional	
Website Development & Hosting	
Resume & Portfolio Expenses	
Other: _____	

Supplies & Other Expenses

Alterations/Repairs (costumes)	
Cleaning (costumes/wardrobe)	
Costumes—Wardrobe (special business)	
Dues—Union & Professional	
Gifts—Business ($25 maximum per person per year)	
Insurance—Equipment	
Interest—Business Loans	
Makeup—Cosmetics (special business)	
Manicure—(special for hand inserts)	
Meals—Business (100% of cost)	
Photocopy—Scripts, etc.	
Postage & Office Supplies	
Props, Stunt Supplies	
Publications—Trade	
Rents—Office, Storage, etc.	
Rents—Equipment, Costumes, etc.	
Repairs—Equipment	
Secretarial & Bookkeeping	
Commissions—Agent/Manager	
Other: _____	

Auto Travel (in miles)

Auditions	
Business Meetings	
Continuing Education	
Job Seeking	
Out-of-Town Business Trips	
Purchasing Job Supplies & Materials	
Professional Society Meetings	
Parking Fees & Tolls	
Other: _____	

Travel—Out of Town

Airfare	
Car Rental	
Parking	
Taxi, Train, Bus, & Subway	
Lodging (do not combine with meals)	
Apartment Rent (jobs lasting less than 1 year)	
Meals (do not combine with lodging)	
Laundry & Porter	
Bridge & Highway Tolls	
Telephone Calls (including home)	
Other: _____	

Communications

Cellular Calls	
FAX, Data, & Other Online Services	
Paging & Call Forwarding Service	
Skype or Other Internet Phone Service	
Land Line	
Other: _____	

Equipment Purchases

Answering Machine	
Smart Phones & Tablets	
Audio Systems	
Musical Instruments	
Pager and Recorder	
Camera & Video Equipment	
Speaker Systems	
Computers, Software, & Printers	
Office Furniture	
Other: _____	

| Form **1040** | Department of the Treasury—Internal Revenue Service   (99) | | | | |
| **U.S. Individual Income Tax Return** | **2015** | OMB No. 1545-0074 | IRS Use Only—Do not write or staple in this space. | | |

For the year Jan. 1–Dec. 31, 2015, or other tax year beginning _____ , 2015, ending _____ , 20 ___   See separate instructions.

Your first name and initial	Last name	Your social security number
Ima	Starr	111-22-3333
If a joint return, spouse's first name and initial	Last name	Spouse's social security number

Home address (number and street). If you have a P.O. box, see instructions. | Apt. no.

5th Ave

▲ Make sure the SSN(s) above and on line 6c are correct.

City, town or post office, state, and ZIP code. If you have a foreign address, also complete spaces below (see instructions).

New York NY 10019

Presidential Election Campaign
Check here if you, or your spouse if filing jointly, want $3 to go to this fund. Checking a box below will not change your tax or refund.   ☐ You ☐ Spouse

Foreign country name	Foreign province/state/county	Foreign postal code

Filing Status

Check only one box.

1 ☒ Single
2 ☐ Married filing jointly (even if only one had income)
3 ☐ Married filing separately. Enter spouse's SSN above and full name here. ▶
4 ☐ Head of household (with qualifying person). (See instructions.) If the qualifying person is a child but not your dependent, enter this child's name here. ▶
5 ☐ Qualifying widow(er) with dependent child

Exemptions

6a ☒ **Yourself.** If someone can claim you as a dependent, **do not** check box 6a . . . .
b ☐ **Spouse** . . . . .

Boxes checked on 6a and 6b   1

c **Dependents:**

(1) First name Last name	(2) Dependent's social security number	(3) Dependent's relationship to you	(4) ✓ If child under age 17 qualifying for child tax credit (see instructions)
			☐
			☐
			☐
			☐

If more than four dependents, see instructions and check here ▶ ☐

No. of children on 6c who:
• lived with you _____
• did not live with you due to divorce or separation (see instructions) _____

Dependents on 6c not entered above _____

Add numbers on lines above ▶ [1]

d   Total number of exemptions claimed

Income

Attach Form(s) W-2 here. Also attach Forms W-2G and 1099-R if tax was withheld.

If you did not get a W-2, see instructions.

7	Wages, salaries, tips, etc. Attach Form(s) W-2	7	49,905.
8a	**Taxable** interest. Attach Schedule B if required	8a	19.
b	Tax-exempt interest. **Do not** include on line 8a . . .	8b	
9a	Ordinary dividends. Attach Schedule B if required . . .	9a	
b	Qualified dividends	9b	
10	Taxable refunds, credits, or offsets of state and local income taxes	10	
11	Alimony received	11	
12	Business income or (loss). Attach Schedule C or C-EZ	12	7,115.
13	Capital gain or (loss). Attach Schedule D if required. If not required, check here ▶ ☐	13	
14	Other gains or (losses). Attach Form 4797	14	
15a	IRA distributions .	15a		b Taxable amount . . .	15b	
16a	Pensions and annuities	16a		b Taxable amount . . .	16b	
17	Rental real estate, royalties, partnerships, S corporations, trusts, etc. Attach Schedule E	17	
18	Farm income or (loss). Attach Schedule F	18	
19	Unemployment compensation	19	
20a	Social security benefits	20a		b Taxable amount . . .	20b	
21	Other income. List type and amount Gambling Winnings	21	1,000.
22	Combine the amounts in the far right column for lines 7 through 21. This is your **total income** ▶	22	58,039.

Adjusted Gross Income

23	Educator expenses . . .	23	
24	Certain business expenses of reservists, performing artists, and fee-basis government officials. Attach Form 2106 or 2106-EZ	24	
25	Health savings account deduction. Attach Form 8889 .	25	
26	Moving expenses. Attach Form 3903 . . .	26	
27	Deductible part of self-employment tax. Attach Schedule SE .	27	503.
28	Self-employed SEP, SIMPLE, and qualified plans . .	28	
29	Self-employed health insurance deduction	29	
30	Penalty on early withdrawal of savings	30	
31a	Alimony paid b Recipient's SSN ▶ _____	31a	
32	IRA deduction	32	
33	Student loan interest deduction	33	
34	Tuition and fees. Attach Form 8917	34	
35	Domestic production activities deduction. Attach Form 8903	35	
36	Add lines 23 through 35	36	503.
37	Subtract line 36 from line 22. This is your **adjusted gross income** . . . . . ▶	37	57,536.

For Disclosure, Privacy Act, and Paperwork Reduction Act Notice, see separate instructions. **BAA**   REV 12/30/15 PRO   Form **1040** (2015)

Form 1040 (2015)   Page **2**

Tax and Credits	38	Amount from line 37 (adjusted gross income)	38	57,536.
	39a	Check if: ☐ **You** were born before January 2, 1951, ☐ Blind. ☐ **Spouse** was born before January 2, 1951, ☐ Blind. } Total boxes checked ▶ 39a ☐		
Standard Deduction for—	b	If your spouse itemizes on a separate return or you were a dual-status alien, check here ▶ 39b ☐		
• People who check any box on line 39a or 39b **or** who can be claimed as a dependent, **see** instructions.	40	**Itemized deductions** (from Schedule A) **or your standard deduction** (see left margin) . .	40	11,769.
	41	Subtract line 40 from line 38	41	45,767.
	42	**Exemptions.** If line 38 is $154,950 or less, multiply $4,000 by the number on line 6d. Otherwise, see instructions	42	4,000.
	43	**Taxable income.** Subtract line 42 from line 41. If line 42 is more than line 41, enter -0- . .	43	41,767.
	44	**Tax** (see instructions). Check if any from: a ☐ Form(s) 8814 b ☐ Form 4972 c ☐ _____	44	6,238.
• All others:	45	**Alternative minimum tax** (see instructions). Attach Form 6251	45	
Single or Married filing separately, $6,300	46	Excess advance premium tax credit repayment. Attach Form 8962	46	
	47	Add lines 44, 45, and 46 . . . . ▶	47	6,238.
Married filing jointly or Qualifying widow(er), $12,600	48	Foreign tax credit. Attach Form 1116 if required	48		
	49	Credit for child and dependent care expenses. Attach Form 2441	49		
	50	Education credits from Form 8863, line 19	50		
Head of household, $9,250	51	Retirement savings contributions credit. Attach Form 8880	51		
	52	Child tax credit. Attach Schedule 8812, if required. . .	52		
	53	Residential energy credits. Attach Form 5695	53		
	54	Other credits from Form: a ☐ 3800 b ☐ 8801 c ☐ ___	54		
	55	Add lines 48 through 54. These are your **total credits**	55	
	56	Subtract line 55 from line 47. If line 55 is more than line 47, enter -0- . . . . ▶	56	6,238.
Other Taxes	57	Self-employment tax. Attach Schedule SE	57	1,005.
	58	Unreported social security and Medicare tax from Form: a ☐ 4137 b ☐ 8919 . .	58	
	59	Additional tax on IRAs, other qualified retirement plans, etc. Attach Form 5329 if required . .	59	
	60a	Household employment taxes from Schedule H	60a	
	b	First-time homebuyer credit repayment. Attach Form 5405 if required	60b	
	61	Health care: individual responsibility (see instructions) Full-year coverage ☒ . .	61	
	62	Taxes from: a ☐ Form 8959 b ☐ Form 8960 c ☐ Instructions; enter code(s) _____	62	
	63	Add lines 56 through 62. This is your **total tax** . . . . ▶	63	7,243.
Payments	64	Federal income tax withheld from Forms W-2 and 1099 .	64	7,530.	
	65	2015 estimated tax payments and amount applied from 2014 return	65		
If you have a qualifying child, attach Schedule EIC.	66a	**Earned income credit (EIC)** . . . No	66a		
	b	Nontaxable combat pay election	66b			
	67	Additional child tax credit. Attach Schedule 8812 . . .	67		
	68	American opportunity credit from Form 8863, line 8 . . .	68		
	69	Net premium tax credit. Attach Form 8962	69		
	70	Amount paid with request for extension to file	70		
	71	Excess social security and tier 1 RRTA tax withheld . . .	71		
	72	Credit for federal tax on fuels. Attach Form 4136 . . .	72		
	73	Credits from Form: a ☐ 2439 b ☐ Reserved c ☐ 8885 d ☐ ___	73		
	74	Add lines 64, 65, 66a, and 67 through 73. These are your **total payments** . . . . . ▶	74	7,530.
Refund	75	If line 74 is more than line 63, subtract line 63 from line 74. This is the amount you **overpaid**	75	287.
	76a	Amount of line 75 you want **refunded to you.** If Form 8888 is attached, check here . ▶ ☐	76a	287.
Direct deposit? ▶ See instructions. ▶	b	Routing number X X X X X X X X X ▶ c Type: ☐ Checking ☐ Savings		
	d	Account number X X X X X X X X X X X X X X X X X		
	77	Amount of line 75 you want **applied to your 2016 estimated tax** ▶	77	
Amount You Owe	78	**Amount you owe.** Subtract line 74 from line 63. For details on how to pay, see instructions ▶	78	
	79	Estimated tax penalty (see instructions)	79		
Third Party Designee		Do you want to allow another person to discuss this return with the IRS (see instructions)? ☐ **Yes. Complete below.** ☒ **No**		
		Designee's name ▶ _____ Phone no. ▶ _____ Personal identification number (PIN) ▶ _____		

Sign Here

Joint return? See instructions.
Keep a copy for your records.

Under penalties of perjury, I declare that I have examined this return and accompanying schedules and statements, and to the best of my knowledge and belief, they are true, correct, and complete. Declaration of preparer (other than taxpayer) is based on all information of which preparer has any knowledge.

Your signature	Date	Your occupation	Daytime phone number
		Performer/Writer	
Spouse's signature. If a joint return, **both** must sign.	Date	Spouse's occupation	If the IRS sent you an Identity Protection PIN, enter it here (see inst.)

Paid Preparer Use Only

Print/Type preparer's name	Preparer's signature	Date	Check ☐ if self-employed	PTIN
Peter Jason Riley CPA	Peter Jason Riley CPA	01/22/2016		P00413102
Firm's name ▶ RILEY & ASSOCIATES, P.C.			Firm's EIN ▶ 04-3577120	
Firm's address ▶ 5 PERRY WAY - P O BOX 157 NEWBURYPORT MA 01950			Phone no. (978)463-9350	

www.irs.gov/form1040   REV 12/30/15 PRO Form **1040** (2015)

SCHEDULE A (Form 1040)		**Itemized Deductions**		OMB No. 1545-0074
Department of the Treasury Internal Revenue Service (99)		► Information about Schedule A and its separate instructions is at *www.irs.gov/schedulea*. ► **Attach to Form 1040.**		20**15** Attachment Sequence No. **07**

Name(s) shown on Form 1040	Your social security number
Ima Starr	111-22-3333

Caution: Do not include expenses reimbursed or paid by others.

Medical and Dental Expenses	1	Medical and dental expenses (see instructions)	1			
	2	Enter amount from Form 1040, line 38 **2**				
	3	Multiply line 2 by 10% (.10). But if either you or your spouse was born before January 2, 1951, multiply line 2 by 7.5% (.075) instead	3			
	4	Subtract line 3 from line 1. If line 3 is more than line 1, enter -0-		4		

Taxes You Paid	5	State and local **(check only one box):**				
		a ☒ Income taxes, **or** }	5		2,854.	
		b ☐ General sales taxes				
	6	Real estate taxes (see instructions)	6			
	7	Personal property taxes	7		204.	
	8	Other taxes. List type and amount ► _____				
			8			
	9	Add lines 5 through 8		9		3,058.

Interest You Paid	10	Home mortgage interest and points reported to you on Form 1098	10			
Note: Your mortgage interest deduction may be limited (see instructions).	11	Home mortgage interest not reported to you on Form 1098. If paid to the person from whom you bought the home, see instructions and show that person's name, identifying no., and address ► _____ _____	11			
	12	Points not reported to you on Form 1098. See instructions for special rules	12			
	13	Mortgage insurance premiums (see instructions)	13			
	14	Investment interest. Attach Form 4952 if required. (See instructions.)	14			
	15	Add lines 10 through 14		15		

Gifts to Charity	16	Gifts by cash or check. If you made any gift of $250 or more, see instructions	16		325.	
If you made a gift and got a benefit for it, see instructions.	17	Other than by cash or check. If any gift of $250 or more, see instructions. You **must** attach Form 8283 if over $500 . . .	17			
	18	Carryover from prior year	18			
	19	Add lines 16 through 18		19		325.

Casualty and Theft Losses	20	Casualty or theft loss(es). Attach Form 4684. (See instructions.)		20		

Job Expenses and Certain Miscellaneous Deductions	21	Unreimbursed employee expenses—job travel, union dues, job education, etc. Attach Form 2106 or 2106-EZ if required. (See instructions.) ► Deductible expenses from Form 2106	21		9,537.	
	22	Tax preparation fees	22			
	23	Other expenses—investment, safe deposit box, etc. List type and amount ► _____ _____	23			
	24	Add lines 21 through 23	24		9,537.	
	25	Enter amount from Form 1040, line 38 **25** 57,536.				
	26	Multiply line 25 by 2% (.02)	26		1,151.	
	27	Subtract line 26 from line 24. If line 26 is more than line 24, enter -0-		27		8,386.

Other Miscellaneous Deductions	28	Other—from list in instructions. List type and amount ► _____ _____		28		

Total Itemized Deductions	29	Is Form 1040, line 38, over $154,950? ☒ **No.** Your deduction is not limited. Add the amounts in the far right column for lines 4 through 28. Also, enter this amount on Form 1040, line 40. ☐ **Yes.** Your deduction may be limited. See the Itemized Deductions Worksheet in the instructions to figure the amount to enter. } . .		29		11,769.
	30	If you elect to itemize deductions even though they are less than your standard deduction, check here . . . . ► ☐				

For Paperwork Reduction Act Notice, see Form 1040 instructions.   **BAA**   REV 12/30/15 PRO   Schedule A (Form 1040) 2015

SCHEDULE C
(Form 1040)

Department of the Treasury
Internal Revenue Service (99)

Profit or Loss From Business
(Sole Proprietorship)

▶ Information about Schedule C and its separate instructions is at *www.irs.gov/schedulec*.
▶ Attach to Form 1040, 1040NR, or 1041; partnerships generally must file Form 1065.

OMB No. 1545-0074

20**15**

Attachment
Sequence No. **09**

Name of proprietor	Social security number (SSN)
Ima Starr	111-22-3333

A	Principal business or profession, including product or service (see instructions)	B Enter code from instructions
	Writer	▶ 7 1 1 5 1 0

C	Business name. If no separate business name, leave blank.	D Employer ID number (EIN), (see instr.)
	Ima Starr	

E	Business address (including suite or room no.) ▶ 5th Ave
	City, town or post office, state, and ZIP code New York, NY 10019

F Accounting method: **(1)** ☒ Cash   **(2)** ☐ Accrual   **(3)** ☐ Other (specify) ▶ _____

G Did you "materially participate" in the operation of this business during 2015? If "No," see instructions for limit on losses . ☒ Yes ☐ No

H If you started or acquired this business during 2015, check here . . . . ▶ ☐

I Did you make any payments in 2015 that would require you to file Form(s) 1099? (see instructions) . . . . . . ☐ Yes ☒ No

J If "Yes," did you or will you file required Forms 1099? . . . . ☐ Yes ☒ No

Part I   Income

1	Gross receipts or sales. See instructions for line 1 and check the box if this income was reported to you on Form W-2 and the "Statutory employee" box on that form was checked . . . . ▶ ☐	1	13,000.
2	Returns and allowances	2	
3	Subtract line 2 from line 1	3	13,000.
4	Cost of goods sold (from line 42)	4	
5	**Gross profit.** Subtract line 4 from line 3	5	13,000.
6	Other income, including federal and state gasoline or fuel tax credit or refund (see instructions)	6	
7	**Gross income.** Add lines 5 and 6 . . . . ▶	7	13,000.

Part II   Expenses. Enter expenses for business use of your home **only** on line 30.

8	Advertising	8		18	Office expense (see instructions)	18	89.
9	Car and truck expenses (see instructions)	9	532.	19	Pension and profit-sharing plans .	19	
				20	Rent or lease (see instructions):		
10	Commissions and fees .	10		a	Vehicles, machinery, and equipment	20a	
11	Contract labor (see instructions)	11		b	Other business property . . .	20b	
12	Depletion	12		21	Repairs and maintenance . . .	21	
13	Depreciation and section 179 expense deduction (not included in Part III) (see instructions)	13	333.	22	Supplies (not included in Part III) .	22	
				23	Taxes and licenses	23	
				24	Travel, meals, and entertainment:		
14	Employee benefit programs (other than on line 19) . .	14		a	Travel	24a	489.
15	Insurance (other than health)	15		b	Deductible meals and entertainment (see instructions) .	24b	32.
16	Interest:			25	Utilities	25	
a	Mortgage (paid to banks, etc.)	16a		26	Wages (less employment credits) .	26	
b	Other	16b		27a	Other expenses (from line 48) .	27a	4,914.
17	Legal and professional services	17	100.	b	**Reserved for future use** . . .	27b	

28	**Total expenses** before expenses for business use of home. Add lines 8 through 27a . . . . . . ▶	28	6,489.
29	Tentative profit or (loss). Subtract line 28 from line 7	29	6,511.
30	Expenses for business use of your home. Do not report these expenses elsewhere. Attach Form 8829 unless using the simplified method (see instructions).
Simplified method filers only: enter the total square footage of: (a) your home: _____ and (b) the part of your home used for business: _____. Use the Simplified Method Worksheet in the instructions to figure the amount to enter on line 30	30	2,653.
31	**Net profit or (loss).** Subtract line 30 from line 29.
• If a profit, enter on both **Form 1040, line 12** (or **Form 1040NR, line 13**) and on **Schedule SE, line 2.** (If you checked the box on line 1, see instructions). Estates and trusts, enter on **Form 1041, line 3.**
• If a loss, you **must** go to line 32.	31	3,858.
32	If you have a loss, check the box that describes your investment in this activity (see instructions).
• If you checked 32a, enter the loss on both **Form 1040, line 12,** (or **Form 1040NR, line 13**) and on **Schedule SE, line 2.** (If you checked the box on line 1, see the line 31 instructions). Estates and trusts, enter on **Form 1041, line 3.**
• If you checked 32b, you **must** attach **Form 6198.** Your loss may be limited.	32a ☒ All investment is at risk.
32b ☐ Some investment is not at risk.

For Paperwork Reduction Act Notice, see the separate instructions.   **BAA**   REV 12/07/15 PRO   Schedule C (Form 1040) 2015

Schedule C (Form 1040) 2015   Page **2**

Part III	**Cost of Goods Sold** (see instructions)

33 Method(s) used to
value closing inventory: **a** ☐ Cost   **b** ☐ Lower of cost or market   **c** ☐ Other (attach explanation)

34 Was there any change in determining quantities, costs, or valuations between opening and closing inventory?
If "Yes," attach explanation . . . . ☐ **Yes**   ☐ **No**

35	Inventory at beginning of year. If different from last year's closing inventory, attach explanation . . .	**35**	
36	Purchases less cost of items withdrawn for personal use	**36**	
37	Cost of labor. Do not include any amounts paid to yourself	**37**	
38	Materials and supplies	**38**	
39	Other costs	**39**	
40	Add lines 35 through 39	**40**	
41	Inventory at end of year	**41**	
42	**Cost of goods sold.** Subtract line 41 from line 40. Enter the result here and on line 4	**42**	

Part IV	**Information on Your Vehicle.** Complete this part **only** if you are claiming car or truck expenses on line 9 and are not required to file Form 4562 for this business. See the instructions for line 13 to find out if you must file Form 4562.

43 When did you place your vehicle in service for business purposes? (month, day, year)   ▶ ----------------------------

44 Of the total number of miles you drove your vehicle during 2015, enter the number of miles you used your vehicle for:

a Business ----------------   **b** Commuting (see instructions) ----------------   **c** Other ----------------

45 Was your vehicle available for personal use during off-duty hours? . . . . ☐ Yes   ☐ No

46 Do you (or your spouse) have another vehicle available for personal use? . . . . ☐ Yes   ☐ No

47a Do you have evidence to support your deduction? . . . . ☐ Yes   ☐ No

   b If "Yes," is the evidence written? . . . . ☐ Yes   ☐ No

Part V	**Other Expenses.** List below business expenses not included on lines 8–26 or line 30.

Education (Columbia)	2,124.
Research (E-Books)	299.
Internet Service	189.
Cell Phone	204.
Agent Commissions	2,000.
Skype Charges	98.

48	**Total other expenses.** Enter here and on line 27a	**48**	4,914.

SCHEDULE C
(Form 1040)

Department of the Treasury
Internal Revenue Service (99)

Profit or Loss From Business
(Sole Proprietorship)

▶ Information about Schedule C and its separate instructions is at *www.irs.gov/schedulec*.
▶ Attach to Form 1040, 1040NR, or 1041; partnerships generally must file Form 1065.

OMB No. 1545-0074

20**15**

Attachment
Sequence No. **09**

Name of proprietor	Social security number (SSN)
Ima Starr	111-22-3333

A Principal business or profession, including product or service (see instructions)
▶ Blue Jazzbos

B Enter code from instructions
▶ 7 1 1 5 1 0

C Business name. If no separate business name, leave blank.
The Blue Jazzbos

D Employer ID number (EIN), (see instr.)

E Business address (including suite or room no.) ▶ 5th Ave
City, town or post office, state, and ZIP code   New York, NY 10019

F Accounting method: (1) ☒ Cash (2) ☐ Accrual (3) ☐ Other (specify) ▶ _____

G Did you "materially participate" in the operation of this business during 2015? If "No," see instructions for limit on losses   ☒ Yes ☐ No

H If you started or acquired this business during 2015, check here . . . . ▶ ☐

I Did you make any payments in 2015 that would require you to file Form(s) 1099? (see instructions) . . . . . ☒ Yes ☐ No

J If "Yes," did you or will you file required Forms 1099? . . . . ☒ Yes ☐ No

Part I Income

1	Gross receipts or sales. See instructions for line 1 and check the box if this income was reported to you on Form W-2 and the "Statutory employee" box on that form was checked . . . . ▶ ☐	1	12,620.
2	Returns and allowances	2	
3	Subtract line 2 from line 1	3	12,620.
4	Cost of goods sold (from line 42)	4	6,179.
5	**Gross profit.** Subtract line 4 from line 3	5	6,441.
6	Other income, including federal and state gasoline or fuel tax credit or refund (see instructions)	6	2,445.
7	**Gross income.** Add lines 5 and 6 . . . . ▶	7	8,886.

Part II Expenses. Enter expenses for business use of your home **only** on line 30.

8	Advertising	8		18	Office expense (see instructions)	18	
9	Car and truck expenses (see instructions)	9		19	Pension and profit-sharing plans .	19	
				20	Rent or lease (see instructions):		
10	Commissions and fees .	10		a	Vehicles, machinery, and equipment	20a	
11	Contract labor (see instructions)	11		b	Other business property . . .	20b	
12	Depletion	12		21	Repairs and maintenance . . .	21	
13	Depreciation and section 179 expense deduction (not included in Part III) (see instructions).	13	759.	22	Supplies (not included in Part III) .	22	204.
				23	Taxes and licenses	23	
				24	Travel, meals, and entertainment:		
14	Employee benefit programs (other than on line 19) . .	14		a	Travel	24a	1,944.
15	Insurance (other than health)	15		b	Deductible meals and entertainment (see instructions) .	24b	362.
16	Interest:			25	Utilities	25	
a	Mortgage (paid to banks, etc.)	16a		26	Wages (less employment credits) .	26	
b	Other	16b		27a	Other expenses (from line 48) . .	27a	2,260.
17	Legal and professional services	17	100.	b	**Reserved for future use** . . .	27b	
28	**Total expenses** before expenses for business use of home. Add lines 8 through 27a . . . . . . ▶					28	5,629.
29	Tentative profit or (loss). Subtract line 28 from line 7					29	3,257.
30	Expenses for business use of your home. Do not report these expenses elsewhere. Attach Form 8829 unless using the simplified method (see instructions). **Simplified method filers only:** enter the total square footage of: (a) your home: _____ and (b) the part of your home used for business: _____. Use the Simplified Method Worksheet in the instructions to figure the amount to enter on line 30					30	
31	**Net profit or (loss).** Subtract line 30 from line 29. • If a profit, enter on both **Form 1040, line 12** (or **Form 1040NR, line 13**) and on **Schedule SE, line 2.** (If you checked the box on line 1, see instructions). Estates and trusts, enter on **Form 1041, line 3.** • If a loss, you **must** go to line 32.					31	3,257.
32	If you have a loss, check the box that describes your investment in this activity (see instructions). • If you checked 32a, enter the loss on both **Form 1040, line 12,** (or **Form 1040NR, line 13**) and on **Schedule SE, line 2.** (If you checked the box on line 1, see the line 31 instructions). Estates and trusts, enter on **Form 1041, line 3.** • If you checked 32b, you **must** attach Form 6198. Your loss may be limited.					32a ☒ All investment is at risk. 32b ☐ Some investment is not at risk.	

For Paperwork Reduction Act Notice, see the separate instructions.   **BAA**   REV 12/07/15 PRO   Schedule C (Form 1040) 2015

Schedule C (Form 1040) 2015   Page **2**

Part III   **Cost of Goods Sold** (see instructions)

33 Method(s) used to value closing inventory: **a** ☐ Cost   **b** ☐ Lower of cost or market   **c** ☐ Other (attach explanation)

34 Was there any change in determining quantities, costs, or valuations between opening and closing inventory? If "Yes," attach explanation . . . . ☐ Yes   ☐ No

35	Inventory at beginning of year. If different from last year's closing inventory, attach explanation	35	
36	Purchases less cost of items withdrawn for personal use	36	
37	Cost of labor. Do not include any amounts paid to yourself	37	5,980.
38	Materials and supplies	38	199.
39	Other costs	39	
40	Add lines 35 through 39	40	6,179.
41	Inventory at end of year	41	
42	**Cost of goods sold.** Subtract line 41 from line 40. Enter the result here and on line 4	42	6,179.

Part IV   **Information on Your Vehicle.** Complete this part **only** if you are claiming car or truck expenses on line 9 and are not required to file Form 4562 for this business. See the instructions for line 13 to find out if you must file Form 4562.

43 When did you place your vehicle in service for business purposes? (month, day, year) ▶ ------------------

44 Of the total number of miles you drove your vehicle during 2015, enter the number of miles you used your vehicle for:

a Business ------------   **b** Commuting (see instructions) ------------   **c** Other ------------

45 Was your vehicle available for personal use during off-duty hours? . . . . ☐ Yes   ☐ No

46 Do you (or your spouse) have another vehicle available for personal use? . . . . ☐ Yes   ☐ No

47a Do you have evidence to support your deduction? . . . . ☐ Yes   ☐ No

b If "Yes," is the evidence written? . . . . ☐ Yes   ☐ No

Part V   **Other Expenses.** List below business expenses not included on lines 8–26 or line 30.

AMORTIZATION	358.
Formal Wear (stage clothes)	304.
Cell Phone	239.
Music Research - Downloads and Streaming	341.
Promo Photos	305.
Trade Publications (Billboard)	299.
Coaching/Education	350.
Skype Charges	64.
48 Total other expenses. Enter here and on line 27a	48	2,260.

REV 12/07/15 PRO   Schedule C (Form 1040) 2015

SCHEDULE SE (Form 1040) Department of the Treasury Internal Revenue Service (99)	**Self-Employment Tax** ▶ Information about Schedule SE and its separate instructions is at *www.irs.gov/schedulese.* ▶ **Attach to Form 1040 or Form 1040NR.**	OMB No. 1545-0074 20**15** Attachment Sequence No. **17**

Name of person with **self-employment** income (as shown on Form 1040 or Form 1040NR) Ima Starr	Social security number of person with **self-employment** income ▶	111-22-3333

Before you begin: To determine if you must file Schedule SE, see the instructions.

May I Use Short Schedule SE or Must I Use Long Schedule SE?

Note. Use this flowchart **only if** you must file Schedule SE. If unsure, see *Who Must File Schedule SE* in the instructions.

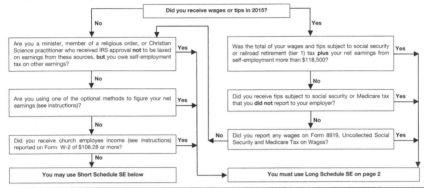

Section A—Short Schedule SE. **Caution.** Read above to see if you can use Short Schedule SE.

1a	Net farm profit or (loss) from Schedule F, line 34, and farm partnerships, Schedule K-1 (Form 1065), box 14, code A	**1a**	
b	If you received social security retirement or disability benefits, enter the amount of Conservation Reserve Program payments included on Schedule F, line 4b, or listed on Schedule K-1 (Form 1065), box 20, code Z	**1b**	( )
2	Net profit or (loss) from Schedule C, line 31; Schedule C-EZ, line 3; Schedule K-1 (Form 1065), box 14, code A (other than farming); and Schedule K-1 (Form 1065-B), box 9, code J1. Ministers and members of religious orders, see instructions for types of income to report on this line. See instructions for other income to report	**2**	7,115.
3	Combine lines 1a, 1b, and 2	**3**	7,115.
4	Multiply line 3 by 92.35% (.9235). If less than $400, you do not owe self-employment tax; **do not** file this schedule unless you have an amount on line 1b . . . . ▶	**4**	6,571.
	Note. If line 4 is less than $400 due to Conservation Reserve Program payments on line 1b, see instructions.		
5	**Self-employment tax.** If the amount on line 4 is: • $118,500 or less, multiply line 4 by 15.3% (.153). Enter the result here and on **Form 1040, line 57,** or **Form 1040NR, line 55** • More than $118,500, multiply line 4 by 2.9% (.029). Then, add $14,694 to the result. Enter the total here and on **Form 1040, line 57,** or **Form 1040NR, line 55**	**5**	1,005.
6	**Deduction for one-half of self-employment tax.** Multiply line 5 by 50% (.50). Enter the result here and on **Form 1040, line 27,** or **Form 1040NR, line 27**	**6**	503.	

For Paperwork Reduction Act Notice, see your tax return instructions. **BAA**   REV 12/04/15 PRO   Schedule SE (Form 1040) 2015

Form **2106-EZ**

Unreimbursed Employee Business Expenses

▶ Attach to Form 1040 or Form 1040NR.

Department of the Treasury
Internal Revenue Service (99)   ▶ Information about Form 2106 and its separate instructions is available at *www.irs.gov/form2106*.

OMB No. 1545-0074

20**15**

Attachment
Sequence No. **129A**

Your name	Occupation in which you incurred expenses	Social security number
Ima Starr	Actress	111-22-3333

You Can Use This Form Only if All of the Following Apply.

• You are an employee deducting ordinary and necessary expenses attributable to your job. An ordinary expense is one that is common and accepted in your field of trade, business, or profession. A necessary expense is one that is helpful and appropriate for your business. An expense does not have to be required to be considered necessary.

• You **do not** get reimbursed by your employer for any expenses (amounts your employer included in box 1 of your Form W-2 are not considered reimbursements for this purpose).

• If you are claiming vehicle expense, you are using the standard mileage rate for 2015.

Caution: *You can use the standard mileage rate for 2015 **only if: (a)** you owned the vehicle and used the standard mileage rate for the first year you placed the vehicle in service, **or (b)** you leased the vehicle and used the standard mileage rate for the portion of the lease period after 1997.*

Part I   **Figure Your Expenses**

1	Complete Part II. Multiply line 8a by 57.5¢ (.575). Enter the result here	**1**	1,097.
2	Parking fees, tolls, and transportation, including train, bus, etc., that **did not** involve overnight travel or commuting to and from work	**2**	306.
3	Travel expense while away from home overnight, including lodging, airplane, car rental, etc. **Do not** include meals and entertainment	**3**	3,866.
4	Business expenses not included on lines 1 through 3. **Do not** include meals and entertainment	**4**	2,652.
5	Meals and entertainment expenses: $ 3,231. × 50% (.50). (Employees subject to Department of Transportation (DOT) hours of service limits: Multiply meal expenses incurred while away from home on business by 80% (.80) instead of 50%. For details, see instructions.)	**5**	1,616.
6	**Total expenses.** Add lines 1 through 5. Enter here and on **Schedule A (Form 1040), line 21** (or on **Schedule A (Form 1040NR), line 7**). (Armed Forces reservists, fee-basis state or local government officials, qualified performing artists, and individuals with disabilities: See the instructions for special rules on where to enter this amount.)	**6**	9,537.

Part II   **Information on Your Vehicle.** Complete this part **only** if you are claiming vehicle expense on line 1.

7   When did you place your vehicle in service for business use? (month, day, year) ▶ 01/01/2011

8   Of the total number of miles you drove your vehicle during 2015, enter the number of miles you used your vehicle for:

a   Business 1,908   **b** Commuting (see instructions) 2,000   **c** Other 7,613

9   Was your vehicle available for personal use during off-duty hours? . . . . ☒ **Yes** ☐ **No**

10   Do you (or your spouse) have another vehicle available for personal use? . . . . ☐ **Yes** ☒ **No**

11a   Do you have evidence to support your deduction? . . . . ☒ **Yes** ☐ **No**

b   If "Yes," is the evidence written? . . . . ☒ **Yes** ☐ **No**

For Paperwork Reduction Act Notice, see your tax return instructions. **BAA**   REV 01/07/16 PRO   Form **2106-EZ** (2015)

Form 8829

Department of the Treasury
Internal Revenue Service (99)

Expenses for Business Use of Your Home

▶ File only with Schedule C (Form 1040). Use a separate Form 8829 for each home you used for business during the year.
▶ Information about Form 8829 and its separate instructions is at *www.irs.gov/form8829*.

OMB No. 1545-0074

2015

Attachment
Sequence No. **176**

Name(s) of proprietor(s)	Your social security number
Ima Starr Writer	111-22-3333

Part I   Part of Your Home Used for Business

1	Area used regularly and exclusively for business, regularly for daycare, or for storage of inventory or product samples (see instructions)	**1**	177
2	Total area of home	**2**	1,241
3	Divide line 1 by line 2. Enter the result as a percentage	**3**	14.26 %

For daycare facilities not used exclusively for business, go to line 4. All others, go to line 7.

4	Multiply days used for daycare during year by hours used per day	**4**		hr.
5	Total hours available for use during the year (365 days x 24 hours) (see instructions)	**5**	8,760	hr.
6	Divide line 4 by line 5. Enter the result as a decimal amount	**6**		
7	Business percentage. For daycare facilities not used exclusively for business, multiply line 6 by line 3 (enter the result as a percentage). All others, enter the amount from line 3 ▶	**7**		14.26 %

Part II   Figure Your Allowable Deduction

8	Enter the amount from Schedule C, line 29, **plus** any gain derived from the business use of your home, **minus** any loss from the trade or business not derived from the business use of your home (see instructions)	**8**	6,511.

See instructions for columns **(a)** and **(b)** before completing lines 9–21.

			(a) Direct expenses	(b) Indirect expenses		
9	Casualty losses (see instructions)	**9**				
10	Deductible mortgage interest (see instructions)	**10**				
11	Real estate taxes (see instructions)	**11**				
12	Add lines 9, 10, and 11	**12**				
13	Multiply line 12, column (b) by line 7		**13**			
14	Add line 12, column (a) and line 13				**14**	
15	Subtract line 14 from line 8. If zero or less, enter -0-				**15**	6,511.
16	Excess mortgage interest (see instructions)	**16**				
17	Insurance	**17**		515.		
18	Rent	**18**		16,500.		
19	Repairs and maintenance	**19**		399.		
20	Utilities	**20**		1,189.		
21	Other expenses (see instructions)	**21**				
22	Add lines 16 through 21	**22**		18,603.		
23	Multiply line 22, column (b) by line 7			**23**	2,653.	
24	Carryover of prior year operating expenses (see instructions)		**24**			
25	Add line 22, column (a), line 23, and line 24				**25**	2,653.
26	Allowable operating expenses. Enter the **smaller** of line 15 or line 25				**26**	2,653.
27	Limit on excess casualty losses and depreciation. Subtract line 26 from line 15				**27**	3,858.
28	Excess casualty losses (see instructions)		**28**			
29	Depreciation of your home from line 41 below		**29**			
30	Carryover of prior year excess casualty losses and depreciation (see instructions)		**30**			
31	Add lines 28 through 30				**31**	
32	Allowable excess casualty losses and depreciation. Enter the **smaller** of line 27 or line 31				**32**	
33	Add lines 14, 26, and 32				**33**	2,653.
34	Casualty loss portion, if any, from lines 14 and 32. Carry amount to **Form 4684** (see instructions)				**34**	
35	**Allowable expenses for business use of your home.** Subtract line 34 from line 33. Enter here and on Schedule C, line 30. If your home was used for more than one business, see instructions ▶				**35**	2,653.

Part III   Depreciation of Your Home

36	Enter the **smaller** of your home's adjusted basis or its fair market value (see instructions)	**36**	
37	Value of land included on line 36	**37**	
38	Basis of building. Subtract line 37 from line 36	**38**	
39	Business basis of building. Multiply line 38 by line 7	**39**	
40	Depreciation percentage (see instructions)	**40**	%
41	Depreciation allowable (see instructions). Multiply line 39 by line 40. Enter here and on line 29 above	**41**	

Part IV   Carryover of Unallowed Expenses to 2016

42	Operating expenses. Subtract line 26 from line 25. If less than zero, enter -0-	**42**	0.
43	Excess casualty losses and depreciation. Subtract line 32 from line 31. If less than zero, enter -0-	**43**	

For Paperwork Reduction Act Notice, see your tax return instructions.   **BAA**   REV 12/04/15 PRO   Form **8829** (2015)

Form **4562**	**Depreciation and Amortization**	OMB No. 1545-0172
	(Including Information on Listed Property)	20**15**
Department of the Treasury Internal Revenue Service (99)	▶ Attach to your tax return. ▶ Information about Form 4562 and its separate instructions is at *www.irs.gov/form4562*.	Attachment Sequence No. **179**
Name(s) shown on return Ima Starr	Business or activity to which this form relates Sch C Writer	Identifying number 111-22-3333

Part I Election To Expense Certain Property Under Section 179

Note: If you have any listed property, complete Part V before you complete Part I.

1	Maximum amount (see instructions)	1	500,000.
2	Total cost of section 179 property placed in service (see instructions)	2	
3	Threshold cost of section 179 property before reduction in limitation (see instructions)	3	2,000,000.
4	Reduction in limitation. Subtract line 3 from line 2. If zero or less, enter -0-	4	
5	Dollar limitation for tax year. Subtract line 4 from line 1. If zero or less, enter -0-. If married filing separately, see instructions	5	

6	(a) Description of property	(b) Cost (business use only)	(c) Elected cost

7	Listed property. Enter the amount from line 29	7	
8	Total elected cost of section 179 property. Add amounts in column (c), lines 6 and 7	8	
9	Tentative deduction. Enter the **smaller** of line 5 or line 8	9	
10	Carryover of disallowed deduction from line 13 of your 2014 Form 4562	10	
11	Business income limitation. Enter the smaller of business income (not less than zero) or line 5 (see instructions)	11	
12	Section 179 expense deduction. Add lines 9 and 10, but do not enter more than line 11	12	
13	Carryover of disallowed deduction to 2016. Add lines 9 and 10, less line 12 ▶	13	

Note: Do not use Part II or Part III below for listed property. Instead, use Part V.

Part II Special Depreciation Allowance and Other Depreciation (Do not include listed property.) (See instructions.)

14	Special depreciation allowance for qualified property (other than listed property) placed in service during the tax year (see instructions)	14	
15	Property subject to section 168(f)(1) election	15	
16	Other depreciation (including ACRS)	16	

Part III MACRS Depreciation (Do not include listed property.) (See instructions.)

Section A

17	MACRS deductions for assets placed in service in tax years beginning before 2015	17	
18	If you are electing to group any assets placed in service during the tax year into one or more general asset accounts, check here . . . . ▶ ☐		

Section B—Assets Placed in Service During 2015 Tax Year Using the General Depreciation System

(a) Classification of property	(b) Month and year placed in service	(c) Basis for depreciation (business/investment use only—see instructions)	(d) Recovery period	(e) Convention	(f) Method	(g) Depreciation deduction
19a 3-year property						
b 5-year property		1,662.	5.0	HY	200 DB	333.
c 7-year property						
d 10-year property						
e 15-year property						
f 20-year property						
g 25-year property			25 yrs.		S/L	
h Residential rental property			27.5 yrs.	MM	S/L	
			27.5 yrs.	MM	S/L	
i Nonresidential real property			39 yrs.	MM	S/L	
				MM	S/L	

Section C—Assets Placed in Service During 2015 Tax Year Using the Alternative Depreciation System

20a Class life					S/L	
b 12-year			12 yrs.		S/L	
c 40-year			40 yrs.	MM	S/L	

Part IV Summary (See instructions.)

21	Listed property. Enter amount from line 28	21	
22	**Total.** Add amounts from line 12, lines 14 through 17, lines 19 and 20 in column (g), and line 21. Enter here and on the appropriate lines of your return. Partnerships and S corporations—see instructions	22	333.
23	For assets shown above and placed in service during the current year, enter the portion of the basis attributable to section 263A costs	23	

For Paperwork Reduction Act Notice, see separate instructions. **BAA**   REV 12/27/15 PRO   Form **4562** (2015)

Form 4562 (2015)   Page **2**

Part V **Listed Property** (Include automobiles, certain other vehicles, certain aircraft, certain computers, and property used for entertainment, recreation, or amusement.)

Note: For any vehicle for which you are using the standard mileage rate or deducting lease expense, complete **only** 24a, 24b, columns (a) through (c) of Section A, all of Section B, and Section C if applicable.

Section A—Depreciation and Other Information (Caution: See the instructions for limits for passenger automobiles.**)**

24a Do you have evidence to support the business/investment use claimed? ☒ Yes ☐ No | 24b If "Yes," is the evidence written? ☒ Yes ☐ No

(a) Type of property (list vehicles first)	(b) Date placed in service	(c) Business/ investment use percentage	(d) Cost or other basis	(e) Basis for depreciation (business/investment use only)	(f) Recovery period	(g) Method/ Convention	(h) Depreciation deduction	(i) Elected section 179 cost
25 Special depreciation allowance for qualified listed property placed in service during the tax year and used more than 50% in a qualified business use (see instructions) .					25			
26 Property used more than 50% in a qualified business use:								
		%						
		%						
		%						
27 Property used 50% or less in a qualified business use:								
Auto	01/01/2010	8.04 %				S/L –		
		%				S/L –		
		%				S/L –		
28 Add amounts in column (h), lines 25 through 27. Enter here and on line 21, page 1 .					28			
29 Add amounts in column (i), line 26. Enter here and on line 7, page 1							29	

Section B—Information on Use of Vehicles

Complete this section for vehicles used by a sole proprietor, partner, or other "more than 5% owner," or related person. If you provided vehicles to your employees, first answer the questions in Section C to see if you meet an exception to completing this section for those vehicles.

		(a) Vehicle 1		(b) Vehicle 2		(c) Vehicle 3		(d) Vehicle 4		(e) Vehicle 5		(f) Vehicle 6	
30 Total business/investment miles driven during the year (**do not** include commuting miles) .		926											
31 Total commuting miles driven during the year		2,000											
32 Total other personal (noncommuting) miles driven		8,595											
33 Total miles driven during the year. Add lines 30 through 32		11,521											
34 Was the vehicle available for personal use during off-duty hours?	Yes	No	Yes	No	Yes	No	Yes	No	Yes	No	Yes	No
		X											
35 Was the vehicle used primarily by a more than 5% owner or related person? . .	X											
36 Is another vehicle available for personal use?			X										

Section C—Questions for Employers Who Provide Vehicles for Use by Their Employees

Answer these questions to determine if you meet an exception to completing Section B for vehicles used by employees who **are not** more than 5% owners or related persons (see instructions).

	Yes	No
37 Do you maintain a written policy statement that prohibits all personal use of vehicles, including commuting, by your employees?		
38 Do you maintain a written policy statement that prohibits personal use of vehicles, except commuting, by your employees? See the instructions for vehicles used by corporate officers, directors, or 1% or more owners . .		
39 Do you treat all use of vehicles by employees as personal use?		
40 Do you provide more than five vehicles to your employees, obtain information from your employees about the use of the vehicles, and retain the information received?		
41 Do you meet the requirements concerning qualified automobile demonstration use? (See instructions.) . . .		

Note: If your answer to 37, 38, 39, 40, or 41 is "Yes," do not complete Section B for the covered vehicles.

Part VI **Amortization**

(a) Description of costs	(b) Date amortization begins	(c) Amortizable amount	(d) Code section	(e) Amortization period or percentage	(f) Amortization for this year
42 Amortization of costs that begins during your 2015 tax year (see instructions):					
43 Amortization of costs that began before your 2015 tax year			43		
44 **Total.** Add amounts in column (f). See the instructions for where to report			44		

REV 12/27/15 PRO   Form **4562** (2015)

Form **4562**	**Depreciation and Amortization**	OMB No. 1545-0172
	(Including Information on Listed Property)	**2015**
Department of the Treasury Internal Revenue Service (99)	▶ Attach to your tax return. ▶ Information about Form 4562 and its separate instructions is at *www.irs.gov/form4562*.	Attachment Sequence No. **179**

Name(s) shown on return	Business or activity to which this form relates	Identifying number
Ima Starr	Sch C Blue Jazzbos	111-22-3333

Part I   **Election To Expense Certain Property Under Section 179**

Note: If you have any listed property, complete Part V before you complete Part I.

1	Maximum amount (see instructions)	**1**	500,000.
2	Total cost of section 179 property placed in service (see instructions)	**2**	
3	Threshold cost of section 179 property before reduction in limitation (see instructions)	**3**	2,000,000.
4	Reduction in limitation. Subtract line 3 from line 2. If zero or less, enter -0-	**4**	
5	Dollar limitation for tax year. Subtract line 4 from line 1. If zero or less, enter -0-. If married filing separately, see instructions	**5**	

6	(a) Description of property	(b) Cost (business use only)	(c) Elected cost		

7	Listed property. Enter the amount from line 29	**7**	
8	Total elected cost of section 179 property. Add amounts in column (c), lines 6 and 7	**8**	
9	Tentative deduction. Enter the **smaller** of line 5 or line 8	**9**	
10	Carryover of disallowed deduction from line 13 of your 2014 Form 4562	**10**	
11	Business income limitation. Enter the smaller of business income (not less than zero) or line 5 (see instructions)	**11**	
12	Section 179 expense deduction. Add lines 9 and 10, but do not enter more than line 11	**12**	
13	Carryover of disallowed deduction to 2016. Add lines 9 and 10, less line 12 ▶	**13**		

Note: Do not use Part II or Part III below for listed property. Instead, use Part V.

Part II   **Special Depreciation Allowance and Other Depreciation (Do not** include listed property.) (See instructions.)

14	Special depreciation allowance for qualified property (other than listed property) placed in service during the tax year (see instructions)	**14**	
15	Property subject to section 168(f)(1) election	**15**	
16	Other depreciation (including ACRS)	**16**	

Part III   **MACRS Depreciation (Do not** include listed property.) (See instructions.)

Section A

17	MACRS deductions for assets placed in service in tax years beginning before 2015	**17**	
18	If you are electing to group any assets placed in service during the tax year into one or more general asset accounts, check here . . . . ▶ ☐		

Section B—Assets Placed in Service During 2015 Tax Year Using the General Depreciation System

(a) Classification of property	(b) Month and year placed in service	(c) Basis for depreciation (business/investment use only—see instructions)	(d) Recovery period	(e) Convention	(f) Method	(g) Depreciation deduction
19a 3-year property						
b 5-year property		3,419.	5.0	HY	200 DB	684.
c 7-year property		524.	7.0	HY	200 DB	75.
d 10-year property						
e 15-year property						
f 20-year property						
g 25-year property			25 yrs.		S/L	
h Residential rental property			27.5 yrs.	MM	S/L	
			27.5 yrs.	MM	S/L	
i Nonresidential real property			39 yrs.	MM	S/L	
				MM	S/L	

Section C—Assets Placed in Service During 2015 Tax Year Using the Alternative Depreciation System

20a Class life					S/L	
b 12-year			12 yrs.		S/L	
c 40-year			40 yrs.	MM	S/L	

Part IV   **Summary** (See instructions.)

21	Listed property. Enter amount from line 28	**21**	
22	**Total.** Add amounts from line 12, lines 14 through 17, lines 19 and 20 in column (g), and line 21. Enter here and on the appropriate lines of your return. Partnerships and S corporations—see instructions .	**22**	759.
23	For assets shown above and placed in service during the current year, enter the portion of the basis attributable to section 263A costs	**23**		

For Paperwork Reduction Act Notice, see separate instructions. **BAA**	REV 12/27/15 PRO	Form **4562** (2015)

Form 4562 (2015)   Page **2**

Part V Listed Property (Include automobiles, certain other vehicles, certain aircraft, certain computers, and property used for entertainment, recreation, or amusement.)

Note: For any vehicle for which you are using the standard mileage rate or deducting lease expense, complete **only** 24a, 24b, columns (a) through (c) of Section A, all of Section B, and Section C if applicable.

Section A—Depreciation and Other Information (Caution: See the instructions for limits for passenger automobiles.**)**

24a Do you have evidence to support the business/investment use claimed? ☐ Yes ☐ No **24b** If "Yes," is the evidence written? ☐ Yes ☐ No

(a) Type of property (list vehicles first)	(b) Date placed in service	(c) Business/ investment use percentage	(d) Cost or other basis	(e) Basis for depreciation (business/investment use only)	(f) Recovery period	(g) Method/ Convention	(h) Depreciation deduction	(i) Elected section 179 cost
25 Special depreciation allowance for qualified listed property placed in service during the tax year and used more than 50% in a qualified business use (see instructions) . **25**								
26 Property used more than 50% in a qualified business use:								
		%						
		%						
		%						
27 Property used 50% or less in a qualified business use:								
		%				S/L –		
		%				S/L –		
		%				S/L –		
28 Add amounts in column (h), lines 25 through 27. Enter here and on line 21, page 1 . **28**								
29 Add amounts in column (i), line 26. Enter here and on line 7, page 1 . . . . **29**								

Section B—Information on Use of Vehicles

Complete this section for vehicles used by a sole proprietor, partner, or other "more than 5% owner," or related person. If you provided vehicles to your employees, first answer the questions in Section C to see if you meet an exception to completing this section for those vehicles.

	(a) Vehicle 1		(b) Vehicle 2		(c) Vehicle 3		(d) Vehicle 4		(e) Vehicle 5		(f) Vehicle 6	
30 Total business/investment miles driven during the year (**do not** include commuting miles) .												
31 Total commuting miles driven during the year												
32 Total other personal (noncommuting) miles driven												
33 Total miles driven during the year. Add lines 30 through 32												
34 Was the vehicle available for personal use during off-duty hours?	Yes	No	Yes	No	Yes	No	Yes	No	Yes	No	Yes	No
35 Was the vehicle used primarily by a more than 5% owner or related person? . .												
36 Is another vehicle available for personal use?												

Section C—Questions for Employers Who Provide Vehicles for Use by Their Employees

Answer these questions to determine if you meet an exception to completing Section B for vehicles used by employees who **are not** more than 5% owners or related persons (see instructions).

		Yes	No
37 Do you maintain a written policy statement that prohibits all personal use of vehicles, including commuting, by your employees?			
38 Do you maintain a written policy statement that prohibits personal use of vehicles, except commuting, by your employees? See the instructions for vehicles used by corporate officers, directors, or 1% or more owners . .			
39 Do you treat all use of vehicles by employees as personal use?			
40 Do you provide more than five vehicles to your employees, obtain information from your employees about the use of the vehicles, and retain the information received?			
41 Do you meet the requirements concerning qualified automobile demonstration use? (See instructions.)			

Note: If your answer to 37, 38, 39, 40, or 41 is "Yes," do not complete Section B for the covered vehicles.

Part VI Amortization

(a) Description of costs	(b) Date amortization begins	(c) Amortizable amount	(d) Code section	(e) Amortization period or percentage	(f) Amortization for this year
42 Amortization of costs that begins during your 2015 tax year (see instructions):					
Website	07/01/2015	2,150.	197	3.00 yrs	358.
43 Amortization of costs that began before your 2015 tax year **43**					
44 Total. Add amounts in column (f). See the instructions for where to report **44**					358.

REV 12/27/15 PRO   Form **4562** (2015)

Ima Starr - 111-22-3333

Schedule C - Other Income (Blue Jazzbos)

Product Endorsement	$550
Modeling Income	$1,895
	$2,445

Schedule C - Other Costs of Goods Sold Blue Jazzbos

Sidemen (1099's Issued)	$5,980
	$5,980

Form 2106 - Acting

Meals - Form 2106 Line 5

Philly	14	$64	$896
LA	6	$64	$384
Cape Cod 1	14	$74	$1,036
London $941 x 30%			$282
Chicago	3	$74	$222
Other Professional Meals			$411
			$3,231

Travel - Form 2106 Line 3

Hotel Philly	$1,346
Airline - LA	$501
Taxi/Car Rental - LA	$324
Ferry - Cape Cod	$52
London $1,949 x 30%	$588
Chicago Audition Airfare	$389
Chicago Hotel	$578
Chicago Taxi	$88
	$3,866

Other Business Expenses - Form 2106

Script Costs	$100
Wardrobe Cleaning	$89
Telephone, Cell & Skype	$568
Research - Streaming Video/DVD	$151
Internet Service	$234
Performance Audit	$385
Union Dues	$689
Trade Publications	$330
Depreciation (Form 4562)	$80
	$2,634

Sch C - The Blue Jazzbos

Depreciation	Acquired	Method	Life	Cost	Accum	Sec 179	Current Expense
Yamaha STAGEPAS	7/1/2015	MACRS	5 Yrs.	$1,249	$0	$0	$250
Video Equipment	7/1/2015	MACRS	5 Yrs.	$1,621	$0	$0	$324
iPhone 6S	7/1/2015	MACRS	5 Yrs.	$299	$0	$0	$43
Sennheiser e945	7/1/2015	MACRS	5 Yrs.	$225	$0	$0	$32
iPad	7/1/2015	MACRS	5 Yrs.	$549	$0	$0	$110
				$3,943	$0	$0	$759
Website	7/1/2015	Amortization	36M	$2,150	$0	$0	$358

Sch C - Writer

Depreciation	Acquired	Method	Life	Cost	Accum	Sec 179	Current Expense
PowerBook & Printer	4/1/2015	MACRS	5 Yrs.	$1,523	$0	$0	$305
Kindle Reader	7/1/2015	MACRS	5 Yrs.	$139	$0	$0	$28
							$333

5

For Musicians and Singers

In this chapter I will look in detail at the activities of our good friend, Sonny Phunky, the kind of income and deductions he had for the year, and how they manifest themselves in his tax return.

To begin, we'll walk through some of the expense items for musicians and singers specifically. I will note in parentheses the type of record keeping the IRS would require:

1. Union dues and professional societies (invoices and payment verifications).

2. Professional fees for agents, attorneys, and accountants (invoices and payment verifications).

3. Professional registries (both printed and on the Internet; invoices, credit card receipt, and payment verifications).

4. Master classes, education, and coaching lessons (invoices and payment verifications).

5. Stage makeup—this does not include street makeup, or what you use going to auditions, but does include makeup for showcases. The IRS can be very aggressive on makeup so write the name of the gig the makeup was used for on the back of the receipt (invoices, credit card receipts, and payment verifications).

6. Hair care—this must be a particular style for a specific gig, not general, looking-for-work upkeep (sales receipts, credit card receipts, and payment verifications).

7. Photographs and résumés—including videos, CDs, CD-ROMs, DVDs, and digital image transfers for use on the Internet or your personal website (sales receipts, credit card receipts, and payment verifications).

8. Stationery and postage (sales receipts and payment verifications).

9. Music books, musical scores, sheet music, batteries, tapes, CDs, etc.—these fall under the heading of supplies and may need to be allocated between employment income and contract income (invoices, credit card receipts, and payment verifications).

10. Communications, Skype, telephone, and cellular phone—actual business calls on your home phone are deductible, but the IRS does not allow the allocation of the base monthly rate. You can deduct only the actual long distance charges. The same rule is true with your cellular phone, online phone, and data service. If you get a second phone line strictly for business then it can be considered 100% deductible (bills and payment verifications).

11. Internet service—for research purposes, business e-mail, and e-mail while on the road. Be sure to allocate some of the costs for personal use (bills, invoices, and credit card receipts).

12. Stage clothes—this refers to professional uniforms, not conventional street wear! The rule says if you can wear it on the street, you can't deduct it. Remember that if the uniform is deductible then the cleaning is as well. A special rule allows musicians to deduct purchase of formal wear (invoices, credit card receipts, and payment verifications).

13. Viewing concerts, performances, and films (live and via DVD, streaming video, and cable)—I often call this expense line item "research"; others refer to it as "performance audit." Whatever you call it, make sure to allocate some of this expense to personal use. After all, you must sometimes take part in these activities for personal enjoyment; it can't be all business. I often quote to clients the old Wall Street saying, "the pigs get fat and the hogs get slaughtered." This is the type of deduction that you must not get piggy with. While the IRS typically hates this deduction, it does clearly acknowledge its validity in its audit guidelines. In an audit you would need to explain specifically what the professional value was (ticket stubs, receipts, and diary entries).

14. Promotional tickets—only your ticket is deductible, not your date's, unless your date is your agent, a band member, a producer, or some other professional colleague (ticket stubs, receipts, and diary entries).

15. Rehearsal hall or club rental (invoices and payment verifications).

16. Accompanist, arranger, sideman, sound or lighting person, personal assistant, etc.—this person must have a defined business purpose. For instance, if your personal assistant is paying your personal bills or engaged in nonbusiness activities, it will not be deductible. Also, if any of these folks are contractors and they receive more than $600 in a calendar year you must issue them a Form 1099-MISC (invoices and payment verifications).

17. Office rent—you must be able to prove you need an outside office (bills, invoices, and payment verifications).

18. Repair of equipment—computers, musical instruments, sound and video equipment (bills, invoices, credit card receipts, and payment verifications).

19. Tax preparation, bookkeeping and accounting fees (bills, invoices, and payment verifications).

20. Demo tapes, videos, DVDs, and commercial prints used in promotional activities (bills, invoices, and payment verifications).

21. Trade advertisements (invoices, credit card receipts, and payment verifications).

22. Trade papers and professional magazines (invoices, credit card receipts, and payment verifications).

23. Travel—hotels, airline, meals (per diem generally), Airbnb, Uber, train, bus, baggage fees, etc. (confirmation and payment verification). Very important: documentation proving the reason for the trip (bills, invoices, and payment verifications).

24. Backstage tips—note: you cannot give these folks gifts (payment verifications and diary entry).

25. Insurance—including riders on your home insurance policy to cover home studio or other business activities (bills, invoices, and payment verifications).

26. Copyright fees (invoices and payment verifications).

27. Equipment purchases—sound equipment, instruments, etc. (bills, invoices, credit card receipts, and payment verifications).

Now, let's see what kind of year our bass player Sonny Phunky had. Luckily for his Certified Public Accountant, he downloaded our Excel spreadsheet for musicians (found at www.artstaxinfo.com), loaded it on his computer at the beginning of the tax year, and carefully tracked his expenses all year!

We will now review Sonny's 1040 income tax return in detail—remember you can download the current year version from our website, www.artstaxinfo.com.

You'll recall that Sonny was hired to play on a national tour with the Butterball Kings rock band (we reviewed his W-2 in Chapter 1). Let's look at some of the expenses that Sonny incurred during this time. Sonny lives in Maine so he had to travel to New York City, where the band rehearsed prior to beginning their tour. Sonny rehearsed with the Butterball Kings for 3 weeks in New York City. He was paid the allowable IRS per diem rate, so those amounts did not alter his income on his W-2. Sonny had depreciation expenses for the new, chartreuse-colored bass he purchased specifically for this gig. During the NYC rehearsal period, Sonny had expenses for supplies, such as new strings, cords, and music books. He purchased a variety of CDs in order to learn some of the music the band played, and he had a local repair shop overhaul his bass amplifier so that it was in good working order for the tour. Sonny used all these above expenses as deductions against the W-2 on Form 2106.

In anticipation of the money he was going to earn on his gig with the Butterball Kings, he splurged almost $15,000 on a rare 1956 Fender Precision electric bass guitar (like Bill Black played with Elvis). His accountant felt that the rare antique instrument might not be deductible until Sonny told him that he had used it on several studio dates and gigs during the year. The fact that this guitar was used in his profession (as opposed to being primarily a collectable piece) will probably make the purchase deductible. His tax advisor told Sonny to get some pictures of him using the guitar in the studio and on stage, in case he was audited. Because Sonny used the guitar on jobs that were mainly contract income, his accountant depreciated the guitar over 7 years as a write-off on Sonny's Schedule C.

During the summer Sonny landed a gig playing for a popular show band in Atlantic City. The band did not offer any monetary reimbursement, but gave the players a place to live there. In this case, Sonny had expenses for meals and incidentals, but obviously not for lodging. Sonny is a terrible record keeper and uses the IRS per diem rates for all his meals and incidentals throughout the year. The daily rate for Atlantic City is $64 a day for 2016. Of course, his mileage driving to New Jersey and his auto use while there were deductible.

In July, Sonny went to the NAMM (National Association of Music Merchandisers) trade show. A luthier he knows asked Sonny to appear in his exhibition booth to endorse and demonstrate a new bass guitar he had designed. The luthier could not pay cash to Sonny for the appearance, so he gave him one of his handmade basses worth an estimated $2,000. The trip did give Sonny a chance to see new products at the show, hand his card and CD out to recording studios, and generally network with other industry and music types. He attended the show for the entire 3 days he was gone. Sonny could clearly show a business purpose and was able to deduct the entire trip. He will declare the $2,000 value of the bass as self-employment income on his Schedule C.

When Sonny is not away from home on gigs he has a standing weekend job at a local bar in Rockridge, Maine. His band, The Over the Hill Gang, is an impromptu one made up of whoever is available that night. The club owner pays Sonny and Sonny in turn pays the band. The club owner issued Sonny a 1099-MISC at the end of the year that included all the funds he had paid Sonny over the year for his band. Sonny then went through his records to obtain a list of all the sidemen to whom he had paid $600 or more during the year. He ended up issuing five 1099-MISC forms to these musicians. To issue a 1099-MISC, Sonny needed each musician's full name, address, and Social Security number. Sonny's accountant had alerted him to this requirement, so Sonny had all his musicians fill out the federal Form W-9 to ensure he would have all this information at year-end. His accountant gave Sonny a pile of W-9 forms to keep in his guitar case. Of course all the sidemen he had paid during the year were deductions against his income on his Schedule C form, even those that made less than $600.

Sonny had one particularly good combination of his The Over the Hill Gang during the year, which he wanted to assemble to make a CD to sell at the gigs and to help promote his own playing. He did not want to front the money for the recording himself, so he used PLEDGEMUSIC.com to raise the money for the recording. This helped Sonny raise part of the $10,000 needed to make the new recording, and this $10,000 (less PLEDGEMUSIC's 15% fee) is included in the bands taxable income this year. It cost him an additional $1,000 to have 500 copies of the CD pressed and covers printed. Offering the CD at gigs and through the mail from such sites as CD Baby, Sonny figured that it would take him 2 years to sell all 500 copies of the disk. He felt there would be income from downloads through iTunes, Bandcamp, and streaming services such as Spotify and Pandora (as well as his website and perhaps ringtones), but that these would not generate substantial income beyond the 2 years. He did not plan on manufacturing any more copies of the disc, which means that he estimated the useful life of the recording to be 2 years. Sonny's accountant will divide the recording costs of $10,000 by 24 (months) and write them off (amortize) over 2 years. The costs of the discs themselves will be expensed on Sonny's Schedule C as "cost of goods sold." Each CD cost $2 to manufacture, so Sonny will expense $2 on his tax return for each CD he sells (or gives away as promotion). Unsold CDs will become inventory. In 2015 Sonny sold 195 CDs at $10 each. This activity is part of Sonny's Schedule C and is found on Line 4 and Part III. Sonny may even have to collect state sales tax on a sale, depending on the regulations of the state in which he is selling.

The CD started to cause some buzz in the music world, so the band decided it needed to hit the road for a short showcase tour to promote the recording. Sonny and the band decided to set up an LLC for the band. They named the LLC "The Lido Shuffle," after one of their favorite songs. They had an attorney set up an LLC entity for them, and Sonny's accountant got a federal tax ID number online (www.irs.gov). Sonny's portion of the band's income from the tour was $3,420 (gross income less touring expenses). The band filed a Federal 1065 Partnership tax return for the LLC and each band member got a Form K-1 for their portion of the net band income. Sonny had some out-of-pocket expenses related to the tour that he was able to take against this income on Schedule E, with the expenses detailed on Statement SBE.

A friend of Sonny's recommended that he spend some time out in Los Angeles to "see what was happening." Sonny flew out to LA and spent a week hearing music and visiting with some musician buddies he had in California. He had a tax-deductible lunch with a studio owner where he discussed the possibility of getting some studio gigs. He even sat in at some clubs, so he got a chance to play. Unfortunately for Sonny, there was little deductible about the trip; he had no income from it and it had no defined, specific business purpose, thus no travel deductions!

Sonny lucked into a gig at the famed Ponderosa Stomp (www.ponderosa stomp.com) in New Orleans. He flew there for 4 days of work (rehearsal and performance) and decided to stay on for 2 extra days to "hang out" and listen to some music. Because the primary reason for the trip was business, he will be able to write off the full cost of the flight. He will be able to deduct meals, lodging, and incidentals only for the 4 days he was employed doing the session work; the extra days will be considered vacation. If the ratio between vacation and workdays were reversed, Sonny would not be able to write off any of his flight down to New Orleans because the trip would shift from being primarily business to primarily personal. The income and expense from this gig are on his Schedule C.

Sonny thought a personal website where he could post his résumé, pictures, mp3s from the new CD by The Over the Hill Gang, and perhaps some video clips from performances would be great (he even purchased a GoPro 4K camcorder). He also wanted to promote his teaching. The costs of setting up the website, registering the domain name, and hosting the site will all be deductible. The IRS stipulates that website development be written off (amortized) over 3 years. So all Sonny's costs of designing and setting up the site will be added up (capitalized) and expensed over 3 years.

When Sonny met with his accountant at year-end to do some tax planning and check on his estimated tax payments for the year, he found he had more income than he had expected. His accountant asked if there were some expenses that he could accelerate into the current year; this way he could get the tax benefit of the deductions in the current year. Sonny decided to purchase a new, smaller bass guitar amplifier before December 31st. By purchasing the amp before year-end he was able to use the section 179 election and write the new amplifier off 100% in the current year. He can do this even if he charges the amp on his credit card and pays it off in the next year, as long as the amp is "in use" before December 31st. Sonny will also have to take a year-end inventory of all the unsold CDs so his accountant can correctly calculate his cost of goods sold.

When he is not on the road, Sonny has a room set up in his house that he uses exclusively to give bass guitar lessons. Sonny has about ten regular students. He uses Form 8829 to take a home office deduction for his music room. He can also deduct the books, instructional videos, and supplies that he uses in his teaching.

Musicians and Singers

Continuing Education

Coaching & Lessons Expense	
Dance Training	
Music—Arrangements	
Tapes, CDs, & Recordings	
Training	
Rents—Rehearsal Hall	
Tickets—Performance Audit/Research	
Voice Training	
Other: _____	

Promotional Expenses

Audition Tapes, Videos, CDs, & DVDs	
Business Cards	
Film & Processing	
Website Development & Hosting	
Mailing Supplies—Envelopes, etc.	
Photos—Professional	
Resume & Portfolio Expenses	
Other: _____	

Supplies & Other Expenses

Uniforms & Formal Wear	
Cleaning (uniforms/formal)	
Recording Studio Costs	
Dues—Union & Professional	
Gifts—Business ($25 maximum per person per year)	
Insurance—Equipment	
Interest—Business Loans	
Strings, Picks, Cords, Reeds, etc.	
Instruments & Musical Supplies	
Meals—Business (enter 100% of cost)	
Photocopy—Music, etc.	

Postage & Office Supplies

Sheet Music

Publications—Trade

Rents—Office, Storage, etc.

Rents—Equipment, etc.

Repairs—Instruments & Equipment

Secretarial & Bookkeeping

Commissions—Agent/Manager

Other: _____

Auto Travel (in miles)

Auditions

Business Meetings

Continuing Education

Job Seeking

Out-of-Town Business Trips

Purchasing Job Supplies & Materials

Professional Society Meetings

Parking Fees & Tolls

Other: _____

Travel—Out of Town

Airfare

Car Rental

Parking

Apartment Rent (jobs lasting less than 1 year)

Taxi, Train, Bus, & Subway

Lodging (do not combine with meals)

Meals (do not combine with lodging)

Laundry & Porter

Bridge & Highway Tolls

Telephone Calls (including home)

Other: _____

Communications Costs

Cellular Calls	
FAX Transmissions, Data, & Other Online Services	
Paging Service & Call Forwarding	
Skype or Other Internet Phone Service	
Land Line	
Other: _____	

Equipment Purchases

Answering Machine	
Smart Phones & Tablets	
Audio Systems & Amplifiers	
Musical Instruments	
Pager & Recorder	
Software	
Speaker Systems	
Computer & Printer	
Tools & Other Music Supplies	
Other: _____	

Form 1040	Department of the Treasury—Internal Revenue Service (99) **U.S. Individual Income Tax Return**	2015	OMB No. 1545-0074	IRS Use Only—Do not write or staple in this space.		

For the year Jan. 1–Dec. 31, 2015, or other tax year beginning ____, 2015, ending ____, 20____ | **See separate instructions.**

Your first name and initial	Last name	Your social security number
Sonny	Phunky	222-33-4444

If a joint return, spouse's first name and initial | Last name | Spouse's social security number

Home address (number and street). If you have a P.O. box, see instructions. | Apt. no.
RR 1

▲ Make sure the SSN(s) above and on line 6c are correct.

City, town or post office, state, and ZIP code. If you have a foreign address, also complete spaces below (see instructions).
Rockridge ME 03905

Presidential Election Campaign
Check here if you, or your spouse if filing jointly, want $3 to go to this fund. Checking a box below will not change your tax or refund. ☐ You ☐ Spouse

Foreign country name | Foreign province/state/county | Foreign postal code

Filing Status
Check only one box.

1 ☒ Single
2 ☐ Married filing jointly (even if only one had income)
3 ☐ Married filing separately. Enter spouse's SSN above and full name here. ▶
4 ☐ Head of household (with qualifying person). (See instructions.) If the qualifying person is a child but not your dependent, enter this child's name here. ▶
5 ☐ Qualifying widow(er) with dependent child

Exemptions

6a ☒ **Yourself.** If someone can claim you as a dependent, **do not** check box 6a . . . . .
b ☐ **Spouse** . . . .

Boxes checked on 6a and 6b **1**
No. of children on 6c who:

c **Dependents:**

(1) First name Last name	(2) Dependent's social security number	(3) Dependent's relationship to you	(4) ✓ if child under age 17 qualifying for child tax credit (see instructions)
			☐
			☐
			☐
			☐

If more than four dependents, see instructions and check here ▶ ☐

• lived with you
• did not live with you due to divorce or separation (see instructions)
Dependents on 6c not entered above

d Total number of exemptions claimed . . . .

Add numbers on lines above ▶ **1**

Income

Attach Form(s) W-2 here. Also attach Forms W-2G and 1099-R if tax was withheld.

If you did not get a W-2, see instructions.

7	Wages, salaries, tips, etc. Attach Form(s) W-2	7	31,071.
8a	**Taxable interest.** Attach Schedule B if required	8a	9.
b	Tax-exempt interest. **Do not** include on line 8a . . .	8b	
9a	Ordinary dividends. Attach Schedule B if required	9a	
b	Qualified dividends	9b	
10	Taxable refunds, credits, or offsets of state and local income taxes	10	
11	Alimony received	11	
12	Business income or (loss). Attach Schedule C or C-EZ	12	5,301.
13	Capital gain or (loss). Attach Schedule D if required. If not required, check here ▶ ☐	13	
14	Other gains or (losses). Attach Form 4797	14	
15a	IRA distributions . 15a	b Taxable amount . . .	15b	
16a	Pensions and annuities 16a	b Taxable amount . . .	16b	
17	Rental real estate, royalties, partnerships, S corporations, trusts, etc. Attach Schedule E	17	1,231.
18	Farm income or (loss). Attach Schedule F	18	
19	Unemployment compensation	19	
20a	Social security benefits 20a	b Taxable amount . . .	20b	
21	Other income. List type and amount _____	21	
22	Combine the amounts in the far right column for lines 7 through 21. This is your **total income** ▶	22	37,612.

Adjusted Gross Income

23	Educator expenses	23	
24	Certain business expenses of reservists, performing artists, and fee-basis government officials. Attach Form 2106 or 2106-EZ	24	
25	Health savings account deduction. Attach Form 8889 .	25	
26	Moving expenses. Attach Form 3903	26	
27	Deductible part of self-employment tax. Attach Schedule SE .	27	462.
28	Self-employed SEP, SIMPLE, and qualified plans . .	28	
29	Self-employed health insurance deduction	29	
30	Penalty on early withdrawal of savings	30	
31a	Alimony paid b Recipient's SSN ▶ _____	31a	
32	IRA deduction	32	
33	Student loan interest deduction	33	
34	Tuition and fees. Attach Form 8917	34	
35	Domestic production activities deduction. Attach Form 8903	35	
36	Add lines 23 through 35	36	462.
37	Subtract line 36 from line 22. This is your **adjusted gross income** . . . . . ▶	37	37,150.

For Disclosure, Privacy Act, and Paperwork Reduction Act Notice, see separate instructions. **BAA** REV 12/30/15 PRO | Form **1040** (2015)

Form 1040 (2015) Page **2**

Tax and Credits	38	Amount from line 37 (adjusted gross income)	38	37,150.
	39a	Check if: ☒ You were born before January 2, 1951, ☐ Blind. ☐ Spouse was born before January 2, 1951, ☐ Blind. **Total boxes checked ▶ 39a**		1
	b	If your spouse itemizes on a separate return or you were a dual-status alien, check here ▶ 39b ☐		
Standard Deduction for—	40	**Itemized deductions** (from Schedule A) **or** your **standard deduction** (see left margin) . .	40	12,175.
• People who check any box on line 39a or 39b **or** who can be claimed as a dependent, see instructions.	41	Subtract line 40 from line 38	41	24,975.
	42	**Exemptions.** If line 38 is $154,950 or less, multiply $4,000 by the number on line 6d. Otherwise, see instructions	42	4,000.
	43	**Taxable income.** Subtract line 42 from line 41. If line 42 is more than line 41, enter -0- . .	43	20,975.
	44	**Tax** (see instructions). Check if any from: a ☐ Form(s) 8814 b ☐ Form 4972 c ☐	44	2,685.
• All others:	45	**Alternative minimum tax** (see instructions). Attach Form 6251	45	
Single or Married filing separately, $6,300	46	Excess advance premium tax credit repayment. Attach Form 8962	46	
	47	Add lines 44, 45, and 46 . . . . ▶	47	2,685.
Married filing jointly or Qualifying widow(er), $12,600	48	Foreign tax credit. Attach Form 1116 if required	48	
	49	Credit for child and dependent care expenses. Attach Form 2441	49	
Head of household, $9,250	50	Education credits from Form 8863, line 19	50	
	51	Retirement savings contributions credit. Attach Form 8880	51	
	52	Child tax credit. Attach Schedule 8812, if required. . .	52	
	53	Residential energy credits. Attach Form 5695 . . .	53	
	54	Other credits from Form: a ☐ 3800 b ☐ 8801 c ☐	54	
	55	Add lines 48 through 54. These are your **total credits**	55	
	56	Subtract line 55 from line 47. If line 55 is more than line 47, enter -0- . . . . . . ▶	56	2,685.
Other Taxes	57	Self-employment tax. Attach Schedule SE	57	923.
	58	Unreported social security and Medicare tax from Form: a ☐ 4137 b ☐ 8919 . .	58	
	59	Additional tax on IRAs, other qualified retirement plans, etc. Attach Form 5329 if required . .	59	
	60a	Household employment taxes from Schedule H	60a	
	b	First-time homebuyer credit repayment. Attach Form 5405 if required	60b	
	61	Health care: individual responsibility (see instructions) Full-year coverage ☒ . . .	61	
	62	Taxes from: a ☐ Form 8959 b ☐ Form 8960 c ☐ Instructions; enter code(s)	62	
	63	Add lines 56 through 62. This is your **total tax** . . . . ▶	63	3,608.
Payments	64	Federal income tax withheld from Forms W-2 and 1099 . .	64	3,462.	
If you have a qualifying child, attach Schedule EIC.	65	2015 estimated tax payments and amount applied from 2014 return	65	
	66a	**Earned income credit (EIC)**	66a	
	b	Nontaxable combat pay election	66b	
	67	Additional child tax credit. Attach Schedule 8812	67	
	68	American opportunity credit from Form 8863, line 8 . . .	68	
	69	Net premium tax credit. Attach Form 8962	69	
	70	Amount paid with request for extension to file	70	
	71	Excess social security and tier 1 RRTA tax withheld . . .	71	
	72	Credit for federal tax on fuels. Attach Form 4136 . . .	72	
	73	Credits from Form: a ☐ 2439 b ☐ Reserved c ☐ 8885 d ☐	73	
	74	Add lines 64, 65, 66a, and 67 through 73. These are your **total payments** . . . . . ▶	74	3,462.
Refund	75	If line 74 is more than line 63, subtract line 63 from line 74. This is the amount you **overpaid**	75	
	76a	Amount of line 75 you want **refunded to you.** If Form 8888 is attached, check here . ▶ ☐	76a	
Direct deposit? ▶ See instructions.	b	Routing number ☐☐☐☐☐☐☐☐☐ ▶ c Type: ☐ Checking ☐ Savings		
	d	Account number ☐☐☐☐☐☐☐☐☐☐☐☐☐☐☐☐☐		
	77	Amount of line 75 you want **applied to your 2016 estimated tax ▶**	77	
Amount You Owe	78	**Amount you owe.** Subtract line 74 from line 63. For details on how to pay, see instructions ▶	78	146.
	79	Estimated tax penalty (see instructions)	79	

Third Party Designee	Do you want to allow another person to discuss this return with the IRS (see instructions)? ☐ **Yes.** Complete below. ☒ **No**
	Designee's name ▶ Phone no. ▶ Personal identification number (PIN) ▶

Sign Here

Under penalties of perjury, I declare that I have examined this return and accompanying schedules and statements, and to the best of my knowledge and belief, they are true, correct, and complete. Declaration of preparer (other than taxpayer) is based on all information of which preparer has any knowledge.

Joint return? See instructions.
Keep a copy for your records.

Your signature	Date	Your occupation Musician	Daytime phone number
Spouse's signature. If a joint return, **both** must sign.	Date	Spouse's occupation	If the IRS sent you an Identity Protection PIN, enter it here (see inst.)

Paid Preparer Use Only	Print/Type preparer's name Peter Jason Riley CPA	Preparer's signature Peter Jason Riley CPA	Date 01/24/2016	Check ☐ if self-employed	PTIN P00413102
	Firm's name ▶ RILEY & ASSOCIATES, P.C.			Firm's EIN ▶	04-3577120
	Firm's address ▶ 5 PERRY WAY – P O BOX 157 NEWBURYPORT MA 01950			Phone no.	(978)463-9350

www.irs.gov/form1040   REV 12/30/15 PRO   Form **1040** (2015)

SCHEDULE A (Form 1040)	**Itemized Deductions**	OMB No. 1545-0074

Department of the Treasury
Internal Revenue Service (99)

▶ Information about Schedule A and its separate instructions is at *www.irs.gov/schedulea*.
▶ Attach to Form 1040.

20**15**

Attachment
Sequence No. **07**

Name(s) shown on Form 1040: Sonny Phunky

Your social security number: 222-33-4444

Medical and Dental Expenses

Caution: Do not include expenses reimbursed or paid by others.

1 Medical and dental expenses (see instructions) . . . . . | 1 |
2 Enter amount from Form 1040, line 38 | 2 |
3 Multiply line 2 by 10% (.10). But if either you or your spouse was born before January 2, 1951, multiply line 2 by 7.5% (.075) instead | 3 |
4 Subtract line 3 from line 1. If line 3 is more than line 1, enter -0- . | 4 |

Taxes You Paid

5 State and local (**check only one box**):
  a ☒ Income taxes, **or**
  b ☐ General sales taxes | 5 | 2,171. |
6 Real estate taxes (see instructions) . . . . | 6 | 1,598. |
7 Personal property taxes . . . . | 7 |
8 Other taxes. List type and amount ▶ _____ | 8 |
9 Add lines 5 through 8 . . . . | 9 | 3,769. |

Interest You Paid

Note:
Your mortgage interest deduction may be limited (see instructions).

10 Home mortgage interest and points reported to you on Form 1098 | 10 | 5,399. |
11 Home mortgage interest not reported to you on Form 1098. If paid to the person from whom you bought the home, see instructions and show that person's name, identifying no., and address ▶ _____ | 11 |
12 Points not reported to you on Form 1098. See instructions for special rules . . . . | 12 |
13 Mortgage insurance premiums (see instructions) . . . . . | 13 |
14 Investment interest. Attach Form 4952 if required. (See instructions.) | 14 |
15 Add lines 10 through 14 . . . . | 15 | 5,399. |

Gifts to Charity

If you made a gift and got a benefit for it, see instructions.

16 Gifts by cash or check. If you made any gift of $250 or more, see instructions . . . . | 16 | 250. |
17 Other than by cash or check. If any gift of $250 or more, see instructions. You **must** attach Form 8283 if over $500 . . . | 17 |
18 Carryover from prior year . . . . | 18 |
19 Add lines 16 through 18 . . . . | 19 | 250. |

Casualty and Theft Losses

20 Casualty or theft loss(es). Attach Form 4684. (See instructions.) . . . . | 20 |

Job Expenses and Certain Miscellaneous Deductions

21 Unreimbursed employee expenses—job travel, union dues, job education, etc. Attach Form 2106 or 2106-EZ if required. (See instructions.) ▶ Deductible expenses from Form 2106 | 21 | 3,500. |
22 Tax preparation fees . . . . | 22 |
23 Other expenses—investment, safe deposit box, etc. List type and amount ▶ _____ | 23 |
24 Add lines 21 through 23 . . . . | 24 | 3,500. |
25 Enter amount from Form 1040, line 38 | 25 | 37,150. |
26 Multiply line 25 by 2% (.02) . . . . | 26 | 743. |
27 Subtract line 26 from line 24. If line 26 is more than line 24, enter -0- . . . . . . | 27 | 2,757. |

Other Miscellaneous Deductions

28 Other—from list in instructions. List type and amount ▶ _____ | 28 |

Total Itemized Deductions

29 Is Form 1040, line 38, over $154,950?
  ☒ **No.** Your deduction is not limited. Add the amounts in the far right column for lines 4 through 28. Also, enter this amount on Form 1040, line 40. | 29 | 12,175. |
  ☐ **Yes.** Your deduction may be limited. See the Itemized Deductions Worksheet in the instructions to figure the amount to enter.
30 If you elect to itemize deductions even though they are less than your standard deduction, check here . . . . ▶ ☐

For Paperwork Reduction Act Notice, see Form 1040 instructions. **BAA**   REV 12/30/15 PRO   Schedule A (Form 1040) 2015

SCHEDULE C
(Form 1040)

Department of the Treasury
Internal Revenue Service (99)

Profit or Loss From Business
(Sole Proprietorship)

▶ Information about Schedule C and its separate instructions is at *www.irs.gov/schedulec.*
▶ **Attach to Form 1040, 1040NR, or 1041; partnerships generally must file Form 1065.**

OMB No. 1545-0074

20**15**

Attachment
Sequence No. **09**

Name of proprietor	Social security number (SSN)
Sonny Phunky	222-33-4444

A	Principal business or profession, including product or service (see instructions)	B Enter code from instructions
	Musician	▶ 7 1 1 5 1 0

C	Business name. If no separate business name, leave blank.	D Employer ID number (EIN), (see instr.)
	Sonny "The Butterball" Phunky	

E Business address (including suite or room no.) ▶ RR 1
   City, town or post office, state, and ZIP code   Rockridge, ME 03905

F Accounting method: (1) ☒ Cash   (2) ☐ Accrual   (3) ☐ Other (specify) ▶ _____

G Did you "materially participate" in the operation of this business during 2015? If "No," see instructions for limit on losses . ☒ Yes ☐ No

H If you started or acquired this business during 2015, check here . . . . ▶ ☐

I Did you make any payments in 2015 that would require you to file Form(s) 1099? (see instructions) . . . . . ☒ Yes ☐ No

J If "Yes," did you or will you file required Forms 1099? . . . . ☒ Yes ☐ No

Part I   Income

1	Gross receipts or sales. See instructions for line 1 and check the box if this income was reported to you on Form W-2 and the "Statutory employee" box on that form was checked . . . . ▶ ☐	1	16,845.
2	Returns and allowances	2	
3	Subtract line 2 from line 1	3	16,845.
4	Cost of goods sold (from line 42)	4	6,455.
5	**Gross profit.** Subtract line 4 from line 3	5	10,390.
6	Other income, including federal and state gasoline or fuel tax credit or refund (see instructions)	6	14,191.
7	**Gross income.** Add lines 5 and 6 . . . . ▶	7	24,581.

Part II   Expenses. Enter expenses for business use of your home **only** on line 30.

8	Advertising	8	341.	18	Office expense (see instructions)	18	104.
9	Car and truck expenses (see instructions)	9	2,215.	19	Pension and profit-sharing plans .	19	
				20	Rent or lease (see instructions):		
10	Commissions and fees .	10		a	Vehicles, machinery, and equipment	20a	
11	Contract labor (see instructions)	11		b	Other business property . . .	20b	
12	Depletion	12		21	Repairs and maintenance . . .	21	114.
13	Depreciation and section 179 expense deduction (not included in Part III) (see instructions).	13	3,282.	22	Supplies (not included in Part III) .	22	474.
				23	Taxes and licenses	23	
				24	Travel, meals, and entertainment:		
14	Employee benefit programs (other than on line 19) . .	14		a	Travel	24a	1,933.
15	Insurance (other than health)	15		b	Deductible meals and entertainment (see instructions) .	24b	1,311.
16	Interest:			25	Utilities	25	
a	Mortgage (paid to banks, etc.)	16a		26	Wages (less employment credits) .	26	
b	Other	16b		27a	Other expenses (from line 48) .	27a	6,504.
17	Legal and professional services	17	350.	b	**Reserved for future use** . . .	27b	

28	**Total expenses** before expenses for business use of home. Add lines 8 through 27a . . . . . . ▶	28	16,628.
29	Tentative profit or (loss). Subtract line 28 from line 7	29	7,953.
30	Expenses for business use of your home. Do not report these expenses elsewhere. Attach Form 8829 unless using the simplified method (see instructions). **Simplified method filers only:** enter the total square footage of: (a) your home: _____ and (b) the part of your home used for business: _____ . Use the Simplified Method Worksheet in the instructions to figure the amount to enter on line 30	30	2,652.
31	**Net profit or (loss).** Subtract line 30 from line 29.		
	• If a profit, enter on both **Form 1040, line 12** (or **Form 1040NR, line 13**) and on **Schedule SE, line 2.** (If you checked the box on line 1, see instructions). Estates and trusts, enter on **Form 1041, line 3.**	31	5,301.
	• If a loss, you **must** go to line 32.		
32	If you have a loss, check the box that describes your investment in this activity (see instructions).		
	• If you checked 32a, enter the loss on both **Form 1040, line 12,** (or **Form 1040NR, line 13**) and on **Schedule SE, line 2.** (If you checked the box on line 1, see the line 31 instructions). Estates and trusts, enter on **Form 1041, line 3.**	32a ☒ All investment is at risk.	
	• If you checked 32b, you **must** attach **Form 6198.** Your loss may be limited.	32b ☐ Some investment is not at risk.	

For Paperwork Reduction Act Notice, see the separate instructions.   **BAA**   REV 12/07/15 PRO   Schedule C (Form 1040) 2015

Part III Cost of Goods Sold (see instructions)

33 Method(s) used to
value closing inventory: **a** ☐ Cost **b** ☒ Lower of cost or market **c** ☐ Other (attach explanation)

34 Was there any change in determining quantities, costs, or valuations between opening and closing inventory?
If "Yes," attach explanation . . . . ☐ Yes ☒ No

35	Inventory at beginning of year. If different from last year's closing inventory, attach explanation . . .	35	
36	Purchases less cost of items withdrawn for personal use	36	1,000.
37	Cost of labor. Do not include any amounts paid to yourself	37	3,640.
38	Materials and supplies	38	
39	Other costs	39	2,425.
40	Add lines 35 through 39	40	7,065.
41	Inventory at end of year	41	610.
42	**Cost of goods sold.** Subtract line 41 from line 40. Enter the result here and on line 4	42	6,455.

Part IV **Information on Your Vehicle.** Complete this part **only** if you are claiming car or truck expenses on line 9 and are not required to file Form 4562 for this business. See the instructions for line 13 to find out if you must file Form 4562.

43 When did you place your vehicle in service for business purposes? (month, day, year) ▶ _____

44 Of the total number of miles you drove your vehicle during 2015, enter the number of miles you used your vehicle for:

a Business _____ **b** Commuting (see instructions) _____ **c** Other _____

45 Was your vehicle available for personal use during off-duty hours? . . . . ☐ Yes ☐ No

46 Do you (or your spouse) have another vehicle available for personal use? . . . . ☐ Yes ☐ No

47a Do you have evidence to support your deduction? . . . . ☐ Yes ☐ No

b If "Yes," is the evidence written? . . . . ☐ Yes ☐ No

Part V **Other Expenses.** List below business expenses not included on lines 8–26 or line 30.

Trade Publications (Billboard)	299.
Research-Streaming Video/Music Downloads	613.
Performance Audit	405.
Internet Service	405.
Cell & Skype Service	372.
Online A&R (Taxi)	300.
CD Baby & other online fees	79.
Instructional DVD's	89.
See Line 48 Other Expenses	3,942.
48 **Total other expenses.** Enter here and on line 27a 48	6,504.

Schedule E (Form 1040) 2015   Attachment Sequence No. **13**   Page **2**

Name(s) shown on return. Do not enter name and social security number if shown on other side.	Your social security number
Sonny Phunky	222-33-4444

Caution. The IRS compares amounts reported on your tax return with amounts shown on Schedule(s) K-1.

Part II   **Income or Loss From Partnerships and S Corporations**   **Note:** If you report a loss from an at-risk activity for which **any** amount is **not** at risk, you **must** check the box in column **(e)** on line 28 and attach Form 6198. See instructions.

27   Are you reporting any loss not allowed in a prior year due to the at-risk, excess farm loss, or basis limitations, a prior year unallowed loss from a passive activity (if that loss was not reported on Form 8582), or unreimbursed partnership expenses? If you answered "Yes," see instructions before completing this section.   ☒ Yes   ☐ No

28	(a) Name	(b) Enter P for partnership; S for S corporation	(c) Check if foreign partnership	(d) Employer identification number	(e) Check if any amount is not at risk
A	The Lido Shuffle	P	☐	26-0000001	☐
B	UPE	P	☐	26-0000001	☐
C			☐		☐
D			☐		☐

	Passive Income and Loss		Nonpassive Income and Loss		
	(f) Passive loss allowed (attach Form 8582 if required)	(g) Passive income from Schedule K-1	(h) Nonpassive loss from Schedule K-1	(i) Section 179 expense deduction from Form 4562	(j) Nonpassive income from Schedule K-1
A					3,420.
B			2,189.		
C					
D					
29a Totals					3,420.
b Totals			2,189.		

30	Add columns (g) and (j) of line 29a	30	3,420.
31	Add columns (f), (h), and (i) of line 29b	31	(2,189.)
32	Total partnership and S corporation income or (loss). Combine lines 30 and 31. Enter the result here and include in the total on line 41 below	32	1,231.

Part III   **Income or Loss From Estates and Trusts**

33	(a) Name	(b) Employer identification number
A		
B		

	Passive Income and Loss		Nonpassive Income and Loss	
	(c) Passive deduction or loss allowed (attach Form 8582 if required)	(d) Passive income from Schedule K-1	(e) Deduction or loss from Schedule K-1	(f) Other income from Schedule K-1
A				
B				
34a Totals				
b Totals				

35	Add columns (d) and (f) of line 34a	35	
36	Add columns (c) and (e) of line 34b	36	( )
37	**Total estate and trust income or (loss).** Combine lines 35 and 36. Enter the result here and include in the total on line 41 below	37	

Part IV   **Income or Loss From Real Estate Mortgage Investment Conduits (REMICs)—Residual Holder**

38	(a) Name	(b) Employer identification number	(c) Excess inclusion from Schedules Q, line 2c (see instructions)	(d) Taxable income (net loss) from Schedules Q, line 1b	(e) Income from Schedules Q, line 3b

39	Combine columns (d) and (e) only. Enter the result here and include in the total on line 41 below	39	

Part V   **Summary**

40	Net farm rental income or (loss) from Form 4835. Also, complete line 42 below	40	
41	**Total income or (loss).** Combine lines 26, 32, 37, 39, and 41. Enter the result here and on Form 1040, line 17, or Form 1040NR, line 18 ▶	41	1,231.

42   **Reconciliation of farming and fishing income.** Enter your **gross** farming and fishing income reported on Form 4835, line 7; Schedule K-1 (Form 1065), box 14, code B; Schedule K-1 (Form 1120S), box 17, code V; and Schedule K-1 (Form 1041), box 14, code F (see instructions) . . | 42 |

43   **Reconciliation for real estate professionals.** If you were a real estate professional (see instructions), enter the net income or (loss) you reported anywhere on Form 1040 or Form 1040NR from all rental real estate activities in which you materially participated under the passive activity loss rules . . | 43 |

REV 12/23/15 PRO   Schedule E (Form 1040) 2015

SCHEDULE SE
(Form 1040)

Department of the Treasury
Internal Revenue Service (99)

Self-Employment Tax

▶ Information about Schedule SE and its separate instructions is at *www.irs.gov/schedulese*.
▶ Attach to Form 1040 or Form 1040NR.

OMB No. 1545-0074

2015

Attachment
Sequence No. **17**

Name of person with **self-employment** income (as shown on Form 1040 or Form 1040NR) Sonny Phunky	Social security number of person with **self-employment** income ▶ 222-33-4444

Before you begin: To determine if you must file Schedule SE, see the instructions.

May I Use Short Schedule SE or Must I Use Long Schedule SE?

Note. Use this flowchart **only if** you must file Schedule SE. If unsure, see *Who Must File Schedule SE* in the instructions.

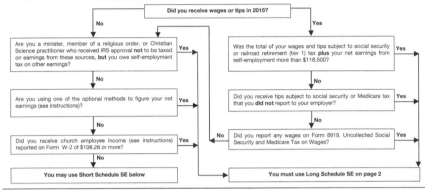

Section A—Short Schedule SE. Caution. Read above to see if you can use Short Schedule SE.

1a	Net farm profit or (loss) from Schedule F, line 34, and farm partnerships, Schedule K-1 (Form 1065), box 14, code A **1a**	
b	If you received social security retirement or disability benefits, enter the amount of Conservation Reserve Program payments included on Schedule F, line 4b, or listed on Schedule K-1 (Form 1065), box 20, code Z **1b** ( )	
2	Net profit or (loss) from Schedule C, line 31; Schedule C-EZ, line 3; Schedule K-1 (Form 1065), box 14, code A (other than farming); and Schedule K-1 (Form 1065-B), box 9, code J1. Ministers and members of religious orders, see instructions for types of income to report on this line. See instructions for other income to report **2**	6,532.
3	Combine lines 1a, 1b, and 2 . . . . **3**	6,532.
4	Multiply line 3 by 92.35% (.9235). If less than $400, you do not owe self-employment tax; **do not** file this schedule unless you have an amount on line 1b . . . . ▶ **4**	6,032.
	Note. If line 4 is less than $400 due to Conservation Reserve Program payments on line 1b, see instructions.	
5	**Self-employment tax.** If the amount on line 4 is:	
	• $118,500 or less, multiply line 4 by 15.3% (.153). Enter the result here and on **Form 1040, line 57,** or **Form 1040NR, line 55**	
	• More than $118,500, multiply line 4 by 2.9% (.029). Then, add $14,694 to the result. Enter the total here and on **Form 1040, line 57,** or **Form 1040NR, line 55** **5**	923.
6	**Deduction for one-half of self-employment tax.** Multiply line 5 by 50% (.50). Enter the result here and on **Form 1040, line 27,** or **Form 1040NR, line 27** . . . . **6** 462.	

For Paperwork Reduction Act Notice, see your tax return instructions.   **BAA**   REV 12/04/15 PRO   Schedule SE (Form 1040) 2015

Form **2106**	**Employee Business Expenses**	OMB No. 1545-0074
Department of the Treasury Internal Revenue Service (99)	▶ Attach to Form 1040 or Form 1040NR. ▶ Information about Form 2106 and its separate instructions is available at *www.irs.gov/form2106*.	20**15** Attachment Sequence No. **129**

Your name	Occupation in which you incurred expenses	Social security number
Sonny Phunky	Musician	222-33-4444

Part I   Employee Business Expenses and Reimbursements

Step 1 Enter Your Expenses

		Column A Other Than Meals and Entertainment	Column B Meals and Entertainment
1	Vehicle expense from line 22 or line 29. (Rural mail carriers: See instructions.) **1**	1,189.	
2	Parking fees, tolls, and transportation, including train, bus, etc., that **did not** involve overnight travel or commuting to and from work . **2**		
3	Travel expense while away from home overnight, including lodging, airplane, car rental, etc. **Do not** include meals and entertainment . **3**	5,082.	
4	Business expenses not included on lines 1 through 3. **Do not** include meals and entertainment **4**	2,311.	
5	Meals and entertainment expenses (see instructions) **5**		1,554.
6	**Total expenses.** In Column A, add lines 1 through 4 and enter the result. In Column B, enter the amount from line 5 . . . . . . **6**	8,582.	1,554.

    Note. *If you were not reimbursed for any expenses in Step 1, skip line 7 and enter the amount from line 6 on line 8.*

Step 2 Enter Reimbursements Received From Your Employer for Expenses Listed in Step 1

7	Enter reimbursements received from your employer that were **not** reported to you in box 1 of Form W-2. Include any reimbursements reported under code "L" in box 12 of your Form W-2 (see instructions). **7**	5,082.	1,554.

Step 3 Figure Expenses To Deduct on Schedule A (Form 1040 or Form 1040NR)

8	Subtract line 7 from line 6. If zero or less, enter -0-. However, if line 7 is greater than line 6 in Column A, report the excess as income on Form 1040, line 7 (or on Form 1040NR, line 8) **8**	3,500.	0.
	Note. *If both columns of line 8 are zero, you cannot deduct employee business expenses. Stop here and attach Form 2106 to your return.*		
9	In Column A, enter the amount from line 8. In Column B, multiply line 8 by 50% (.50). (Employees subject to Department of Transportation (DOT) hours of service limits: Multiply meal expenses incurred while away from home on business by 80% (.80) instead of 50%. For details, see instructions.) **9**	3,500.	0.
10	Add the amounts on line 9 of both columns and enter the total here. **Also, enter the total on Schedule A (Form 1040), line 21** (or on **Schedule A (Form 1040NR), line 7**). (Armed Forces reservists, qualified performing artists, fee-basis state or local government officials, and individuals with disabilities: See the instructions for special rules on where to enter the total.) . . . . . ▶ **10**		3,500.

For Paperwork Reduction Act Notice, see your tax return instructions. **BAA**   REV 01/06/16 PRO   Form **2106** (2015)

Form 2106 (2015)   Page **2**

Part II Vehicle Expenses

Section A—General Information (You must complete this section if you are claiming vehicle expenses.)

			(a) Vehicle 1	**(b)** Vehicle 2
11	Enter the date the vehicle was placed in service	11	01/01/2013	
12	Total miles the vehicle was driven during 2015	12	15,941 miles	miles
13	Business miles included on line 12	13	2,067 miles	miles
14	Percent of business use. Divide line 13 by line 12	14	12.97 %	%
15	Average daily roundtrip commuting distance	15	miles	miles
16	Commuting miles included on line 12	16	miles	miles
17	Other miles. Add lines 13 and 16 and subtract the total from line 12 . .	17	13,874 miles	miles
18	Was your vehicle available for personal use during off-duty hours?		☒ Yes ☐ No	
19	Do you (or your spouse) have another vehicle available for personal use?		☐ Yes ☒ No	
20	Do you have evidence to support your deduction?		☒ Yes ☐ No	
21	If "Yes," is the evidence written?		☒ Yes ☐ No	

Section B—Standard Mileage Rate (See the instructions for Part II to find out whether to complete this section or Section C.)

22	Multiply line 13 by 57.5¢ (.575). Enter the result here and on line 1	22	1,189.

Section C—Actual Expenses

			(a) Vehicle 1	**(b)** Vehicle 2
23	Gasoline, oil, repairs, vehicle insurance, etc.	23		
24a	Vehicle rentals	24a		
b	Inclusion amount (see instructions) .	24b		
c	Subtract line 24b from line 24a .	24c		
25	Value of employer-provided vehicle (applies only if 100% of annual lease value was included on Form W-2—see instructions)	25		
26	Add lines 23, 24c, and 25 . . .	26		
27	Multiply line 26 by the percentage on line 14	27		
28	Depreciation (see instructions) . .	28		
29	Add lines 27 and 28. Enter total here and on line 1	29		

Section D—Depreciation of Vehicles (Use this section only if you owned the vehicle and are completing Section C for the vehicle.)

			(a) Vehicle 1	**(b)** Vehicle 2
30	Enter cost or other basis (see instructions)	30		
31	Enter section 179 deduction and special allowance (see instructions)	31		
32	Multiply line 30 by line 14 (see instructions if you claimed the section 179 deduction or special allowance)	32		
33	Enter depreciation method and percentage (see instructions) .	33		
34	Multiply line 32 by the percentage on line 33 (see instructions) . .	34		
35	Add lines 31 and 34	35		
36	Enter the applicable limit explained in the line 36 instructions . . .	36		
37	Multiply line 36 by the percentage on line 14	37		
38	Enter the **smaller** of line 35 or line 37. If you skipped lines 36 and 37, enter the amount from line 35. Also enter this amount on line 28 above	38		

REV 01/06/16 PRO   Form **2106** (2015)

Form 8829

Department of the Treasury
Internal Revenue Service (99)

Expenses for Business Use of Your Home

▶ File only with Schedule C (Form 1040). Use a separate Form 8829 for each home you used for business during the year.
▶ Information about Form 8829 and its separate instructions is at *www.irs.gov/form8829*.

OMB No. 1545-0074

2015

Attachment
Sequence No. **176**

Name(s) of proprietor(s)	Your social security number
Sonny Phunky	222-33-4444

Part I   Part of Your Home Used for Business   Musician

1 Area used regularly and exclusively for business, regularly for daycare, or for storage of inventory or product samples (see instructions)	1	208
2 Total area of home	2	1,321
3 Divide line 1 by line 2. Enter the result as a percentage	3	15.75 %

For daycare facilities not used exclusively for business, go to line 4. All others, go to line 7.

4 Multiply days used for daycare during year by hours used per day	4		hr.
5 Total hours available for use during the year (365 days x 24 hours) (see instructions)	5	8,760	hr.
6 Divide line 4 by line 5. Enter the result as a decimal amount . . .	6		

7 Business percentage. For daycare facilities not used exclusively for business, multiply line 6 by line 3 (enter the result as a percentage). All others, enter the amount from line 3 . . . . . ▶	7	15.75 %

Part II   Figure Your Allowable Deduction

8 Enter the amount from Schedule C, line 29, **plus** any gain derived from the business use of your home, **minus** any loss from the trade or business not derived from the business use of your home (see instructions)	8	7,953.

See instructions for columns (a) and (b) before completing lines 9–21.

		(a) Direct expenses	(b) Indirect expenses		
9 Casualty losses (see instructions)	9				
10 Deductible mortgage interest (see instructions)	10		6,408.		
11 Real estate taxes (see instructions)	11		1,897.		
12 Add lines 9, 10, and 11	12		8,305.		
13 Multiply line 12, column (b) by line 7		13	1,308.		
14 Add line 12, column (a) and line 13				14	1,308.
15 Subtract line 14 from line 8. If zero or less, enter -0-				15	6,645.
16 Excess mortgage interest (see instructions) .	16				
17 Insurance	17		478.		
18 Rent	18				
19 Repairs and maintenance	19		199.		
20 Utilities	20		2,977.		
21 Other expenses (see instructions).	21				
22 Add lines 16 through 21	22		3,654.		
23 Multiply line 22, column (b) by line 7		23	576.		
24 Carryover of prior year operating expenses (see instructions) . .		24			
25 Add line 22, column (a), line 23, and line 24				25	576.
26 Allowable operating expenses. Enter the **smaller** of line 15 or line 25				26	576.
27 Limit on excess casualty losses and depreciation. Subtract line 26 from line 15				27	6,069.
28 Excess casualty losses (see instructions)		28			
29 Depreciation of your home from line 41 below		29	768.		
30 Carryover of prior year excess casualty losses and depreciation (see instructions)		30			
31 Add lines 28 through 30				31	768.
32 Allowable excess casualty losses and depreciation. Enter the **smaller** of line 27 or line 31 . .				32	768.
33 Add lines 14, 26, and 32.				33	2,652.
34 Casualty loss portion, if any, from lines 14 and 32. Carry amount to **Form 4684** (see instructions)				34	
35 **Allowable expenses for business use of your home.** Subtract line 34 from line 33. Enter here and on Schedule C, line 30. If your home was used for more than one business, see instructions ▶				35	2,652.

Part III   Depreciation of Your Home

36 Enter the **smaller** of your home's adjusted basis or its fair market value (see instructions) . .	36	225,000.
37 Value of land included on line 36	37	35,000.
38 Basis of building. Subtract line 37 from line 36	38	190,000.
39 Business basis of building. Multiply line 38 by line 7.	39	29,925.
40 Depreciation percentage (see instructions).	40	2.5641 %
41 Depreciation allowable (see instructions). Multiply line 39 by line 40. Enter here and on line 29 above	41	768.

Part IV   Carryover of Unallowed Expenses to 2016

42 Operating expenses. Subtract line 26 from line 25. If less than zero, enter -0-	42	0.
43 Excess casualty losses and depreciation. Subtract line 32 from line 31. If less than zero, enter -0-	43	0.

For Paperwork Reduction Act Notice, see your tax return instructions.   **BAA**   REV 12/04/15 PRO   Form **8829** (2015)

Form **4562**	**Depreciation and Amortization**	OMB No. 1545-0172
Department of the Treasury Internal Revenue Service (99)	(Including Information on Listed Property) ▶ Attach to your tax return. ▶ Information about Form 4562 and its separate instructions is at *www.irs.gov/form4562*.	20**15** Attachment Sequence No. **179**

Name(s) shown on return	Business or activity to which this form relates	Identifying number
Sonny Phunky	Sch C Musician	222-33-4444

Part I Election To Expense Certain Property Under Section 179
Note: If you have any listed property, complete Part V before you complete Part I.

1	Maximum amount (see instructions)	1	500,000.
2	Total cost of section 179 property placed in service (see instructions)	2	21,665.
3	Threshold cost of section 179 property before reduction in limitation (see instructions)	3	2,000,000.
4	Reduction in limitation. Subtract line 3 from line 2. If zero or less, enter -0-	4	0.
5	Dollar limitation for tax year. Subtract line 4 from line 1. If zero or less, enter -0-. If married filing separately, see instructions	5	500,000.

6	(a) Description of property	(b) Cost (business use only)	(c) Elected cost
	Gallien-Krueger Amplifier	799.	799.

7	Listed property. Enter the amount from line 29	7	
8	Total elected cost of section 179 property. Add amounts in column (c), lines 6 and 7	8	799.
9	Tentative deduction. Enter the **smaller** of line 5 or line 8	9	799.
10	Carryover of disallowed deduction from line 13 of your 2014 Form 4562	10	
11	Business income limitation. Enter the smaller of business income (not less than zero) or line 5 (see instructions)	11	38,402.
12	Section 179 expense deduction. Add lines 9 and 10, but do not enter more than line 11	12	799.
13	Carryover of disallowed deduction to 2016. Add lines 9 and 10, less line 12 ▶	13	0.

Note: Do not use Part II or Part III below for listed property. Instead, use Part V.

Part II Special Depreciation Allowance and Other Depreciation (Do not include listed property.) (See instructions.)

14	Special depreciation allowance for qualified property (other than listed property) placed in service during the tax year (see instructions)	14	200.
15	Property subject to section 168(f)(1) election	15	
16	Other depreciation (including ACRS)	16	

Part III MACRS Depreciation (Do not include listed property.) (See instructions.)

Section A

17	MACRS deductions for assets placed in service in tax years beginning before 2015	17	768.
18	If you are electing to group any assets placed in service during the tax year into one or more general asset accounts, check here . . . . ▶ ☐		

Section B—Assets Placed in Service During 2015 Tax Year Using the General Depreciation System

(a) Classification of property	(b) Month and year placed in service	(c) Basis for depreciation (business/investment use only—see instructions)	(d) Recovery period	(e) Convention	(f) Method	(g) Depreciation deduction
19a 3-year property						
b 5-year property		698.	5.0	HY	200 DB	140.
c 7-year property		15,000.	7.0	HY	200 DB	2,143.
d 10-year property						
e 15-year property						
f 20-year property						
g 25-year property			25 yrs.		S/L	
h Residential rental property			27.5 yrs.	MM	S/L	
			27.5 yrs.	MM	S/L	
i Nonresidential real property			39 yrs.	MM	S/L	
				MM	S/L	

Section C—Assets Placed in Service During 2015 Tax Year Using the Alternative Depreciation System

20a Class life					S/L	
b 12-year			12 yrs.		S/L	
c 40-year			40 yrs.	MM	S/L	

Part IV Summary (See instructions.)

21	Listed property. Enter amount from line 28	21	
22	**Total.** Add amounts from line 12, lines 14 through 17, lines 19 and 20 in column (g), and line 21. Enter here and on the appropriate lines of your return. Partnerships and S corporations—see instructions	22	4,050.
23	For assets shown above and placed in service during the current year, enter the portion of the basis attributable to section 263A costs	23	

For Paperwork Reduction Act Notice, see separate instructions. **BAA**   REV 12/27/15 PRO   Form **4562** (2015)

Form 4562 (2015)　　　　　　　　　　　　　　　　　　　　　　　　　　　　　　　　　　　　Page **2**

Part V **Listed Property** (Include automobiles, certain other vehicles, certain aircraft, certain computers, and property used for entertainment, recreation, or amusement.)

Note: For any vehicle for which you are using the standard mileage rate or deducting lease expense, complete **only** 24a, 24b, columns (a) through (c) of Section A, all of Section B, and Section C if applicable.

Section A—Depreciation and Other Information (Caution: See the instructions for limits for passenger automobiles.**)**

24a Do you have evidence to support the business/investment use claimed? ☒ Yes ☐ No | 24b If "Yes," is the evidence written? ☒ Yes ☐ No

(a) Type of property (list vehicles first)	(b) Date placed in service	(c) Business/investment use percentage	(d) Cost or other basis	(e) Basis for depreciation (business/investment use only)	(f) Recovery period	(g) Method/ Convention	(h) Depreciation deduction	(i) Elected section 179 cost
25 Special depreciation allowance for qualified listed property placed in service during the tax year and used more than 50% in a qualified business use (see instructions) .					25			
26 Property used more than 50% in a qualified business use:								
		%						
		%						
		%						
27 Property used 50% or less in a qualified business use:								
Vehicle	01/01/2010	24.17 %				S/L –		
		%				S/L –		
		%				S/L –		
28 Add amounts in column (h), lines 25 through 27. Enter here and on line 21, page 1 .					28			
29 Add amounts in column (i), line 26. Enter here and on line 7, page 1							29	

Section B—Information on Use of Vehicles

Complete this section for vehicles used by a sole proprietor, partner, or other "more than 5% owner," or related person. If you provided vehicles to your employees, first answer the questions in Section C to see if you meet an exception to completing this section for those vehicles.

	(a) Vehicle 1		(b) Vehicle 2		(c) Vehicle 3		(d) Vehicle 4		(e) Vehicle 5		(f) Vehicle 6	
30 Total business/investment miles driven during the year (**do not** include commuting miles) .	3,853											
31 Total commuting miles driven during the year												
32 Total other personal (noncommuting) miles driven	12,088											
33 Total miles driven during the year. Add lines 30 through 32	15,941											
34 Was the vehicle available for personal use during off-duty hours?	Yes	No	Yes	No	Yes	No	Yes	No	Yes	No	Yes	No
	✕											
35 Was the vehicle used primarily by a more than 5% owner or related person? . .	✕											
36 Is another vehicle available for personal use?		✕										

Section C—Questions for Employers Who Provide Vehicles for Use by Their Employees

Answer these questions to determine if you meet an exception to completing Section B for vehicles used by employees who **are not** more than 5% owners or related persons (see instructions).

		Yes	No
37 Do you maintain a written policy statement that prohibits all personal use of vehicles, including commuting, by your employees?			
38 Do you maintain a written policy statement that prohibits personal use of vehicles, except commuting, by your employees? See the instructions for vehicles used by corporate officers, directors, or 1% or more owners . .			
39 Do you treat all use of vehicles by employees as personal use?			
40 Do you provide more than five vehicles to your employees, obtain information from your employees about the use of the vehicles, and retain the information received?			
41 Do you meet the requirements concerning qualified automobile demonstration use? (See instructions.) . . .			

Note: If your answer to 37, 38, 39, 40, or 41 is "Yes," do not complete Section B for the covered vehicles.

Part VI **Amortization**

(a) Description of costs	(b) Date amortization begins	(c) Amortizable amount	(d) Code section	(e) Amortization period or percentage	(f) Amortization for this year
42 Amortization of costs that begins during your 2015 tax year (see instructions):					
CD Production	07/01/2015	10,000.	197	2.00 yrs	2,500.
Website	08/09/2015	2,841.	197	3.00 yrs	947.
43 Amortization of costs that began before your 2015 tax year				43	
44 **Total.** Add amounts in column (f). See the instructions for where to report				44	3,447.

REV 12/27/15 PRO　　　　　　　　　　　　　　　　　　　　　　　　　　　Form **4562** (2015)

Form **4562**	**Depreciation and Amortization**	OMB No. 1545-0172
	(Including Information on Listed Property)	20**15**
Department of the Treasury Internal Revenue Service (99)	▶ Attach to your tax return. ▶ Information about Form 4562 and its separate instructions is at *www.irs.gov/form4562*.	Attachment Sequence No. **179**

Name(s) shown on return	Business or activity to which this form relates	Identifying number
Sonny Phunky	K1 Partnership SBE The Lido Shuffle	222-33-4444

Part I   **Election To Expense Certain Property Under Section 179**
    Note: If you have any listed property, complete Part V before you complete Part I.

1	Maximum amount (see instructions)	**1**	500,000.
2	Total cost of section 179 property placed in service (see instructions)	**2**	
3	Threshold cost of section 179 property before reduction in limitation (see instructions)	**3**	2,000,000.
4	Reduction in limitation. Subtract line 3 from line 2. If zero or less, enter -0-	**4**	
5	Dollar limitation for tax year. Subtract line 4 from line 1. If zero or less, enter -0-. If married filing separately, see instructions	**5**	

6	(a) Description of property	(b) Cost (business use only)	(c) Elected cost		

7	Listed property. Enter the amount from line 29	**7**	
8	Total elected cost of section 179 property. Add amounts in column (c), lines 6 and 7	**8**	
9	Tentative deduction. Enter the **smaller** of line 5 or line 8	**9**	
10	Carryover of disallowed deduction from line 13 of your 2014 Form 4562	**10**	
11	Business income limitation. Enter the smaller of business income (not less than zero) or line 5 (see instructions)	**11**	
12	Section 179 expense deduction. Add lines 9 and 10, but do not enter more than line 11	**12**	
13	Carryover of disallowed deduction to 2016. Add lines 9 and 10, less line 12 ▶	**13**	

Note: Do not use Part I or Part III below for listed property. Instead, use Part V.

Part II   **Special Depreciation Allowance and Other Depreciation (Do not** include listed property.) (See instructions.)

14	Special depreciation allowance for qualified property (other than listed property) placed in service during the tax year (see instructions)	**14**	
15	Property subject to section 168(f)(1) election	**15**	
16	Other depreciation (including ACRS)	**16**	

Part III   **MACRS Depreciation (Do not** include listed property.) (See instructions.)

Section A

17	MACRS deductions for assets placed in service in tax years beginning before 2015	**17**	
18	If you are electing to group any assets placed in service during the tax year into one or more general asset accounts, check here . . . . ▶ ☐		

Section B—Assets Placed in Service During 2015 Tax Year Using the General Depreciation System

(a) Classification of property	(b) Month and year placed in service	(c) Basis for depreciation (business/investment use only—see instructions)	(d) Recovery period	(e) Convention	(f) Method	(g) Depreciation deduction
19a 3-year property						
b 5-year property						
c 7-year property						
d 10-year property						
e 15-year property						
f 20-year property						
g 25-year property			25 yrs.		S/L	
h Residential rental property			27.5 yrs.	MM	S/L	
			27.5 yrs.	MM	S/L	
i Nonresidential real property			39 yrs.	MM	S/L	
				MM	S/L	

Section C—Assets Placed in Service During 2015 Tax Year Using the Alternative Depreciation System

20a Class life					S/L	
b 12-year			12 yrs.		S/L	
c 40-year			40 yrs.	MM	S/L	

Part IV   **Summary** (See instructions.)

21	Listed property. Enter amount from line 28	**21**	
22	**Total.** Add amounts from line 12, lines 14 through 17, lines 19 and 20 in column (g), and line 21. Enter here and on the appropriate lines of your return. Partnerships and S corporations—see instructions .	**22**	
23	For assets shown above and placed in service during the current year, enter the portion of the basis attributable to section 263A costs	**23**	

For Paperwork Reduction Act Notice, see separate instructions. **BAA**   REV 12/27/15 PRO   Form **4562** (2015)

Form 4562 (2015)   Page **2**

Part V **Listed Property** (Include automobiles, certain other vehicles, certain aircraft, certain computers, and property used for entertainment, recreation, or amusement.)

Note: For any vehicle for which you are using the standard mileage rate or deducting lease expense, complete **only** 24a, 24b, columns (a) through (c) of Section A, all of Section B, and Section C if applicable.

Section A—Depreciation and Other Information (Caution: See the instructions for limits for passenger automobiles.)

24a Do you have evidence to support the business/investment use claimed?   ☒ Yes ☐ No   **24b** If "Yes," is the evidence written? ☒ Yes ☐ No

(a) Type of property (list vehicles first)	(b) Date placed in service	(c) Business/ investment use percentage	(d) Cost or other basis	(e) Basis for depreciation (business/investment use only)	(f) Recovery period	(g) Method/ Convention	(h) Depreciation deduction	(i) Elected section 179 cost
25 Special depreciation allowance for qualified listed property placed in service during the tax year and used more than 50% in a qualified business use (see instructions) .					**25**			
26 Property used more than 50% in a qualified business use:								
		%						
		%						
		%						
27 Property used 50% or less in a qualified business use:								
Vehicle	01/01/2011	6.03 %				S/L –		
		%				S/L –		
		%				S/L –		
28 Add amounts in column (h), lines 25 through 27. Enter here and on line 21, page 1 .					**28**			
29 Add amounts in column (i), line 26. Enter here and on line 7, page 1							**29**	

Section B—Information on Use of Vehicles

Complete this section for vehicles used by a sole proprietor, partner, or other "more than 5% owner," or related person. If you provided vehicles to your employees, first answer the questions in Section C to see if you meet an exception to completing this section for those vehicles.

	(a) Vehicle 1		(b) Vehicle 2		(c) Vehicle 3		(d) Vehicle 4		(e) Vehicle 5		(f) Vehicle 6	
30 Total business/investment miles driven during the year (**do not** include commuting miles) .	962											
31 Total commuting miles driven during the year												
32 Total other personal (noncommuting) miles driven	14,979											
33 Total miles driven during the year. Add lines 30 through 32	15,941											
34 Was the vehicle available for personal use during off-duty hours?	Yes ✗	No	Yes	No	Yes	No	Yes	No	Yes	No	Yes	No
35 Was the vehicle used primarily by a more than 5% owner or related person? . .	✗											
36 Is another vehicle available for personal use?		✗										

Section C—Questions for Employers Who Provide Vehicles for Use by Their Employees

Answer these questions to determine if you meet an exception to completing Section B for vehicles used by employees who **are not** more than 5% owners or related persons (see instructions).

	Yes	No
37 Do you maintain a written policy statement that prohibits all personal use of vehicles, including commuting, by your employees?		
38 Do you maintain a written policy statement that prohibits personal use of vehicles, except commuting, by your employees? See the instructions for vehicles used by corporate officers, directors, or 1% or more owners . .		
39 Do you treat all use of vehicles by employees as personal use?		
40 Do you provide more than five vehicles to your employees, obtain information from your employees about the use of the vehicles, and retain the information received?		
41 Do you meet the requirements concerning qualified automobile demonstration use? (See instructions.) . . .		

Note: If your answer to 37, 38, 39, 40, or 41 is "Yes," do not complete Section B for the covered vehicles.

Part VI **Amortization**

(a) Description of costs	(b) Date amortization begins	(c) Amortizable amount	(d) Code section	(e) Amortization period or percentage	(f) Amortization for this year
42 Amortization of costs that begins during your 2015 tax year (see instructions):					
43 Amortization of costs that began before your 2015 tax year			**43**		
44 Total. Add amounts in column (f). See the instructions for where to report			**44**		

REV 12/27/15 PRO   Form **4562** (2015)

Form **4562**	**Depreciation and Amortization**	OMB No. 1545-0172
	(Including Information on Listed Property)	20**15**
Department of the Treasury Internal Revenue Service (99)	► Attach to your tax return. ► Information about Form 4562 and its separate instructions is at *www.irs.gov/form4562*.	Attachment Sequence No. **179**

Name(s) shown on return	Business or activity to which this form relates	Identifying number
Sonny Phunky	Form 2106 Musician	222-33-4444

Part I Election To Expense Certain Property Under Section 179
Note: If you have any listed property, complete Part V before you complete Part I.

1	Maximum amount (see instructions)	1	500,000.
2	Total cost of section 179 property placed in service (see instructions)	2	
3	Threshold cost of section 179 property before reduction in limitation (see instructions)	3	2,000,000.
4	Reduction in limitation. Subtract line 3 from line 2. If zero or less, enter -0-	4	
5	Dollar limitation for tax year. Subtract line 4 from line 1. If zero or less, enter -0-. If married filing separately, see instructions	5	

6	(a) Description of property	(b) Cost (business use only)	(c) Elected cost	

7	Listed property. Enter the amount from line 29	7	
8	Total elected cost of section 179 property. Add amounts in column (c), lines 6 and 7	8	
9	Tentative deduction. Enter the **smaller** of line 5 or line 8	9	
10	Carryover of disallowed deduction from line 13 of your 2014 Form 4562	10	
11	Business income limitation. Enter the smaller of business income (not less than zero) or line 5 (see instructions)	11	
12	Section 179 expense deduction. Add lines 9 and 10, but do not enter more than line 11	12	
13	Carryover of disallowed deduction to 2016. Add lines 9 and 10, less line 12 ►	13	

Note: Do not use Part II or Part III below for listed property. Instead, use Part V.

Part II Special Depreciation Allowance and Other Depreciation (Do not include listed property.) (See instructions.)

14	Special depreciation allowance for qualified property (other than listed property) placed in service during the tax year (see instructions)	14	
15	Property subject to section 168(f)(1) election	15	
16	Other depreciation (including ACRS)	16	

Part III MACRS Depreciation (Do not include listed property.) (See instructions.)

Section A

17	MACRS deductions for assets placed in service in tax years beginning before 2015	17	
18	If you are electing to group any assets placed in service during the tax year into one or more general asset accounts, check here . . . . ► ☐		

Section B—Assets Placed in Service During 2015 Tax Year Using the General Depreciation System

(a) Classification of property	(b) Month and year placed in service	(c) Basis for depreciation (business/investment use only—see instructions)	(d) Recovery period	(e) Convention	(f) Method	(g) Depreciation deduction
19a 3-year property						
b 5-year property		4,968.	5.0	HY	200 DB	994.
c 7-year property						
d 10-year property						
e 15-year property						
f 20-year property						
g 25-year property			25 yrs.		S/L	
h Residential rental property			27.5 yrs.	MM	S/L	
			27.5 yrs.	MM	S/L	
i Nonresidential real property			39 yrs.	MM	S/L	
				MM	S/L	

Section C—Assets Placed in Service During 2015 Tax Year Using the Alternative Depreciation System

20a Class life					S/L	
b 12-year			12 yrs.		S/L	
c 40-year			40 yrs.	MM	S/L	

Part IV Summary (See instructions.)

21	Listed property. Enter amount from line 28	21	
22	**Total.** Add amounts from line 12, lines 14 through 17, lines 19 and 20 in column (g), and line 21. Enter here and on the appropriate lines of your return. Partnerships and S corporations—see instructions .	22	994.
23	For assets shown above and placed in service during the current year, enter the portion of the basis attributable to section 263A costs	23	

For Paperwork Reduction Act Notice, see separate instructions. **BAA**	REV 12/27/15 PRO	Form **4562** (2015)

Schedule E Line 28	**Supplemental Business Expenses Worksheet**	**2015**

Your Name	Social Security Number
Sonny Phunky	222-33-4444

Partnership
The Lido Shuffle

Expenses

1	Vehicle expenses	1	706.
2	Vehicle rentals	2	0.
3	Travel expense while away from home overnight, including lodging, airplane, car rental, etc. **Do not** include meals and entertainment	3	412.
4	Business gifts	4	
5	Education	5	
6	Office supplies and expenses	6	
7	Telephone, fax, pager, etc	7	
8	Trade publications	8	
9	Depreciation and amortization	9	
10	Other (enter meals and entertainment on line 12):	10	
	Supplies		294.
	Cell Phone		39.
	. . . .		
	. . . .		
11	Total expenses other than meals and entertainment. Add lines 1 through 10 . .	11	1,451.
12	Meals and entertainment expenses	12	1,836.

Reimbursements & Deductible Expenses

13	Reimbursements for other than meals and entertainment	13	
14	Reimbursements for meals and entertainment	14	360.
15	Deductible exp other than meals and ent. Subtract line 13 from line 11	15	1,451.
16	Subtract line 14 from line 12	16	1,476.
17	Deductible meals and entertainment expenses. Enter 50% of line 16	17	738.
18	**Total expenses**. Add line 15 and line 17	18	2,189.

Self-Employed Income Reconciliation

19	Net earnings (loss) from self-employment from Sch K-1 Wks, Part III, line 14 . .	19	3,420.
20	Expenses from line 18	20	2,189.
21	Allowed section 179 expense from Schedule K-1 Additional Info 1, Box 12, line 2 (if applicable)	21	
22	Net self-employment income. Subtract lines 20 and 21 from line 19	22	1,231.

Sonny Phunky   222-33-4444

Schedule C (line 6) - Other Income

Endorsement (value of bass)	$2,000
Sales of CDs	$1,950
Royalties	$241
PLEDGEMUSIC Income	$10,000
	$14,191

Schedule C - Meals Detail Line 24B

Atlantic City	14	$97	$1,358
New Orleans	6	$64	$384
Nashville (NAMM)	3	$59	$177
Other professional meals			$704
			$2,623 (only 50% deductible)

Schedule C Travel Line 24A

New Orleans Hotel and Airline	$1,446
Nashville (NAMM) hotel	$487
	$1,933

Schedule C - Other Expenses

Trade Publications (Billboard)	$299
Research & Music Downloads	$613
Performance Audit	$405
Internet Service	$405
Cell & Skype Phone Service	$372
Online A&R (Taxi)	$300
CD Baby and other online fees	$79
Instructional DVD's	$89
Sheet Music	$161
Promo Photos	$285
Printing	$49
Amortization	$3,447
	$6,504

Schedule C (line 40/Pt III) - Other Costs of Goods Sold

Sidemen (1099's issued)	$3,640
500 CD's pressed	$1,000
1099 Income not received until 2012	$925
PLEDGEMUSIC commission	$1,500
	$7,065

Form 2106 - Deducted on Sch A - Line 21

Travel (line 3) NYC	21	$316		$6,636
Supplies				
Research CD's & downloads				$818
Instrument Repairs				$399
Professional Fees				$100
Depreciation (chartreuse bass, Pono Player & Ampeg)				$994
				$2,311
Meals (form 2106) NYC 21 days @ $71				$1,491

Supplemental Business Expenses
The Lido Shuffle Form K-1 (Schedule E)

Vehicle expense		$553
Parking		$153
Travel		$412
Music Supplies		$294
Cell Phone		$39
		$1,451

Meals		
36 days @ $51 (per deim)		$1,836
Reimbursement by band		-$360
	100%	$1,476
Half deductible	50%	$738
Total deduction		$2,189

Depreciation (Sch C)

	Acquired	Method	Life	Cost	Accum	Sec 179	Current Expense
CD Production	7/1/2015	Amortization	24M	$10,000	$0	$0	$2,500
Website	8/9/2015	Amortization	36M	$2,841	$0	$0	$947
							$3,447
Fender Bass 1956	7/1/2015	MACRS	7 Yrs.	$15,000	$0	$0	$2,143
Gallien-Krueger Amp	9/15/2015	MACRS	5 Yrs.	$799	$0	$799	$799
GoPro 4K Video	7/1/2015	MACRS	5 Yrs.	$499	$0	$0	$100
iPhone 6	7/1/2015	MACRS	5 Yrs.	$399	$0	$0	$240
				$16,697	$0	$799	$3,282

6

For Visual Artists

In this chapter I will look in detail at the activities of our good friend, Liz Brushstroke, and the kind of income and deductions she had for the year.

First, let's walk through some of the expense items for visual artists specifically. I will note in parentheses the type of record keeping the IRS would require:

1. Union dues, professional societies, and organizations (invoices and payment verification).

2. Professional fees for agents, attorneys, and accountants (invoices and payment verification).

3. Artist registries—both printed and on the Internet (bills, invoices, credit card receipts, or payment verification).

4. Master classes, education, and seminars (bills, invoices, credit card receipts, or payment verification).

5. Personal photographs and resumes—including videos, CDs, CD-ROMs, USB drives, DVDs, scans and digital image transfers for use on the Internet or your personal website (bills, invoices, credit card receipts, or payment verification).

6. Slides of artwork—including all photographers' fees, developing, slide copies, and digital image transfers to CDs (invoices and payment verification).

7. Costs of printmaking—having Giclée or other types of printing done (bills, invoices, payment verification, or credit card receipts).

8. Stationery and postage (sales receipts, credit card receipts, and payment verification).

9. Printing of brochures (invoices and payment verification).

10. Art books—these may need to be allocated between employment income and contract income (sales receipts, credit card receipts, and payment verification).

11. Telephone, Internet communications, and cellular phone—actual business calls on your home phone are deductible, but the IRS does not allow the allocation of the base monthly rate. You can deduct only the actual long distance charges. The same rule is true with your cellular phone or Skype service. If you get a second phone line strictly for business, then it can be considered 100% deductible (bills and payment verification).

12. Travel—hotels, airline, meals (per diem generally), Airbnb, Uber, train, bus, baggage fees, etc. (confirmation and payment verification). Very important: documentation proving the reason for the trip (invoice, confirmations, and payment verification).

13. Internet, data, and cloud services—for research purposes, business e-mail, and e-mail while traveling. Be sure to allocate some of the costs for personal use (bills, invoices, and credit card receipts).

14. Visiting galleries and museums to view artwork—I often call this expense line item "research"; others refer to it as "auditing." Whatever you call it, make sure to allocate some of this expense to personal use. After all, you must sometimes take part in these activities for personal enjoyment; it can't be all business. I quote to clients the old Wall Street saying, "the pigs get fat and the hogs get slaughtered." This is the type of deduction that you must not get piggy with. While the IRS typically hates this deduction, you can easily argue that the visual artist must engage in these viewings for educational reasons and to keep abreast of trends and dynamics within their profession. In an audit you would need to explain what the specific professional value was (museum admission stubs, business cards from the gallery, and diary entries).

15. Gallery rents or memberships (invoices and payment verification).

16. Studio rent—you must be able to prove you need an outside studio, and note: you cannot maintain a tax-deductible home studio if you rent outside space (bills, invoices, and payment verification).

17. Repair of equipment—computers, presses, sculpting tools and equipment, photography equipment, etc. (bills, invoices, and payment verification).

18. Tax preparation, bookkeeping and accounting fees (bills, invoices, and payment verification).

19. Entry fees into juried show (copy of entry and payment verification).

20. Advertisement and listing in arts publications (bills, invoices, credit card receipts, or payment verification).

21. Professional magazines (bills, invoices, credit card receipts, or payment verification).

22. Insurance—this can include riders on your home policy that relate directly to your home studio (bills, invoices, and payment verification).

23. Copyright fees (invoices and payment verification).

24. Equipment purchases—tools, presses, tablet computers, smartphones, camera and video equipment, welders, computers, printers, etc. (bills, invoices, credit card receipts, or payment verification).

25. Framing and displaying costs—you can only deduct for the costs of artwork you actually sold, other costs related to unsold work become inventory at year-end (bills, invoices, credit card receipts, or payment verification).

26. Supplies—like the framing costs listed above, keep in mind that you can only deduct for the costs of artwork you actually sold. Other costs related to unsold work become inventory at year-end (bills, invoices, credit card receipts, or payment verification).

27. Studio supplies and fixtures (bills, invoices, credit card receipts, or payment verification).

Now, let's see what kind of year our artist, Liz, had.

Luckily for her tax preparer, Liz downloaded our Excel spreadsheet for visual artists (found on www.artstaxinfo.com), loaded it on her notebook computer at the beginning of the tax year, and carefully tracked her expenses all year!

We will now review Liz's 1040 income tax return in detail—and remember you can download the current year version from our website—www.artstaxinfo.com.

Liz's primary income is from her teaching position at the Independent Art Institute. This income is reported on her W-2 and is found in Box 7 of her 1040.

During the winter she had a one-artist show of her work at a Dublin gallery. She had to arrange for shipping her artwork to Ireland. She planned to go over to Ireland for the show opening, as the artist's presence generally increases sales, and the gallery owner had arranged for her to give a talk on her artwork while she was there. Liz wanted to make sure the trip would be 100% deductible, so she discussed it with her accountant in advance. Her trip was going to last 8 days; as it was outside the continental United States, she learned that any personal and/or vacation time would have to be limited to no more than 25%. Liz realized she would need to arrange some other business activities beyond the gallery exhibit and talk. Using an online search of some schools in Dublin to see if they were offering a class or seminar that she could attend, she signed up for a seminar being given by a famous Irish art historian on the history of Irish art. She also arranged a studio visit with an Irish landscape painter she admired, and she prearranged appointments with some gallery owners who owned galleries in Europe to see what opportunities might be available beyond Ireland. These other business activities helped Liz to make the entire trip deductible and still have some time for tourist activity. She could deduct her flight, the shipping of the artwork to Ireland and back, the 50% allowed for meals, all her hotel costs during the business portion of the trip, her auto rental there, laundry, phone calls home, etc. She will also deduct the costs of the artwork sold, including framing costs, as a "cost of goods sold" on her Schedule C. She did not want to be bothered to keep receipts of meals, so she decided to use the Internal Revenue Service approved foreign per diem rates (OCONUS) published by the Department of Defense (find link at www.artstaxinfo.com). The rate for Dublin in 2016 is $126 for meals and incidentals. Liz was sad to sell one of her personal favorite paintings, "Sunlight on the Brook." Of course, the income from the art she sold will be self-employment income on her Schedule C.

Here we must pause to discuss the issue of inventory. Inventory is problematic for many artists; I often get blank stares when I ask the question at tax time. The inquiry concerns the cost at year-end of the artwork that has not yet been sold—this is the artist's inventory.

Not to get too technical, the calculation of inventory is primary in arriving at "cost of goods sold." In other words, my direct materials deduction for tax purposes is (1) the direct *cost* of all materials used in the production of finished artwork (materials, framing, printing, etc.) *less* (2) the finished artwork held at the end of the year (ending inventory). Please note: the IRS specifically exempts visual and other artists from the onerous "Uniform Capitalization

Rules" regarding the application of direct and indirect overhead costs, but the artists still have to account for the actual costs of work they have created. Some artists (being cash-based taxpayers) can ignore this process altogether because the direct product costs are relatively minor (a potter comes to mind), but for most fine artists, photographers, etc., the cost of framing alone can be sizable enough to require addressing ending inventory.

On the tax return the calculation looks something like this (Schedule C, Part III):

Beginning inventory (beginning of year—from all prior years)	$5,000
Materials purchased during the current year	$3,000
Printing done during the current year	$2,000
Framing done during the current year	$6,000
Total inventory available for sale in the current year	$16,000
Ending inventory (end of year)	−$5,500
Cost of goods sold	$10,500

In this example, Liz started the year with $5,000 of value (stretchers, printing, materials costs, framing, prints, etc.) in "unsold" artwork from prior years. During the year she purchased $3,000 of materials, had $2,000 in printing costs, and spent $6,000 on framing so that during the year she spent $11,000 producing new, finished artwork. The $11,000 added to the $5,000 beginning number yielded $16,000 of direct costs in finished art for the year. Finally, at year-end she had $5,500 (in cost) of unsold artwork; this was her ending inventory. According to this example, Liz had deductible, direct cost of artwork sold during the year of $10,500. You will see on Liz's Schedule C Line 4 and Part III how this worked out on her 1040 income tax return.

In the spring, Liz attended the annual conference of a national women's art organization in Phoenix, Arizona. As an officer in the local chapter of this organization, Liz was expected to be there. The trip gave her a chance to network with fellow artists, an opportunity to see new products that art supply dealers displayed, and the occasion to show her portfolio to some gallery owners. She even discussed with a fellow artist the possibility of using Kickstarter as a way to fund the publishing of a book or an iPad app of their work. The organization held educational events for the participants every day and an afternoon of gallery tours. Liz was at the conference for the entire 3 days she was gone. She made sure that she brought home the convention schedule and related literature and noted which events she attended and when. Liz clearly showed a business purpose and she will be able to deduct the entire trip.

A friend of Liz recommended that she spend some time in New York City to "see what was happening" in the art scene there. Liz flew to the city and spent a week visiting galleries and museums, staying with artist friends she had in New York. She even did some studio visits with other artists. While she may be able to claim some business entertainment expense for lunch with a gallery owner, and perhaps to deduct the costs of attending the museums, unfortunately for Liz, there will probably be little to deduct on this trip. She had no income from it, and as far as the IRS is concerned, it had no well-defined, specific business purpose, thus few deductions!

Liz was invited to be the juror for a local art show. A small art nonprofit decided to have its own juried art show in order to attract more artists from around the region. Liz received a small stipend from the organization. Other than some car mileage, she probably didn't have other expenses connected with this activity.

After her opening in Dublin, Liz decided that she wanted to set up a personal website so she could link to her popular blog where she writes about art, posts her résumé, art images, artist statement, etc. She was also using Instagram and Facebook to post her most current work. If she were going to expand into Europe, it would be very helpful to have an online presence for gallery owners to be able to visit and see her latest work. The costs of setting up the website, registering the domain name, and hosting the site will all be deductible. She will be able to deduct the costs of having photos taken and transferred to digital images or possibly scanned for use on the site. The IRS stipulates that website development is written off (amortized) over 3 years. So all the costs of designing and setting up the site will be added up (capitalized) and expensed over 3 years.

The look of her new website pleased Liz so much that she decided to have business cards, stationery, and a digital brochure designed and printed to capitalize on and promote the site. To let folks know the website and social media campaign was up and running, she did a postcard and e-mail marketing campaign. She had some custom USB drives prepared that were preloaded with her digital brochure, as well as a selection of images of her artwork and a link to her website to give to potential clients and gallery owners. All the costs of printing the postcards, purchasing the e-mail list, the USB drives, and postage were fully deductible on Liz's Schedule C. Any of these materials remaining unsent (if significant) at year-end may have to be added to her year-end inventory.

Near the end of the year Liz was in a group show at the New York City gallery that represents her. As flying was not as time-effective as it once had been, she decided to drive to NYC to attend the opening. She spent the following day at the gallery and in the evening had dinner with the gallery owner to discuss possibilities of future shows. The next day she drove back home. Her entire trip will be deductible, including mileage, tolls, parking, hotel and meals (50%), etc. Sales of artwork in NYC are subject to sales tax, but since the gallery is the entity actually selling Liz's work, they would have the responsibility for handling this tax.

During the year, Liz entered her work into several juried art shows throughout the country. The entry fees, photographer, costs of developing and sending slides, and shipping artwork would all be deductible business expenses on her Schedule C. To provide evidence of her ongoing effort to market and sell artwork, Liz saves scans of all her entries. These could be very important if Liz is hit with a "hobby loss" audit, as we discussed in Chapter 3.

Liz set up a large room in her home as a studio that she uses exclusively to make art. She takes a home office deduction for the studio on Form 8829. This form allows her to take a portion of all her general home expenses as a deduction against her art income. If she makes alterations to the room specifically for the production of art, she can take those expenses 100%. This year Liz installed an air venting system to help extract the paint fumes from the studio when she is working. She also upgraded her electrical system. Liz's accountant will depreciate both of these items.

When she met with her accountant at year-end to do some tax planning and payment verification on her estimated tax payments for the year, she had more income than she had anticipated. Her accountant asked if there were some expenses that she could accelerate into the current year; this way she would get the tax benefit of the deductions in the current year. Liz needed more places to store artwork and wanted some new flat files. She also needed a new digital camera to take pictures of subjects she wanted to paint in her studio, as well as to take pictures of her artwork. She decided to purchase the new files and the camera before December 31st. By purchasing these before year-end, she was able to use the Section 179 election and write them off 100% in the current year. She can do this even if she charges the files and/or camera on her credit card and pays it off in the next year, as long as the files are "in use" before December 31st.

Painters, Photographers, & Other Visual Artists

Continuing Education

Private Lessons	
Master Classes & Apprenticeships	
Schools & Conferences	
Tickets to Special Exhibits	
Gallery Visits & Talks	
Museum Memberships	
Other: _____	

Promotional Expenses

Portfolio Costs	
Business Cards & Resume	
Website Development & Hosting	
Postage & Shipping	
Slide & Photographer Fees	
Printing of Show Announcement Cards	
Shows & Exhibits	
Printing Costs	
Other: _____	

Supplies & Other Expenses

Gallery Membership & Dues	
Brushes & Cleaning Supplies	
Paint, Film, Papers, etc.	
Dues—Union & Professional	
Gifts—Business ($25 maximum per person per year)	
Chemicals for Film Processing	
Museum Dues & Memberships	
Canvas & Stretchers	
Framing Costs	
Meals—Business (enter 100% of cost)	
Slide & Film Processing	
Stationary & Office Supplies	

Rent—Studio & Gallery Space

Art Magazines & Books

Legal & Accounting Fees

Rents & Repairs of Equipment

Sculpture Supplies & Hardware

Food & Wine—Gallery Openings

Modeling Fees & Props

Commissions—Agent/Manager

Other: _____

Auto Travel (in miles)

Museum & Gallery Visits

Client & Business Meetings

Continuing Education

Gallery Interviews (Potential Shows)

Out-of-Town Business Trips

Purchasing Art Supplies & Materials

Professional Society Meetings

Parking Fees & Tolls

Other: _____

Travel—Out of Town

Airfare & Auto Rental

Van Rental for Moving of Artwork

Parking

Taxi, Train, Bus, & Subway

Lodging (do not combine with meals)

Meals (enter 100% of expense)

Laundry, Maid, & Porter

Tolls

Telephone Calls (including home)

Other: _____

Communications Costs

Skype or Other Internet Phone Service

Internet & Online Services

Land Line

Cellular Phone

Other: _____

Equipment Purchases

Phone & Answering Machine

Computer, Peripherals, & Software

Press, Easel, & Paint Box

Darkroom Equipment

Camera (Digital & Traditional) & Lenses

Safety Equipment & Fixtures

Kiln & Foundry

Framing Apparatus

Power & Hand Tools

Sculpting Tools & Equipment

Other: _____

Form **1040**	Department of the Treasury—Internal Revenue Service (99) **U.S. Individual Income Tax Return**	2015	OMB No. 1545-0074	IRS Use Only—Do not write or staple in this space.

For the year Jan. 1–Dec. 31, 2015, or other tax year beginning ____ , 2015, ending ____ , 20 ____ See separate instructions.

Your first name and initial	Last name	Your social security number
Liz	Brushstroke	333-44-5555

If a joint return, spouse's first name and initial	Last name	Spouse's social security number

Home address (number and street). If you have a P.O. box, see instructions. **Apt. no.**
Commonwealth Ave   5

City, town or post office, state, and ZIP code. If you have a foreign address, also complete spaces below (see instructions).
Chestnut Hill MA 02467

▲ Make sure the SSN(s) above and on line 6c are correct.

Presidential Election Campaign
Check here if you, or your spouse if filing jointly, want $3 to go to this fund. Checking a box below will not change your tax or refund. ☐ You ☐ Spouse

Foreign country name	Foreign province/state/county	Foreign postal code

Filing Status

Check only one box.

1 ☒ Single
2 ☐ Married filing jointly (even if only one had income)
3 ☐ Married filing separately. Enter spouse's SSN above and full name here. ▶
4 ☐ Head of household (with qualifying person). (See instructions.) If the qualifying person is a child but not your dependent, enter this child's name here. ▶
5 ☐ Qualifying widow(er) with dependent child

Exemptions

6a ☒ **Yourself.** If someone can claim you as a dependent, **do not** check box 6a . . . . .
b ☐ **Spouse** . . . .

c **Dependents:**

(1) First name Last name	(2) Dependent's social security number	(3) Dependent's relationship to you	(4) ✓ if child under age 17 qualifying for child tax credit (see instructions)
			☐
			☐
			☐
			☐

If more than four dependents, see instructions and check here ▶ ☐

d   Total number of exemptions claimed . . . .

Boxes checked on 6a and 6b   **1**
No. of children on 6c who:
• lived with you ____
• did not live with you due to divorce or separation (see instructions) ____
Dependents on 6c not entered above ____
Add numbers on lines above ▶ **1**

Income

Attach Form(s) W-2 here. Also attach Forms W-2G and 1099-R if tax was withheld.

If you did not get a W-2, see instructions.

7	Wages, salaries, tips, etc. Attach Form(s) W-2	7	53,211.
8a	Taxable interest. Attach Schedule B if required	8a	
b	Tax-exempt interest. **Do not** include on line 8a . . .	8b	
9a	Ordinary dividends. Attach Schedule B if required	9a	
b	Qualified dividends	9b	
10	Taxable refunds, credits, or offsets of state and local income taxes	10	
11	Alimony received	11	
12	Business income or (loss). Attach Schedule C or C-EZ	12	1,171.
13	Capital gain or (loss). Attach Schedule D if required. If not required, check here ▶ ☐	13	
14	Other gains or (losses). Attach Form 4797	14	
15a	IRA distributions .	15a		b Taxable amount . . .	15b	
16a	Pensions and annuities	16a		b Taxable amount . . .	16b	
17	Rental real estate, royalties, partnerships, S corporations, trusts, etc. Attach Schedule E	17	
18	Farm income or (loss). Attach Schedule F	18	
19	Unemployment compensation	19	
20a	Social security benefits	20a		b Taxable amount . . .	20b	
21	Other income. List type and amount	21	
22	Combine the amounts in the far right column for lines 7 through 21. This is your **total income** ▶	22	54,382.

Adjusted Gross Income

23	Educator expenses	23	
24	Certain business expenses of reservists, performing artists, and fee-basis government officials. Attach Form 2106 or 2106-EZ	24	
25	Health savings account deduction. Attach Form 8889 .	25	
26	Moving expenses. Attach Form 3903	26	
27	Deductible part of self-employment tax. Attach Schedule SE .	27	83.
28	Self-employed SEP, SIMPLE, and qualified plans .	28	
29	Self-employed health insurance deduction . . .	29	
30	Penalty on early withdrawal of savings	30	
31a	Alimony paid b Recipient's SSN ▶	31a	
32	IRA deduction	32	
33	Student loan interest deduction	33	
34	Tuition and fees. Attach Form 8917	34	
35	Domestic production activities deduction. Attach Form 8903	35	
36	Add lines 23 through 35	36	83.
37	Subtract line 36 from line 22. This is your **adjusted gross income** . . . . . ▶	37	54,299.

For Disclosure, Privacy Act, and Paperwork Reduction Act Notice, see separate instructions. **BAA**   REV 12/30/15 PRO   Form **1040** (2015)

Form 1040 (2015)   Page **2**

Tax and Credits	38	Amount from line 37 (adjusted gross income)	38	54,299.
	39a	Check if: ☐ **You** were born before January 2, 1951, ☐ Blind. } Total boxes ☐ **Spouse** was born before January 2, 1951, ☐ Blind. } checked ▶ 39a ☐		
	b	If your spouse itemizes on a separate return or you were a dual-status alien, check here ▶ 39b ☐		
Standard Deduction for— • People who check any box on line 39a or 39b **or** who can be claimed as a dependent, see instructions. • All others: Single or Married filing separately, $6,300 Married filing jointly or Qualifying widow(er), $12,600 Head of household, $9,250	40	**Itemized deductions** (from Schedule A) **or** your **standard deduction** (see left margin) . .	40	6,300.
	41	Subtract line 40 from line 38	41	47,999.
	42	**Exemptions.** If line 38 is $154,950 or less, multiply $4,000 by the number on line 6d. Otherwise, see instructions	42	4,000.
	43	**Taxable income.** Subtract line 42 from line 41. If line 42 is more than line 41, enter -0- . .	43	43,999.
	44	**Tax** (see instructions). Check if any from: **a** ☐ Form(s) 8814 **b** ☐ Form 4972 **c** ☐	44	6,788.
	45	**Alternative minimum tax** (see instructions). Attach Form 6251	45	
	46	Excess advance premium tax credit repayment. Attach Form 8962	46	
	47	Add lines 44, 45, and 46 . . . . ▶	47	6,788.
	48	Foreign tax credit. Attach Form 1116 if required . .	48		
	49	Credit for child and dependent care expenses. Attach Form 2441	49		
	50	Education credits from Form 8863, line 19	50		
	51	Retirement savings contributions credit. Attach Form 8880	51		
	52	Child tax credit. Attach Schedule 8812, if required . . .	52		
	53	Residential energy credits. Attach Form 5695 . . .	53		
	54	Other credits from Form: **a** ☐ 3800 **b** ☐ 8801 **c** ☐	54		
	55	Add lines 48 through 54. These are your **total credits**	55	
	56	Subtract line 55 from line 47. If line 55 is more than line 47, enter -0- . . . . ▶	56	6,788.
Other Taxes	57	Self-employment tax. Attach Schedule SE	57	165.
	58	Unreported social security and Medicare tax from Form: **a** ☐ 4137 **b** ☐ 8919	58	
	59	Additional tax on IRAs, other qualified retirement plans, etc. Attach Form 5329 if required . .	59	
	60a	Household employment taxes from Schedule H	60a	
	b	First-time homebuyer credit repayment. Attach Form 5405 if required	60b	
	61	Health care: individual responsibility (see instructions) Full-year coverage ☒	61	
	62	Taxes from: **a** ☐ Form 8959 **b** ☐ Form 8960 **c** ☐ Instructions; enter code(s)	62	
	63	Add lines 56 through 62. This is your **total tax** . . . . ▶	63	6,953.
Payments If you have a qualifying child, attach Schedule EIC.	64	Federal income tax withheld from Forms W-2 and 1099 . .	64	7,144.	
	65	2015 estimated tax payments and amount applied from 2014 return	65		
	66a	**Earned income credit (EIC)** No	66a		
	b	Nontaxable combat pay election	66b		
	67	Additional child tax credit. Attach Schedule 8812	67		
	68	American opportunity credit from Form 8863, line 8 . . .	68		
	69	Net premium tax credit. Attach Form 8962	69		
	70	Amount paid with request for extension to file	70		
	71	Excess social security and tier 1 RRTA tax withheld . . .	71		
	72	Credit for federal tax on fuels. Attach Form 4136 . . .	72		
	73	Credits from Form: **a** ☐ 2439 **b** ☐ Reserved **c** ☐ 8885 **d** ☐	73		
	74	Add lines 64, 65, 66a, and 67 through 73. These are your **total payments** . . . . . ▶	74	7,144.
Refund Direct deposit? ▶ See instructions.	75	If line 74 is more than line 63, subtract line 63 from line 74. This is the amount you **overpaid**	75	191.
	76a	Amount of line 75 you want **refunded to you.** If Form 8888 is attached, check here . ▶ ☐	76a	191.
	b	Routing number X X X X X X X X X ▶ **c** Type: ☐ Checking ☐ Savings		
	d	Account number X X X X X X X X X X X X X X X X X		
	77	Amount of line 75 you want **applied to your 2016 estimated tax** ▶ 77		
Amount You Owe	78	**Amount you owe.** Subtract line 74 from line 63. For details on how to pay, see instructions ▶	78	
	79	Estimated tax penalty (see instructions) 79		
Third Party Designee		Do you want to allow another person to discuss this return with the IRS (see instructions)? ☐ **Yes.** Complete below. ☒ **No**		

Designee's name ▶   Phone no. ▶   Personal identification number (PIN) ▶

Sign Here Joint return? See instructions. Keep a copy for your records.	Under penalties of perjury, I declare that I have examined this return and accompanying schedules and statements, and to the best of my knowledge and belief, they are true, correct, and complete. Declaration of preparer (other than taxpayer) is based on all information of which preparer has any knowledge.

Your signature	Date	Your occupation	Daytime phone number
		Professor/Artist	
Spouse's signature. If a joint return, **both** must sign.	Date	Spouse's occupation	If the IRS sent you an Identity Protection PIN, enter it here (see inst.)

Paid Preparer Use Only	Print/Type preparer's name	Preparer's signature	Date	Check ☐ if self-employed	PTIN
	Peter Jason Riley CPA	Peter Jason Riley CPA	01/24/2016		P00413102
	Firm's name ▶ RILEY & ASSOCIATES, P.C.			Firm's EIN ▶ 04-3577120	
	Firm's address ▶ 5 PERRY WAY - P O BOX 157 NEWBURYPORT MA 01950			Phone no. (978)463-9350	

www.irs.gov/form1040   REV 12/30/15 PRO Form **1040** (2015)

SCHEDULE C
(Form 1040)

Department of the Treasury
Internal Revenue Service (99)

Profit or Loss From Business
(Sole Proprietorship)

▶ Information about Schedule C and its separate instructions is at *www.irs.gov/schedulec.*
▶ Attach to Form 1040, 1040NR, or 1041; partnerships generally must file Form 1065.

OMB No. 1545-0074

Attachment
Sequence No. **09**

Name of proprietor	Social security number (SSN)
Liz Brushstroke	333-44-5555

A Principal business or profession, including product or service (see instructions)
Visual Artist

B Enter code from instructions
▶ 7 1 1 5 1 0

C Business name. If no separate business name, leave blank.
Big Orb Art Studio

D Employer ID number (EIN), (see instr.)

E Business address (including suite or room no.) ▶ Commonwealth Ave
City, town or post office, state, and ZIP code   Chestnut Hill, MA 02467

F Accounting method: (1) ☒ Cash   (2) ☐ Accrual   (3) ☐ Other (specify) ▶

G Did you "materially participate" in the operation of this business during 2015? If "No," see instructions for limit on losses ☒ Yes ☐ No

H If you started or acquired this business during 2015, check here . . . . ▶ ☐

I Did you make any payments in 2015 that would require you to file Form(s) 1099? (see instructions) . . . . ☐ Yes ☒ No

J If "Yes," did you or will you file required Forms 1099? . . . . ☐ Yes ☐ No

Part I   Income

1	Gross receipts or sales. See instructions for line 1 and check the box if this income was reported to you on Form W-2 and the "Statutory employee" box on that form was checked . . . . ▶ ☐	1	29,540.
2	Returns and allowances	2	
3	Subtract line 2 from line 1	3	29,540.
4	Cost of goods sold (from line 42)	4	10,500.
5	**Gross profit.** Subtract line 4 from line 3	5	19,040.
6	Other income, including federal and state gasoline or fuel tax credit or refund (see instructions)	6	
7	**Gross income.** Add lines 5 and 6 . . . . ▶	7	19,040.

Part II   Expenses. Enter expenses for business use of your home **only** on line 30.

8	Advertising	8		18	Office expense (see instructions)	18	104.
9	Car and truck expenses (see instructions).	9	2,379.	19	Pension and profit-sharing plans .	19	
				20	Rent or lease (see instructions):		
10	Commissions and fees .	10		a	Vehicles, machinery, and equipment	20a	
11	Contract labor (see instructions)	11		b	Other business property . . .	20b	
12	Depletion	12		21	Repairs and maintenance . . .	21	
13	Depreciation and section 179 expense deduction (not included in Part III) (see instructions)	13	845.	22	Supplies (not included in Part III) .	22	207.
				23	Taxes and licenses	23	
				24	Travel, meals, and entertainment:		
14	Employee benefit programs (other than on line 19) . .	14		a	Travel	24a	3,835.
15	Insurance (other than health)	15		b	Deductible meals and entertainment (see instructions)	24b	888.
16	Interest:			25	Utilities	25	
a	Mortgage (paid to banks, etc.)	16a		26	Wages (less employment credits) .	26	
b	Other	16b		27a	Other expenses (from line 48) . .	27a	5,831.
17	Legal and professional services	17	250.	b	**Reserved for future use** . . .	27b	

28	**Total expenses** before expenses for business use of home. Add lines 8 through 27a . . . . . ▶	28	14,339.
29	Tentative profit or (loss). Subtract line 28 from line 7	29	4,701.
30	Expenses for business use of your home. Do not report these expenses elsewhere. Attach Form 8829 unless using the simplified method (see instructions). **Simplified method filers only:** enter the total square footage of: (a) your home: _____ and (b) the part of your home used for business: _____ . Use the Simplified Method Worksheet in the instructions to figure the amount to enter on line 30	30	3,530.
31	**Net profit or (loss).** Subtract line 30 from line 29. • If a profit, enter on both **Form 1040, line 12** (or **Form 1040NR, line 13**) and on **Schedule SE, line 2.** (If you checked the box on line 1, see instructions). Estates and trusts, enter on **Form 1041, line 3.** • If a loss, you **must** go to line 32.	31	1,171.
32	If you have a loss, check the box that describes your investment in this activity (see instructions). • If you checked 32a, enter the loss on both **Form 1040, line 12,** (or **Form 1040NR, line 13**) and on **Schedule SE, line 2.** (If you checked the box on line 1, see the line 31 instructions). Estates and trusts, enter on **Form 1041, line 3.** • If you checked 32b, you **must** attach **Form 6198.** Your loss may be limited.	32a ☒ All investment is at risk. 32b ☐ Some investment is not at risk.	

For Paperwork Reduction Act Notice, see the separate instructions.   **BAA**   REV 12/07/15 PRO   Schedule C (Form 1040) 2015

Part III　　**Cost of Goods Sold**　(see instructions)

33	Method(s) used to value closing inventory:　**a** ☐ Cost　**b** ☒ Lower of cost or market　**c** ☐ Other (attach explanation)		
34	Was there any change in determining quantities, costs, or valuations between opening and closing inventory?　If "Yes," attach explanation		☐ Yes　☒ No
35	Inventory at beginning of year. If different from last year's closing inventory, attach explanation . . .	**35**	5,000.
36	Purchases less cost of items withdrawn for personal use	**36**	
37	Cost of labor. Do not include any amounts paid to yourself	**37**	
38	Materials and supplies	**38**	3,000.
39	Other costs	**39**	8,000.
40	Add lines 35 through 39	**40**	16,000.
41	Inventory at end of year	**41**	5,500.
42	**Cost of goods sold.** Subtract line 41 from line 40. Enter the result here and on line 4	**42**	10,500.

Part IV　　**Information on Your Vehicle.**　Complete this part **only** if you are claiming car or truck expenses on line 9 and are not required to file Form 4562 for this business. See the instructions for line 13 to find out if you must file Form 4562.

43　When did you place your vehicle in service for business purposes? (month, day, year)　▶ ....

44　Of the total number of miles you drove your vehicle during 2015, enter the number of miles you used your vehicle for:

　a　Business ....　**b** Commuting (see instructions) ....　**c** Other ....

45	Was your vehicle available for personal use during off-duty hours?	☐ Yes	☐ No
46	Do you (or your spouse) have another vehicle available for personal use?	☐ Yes	☐ No
47a	Do you have evidence to support your deduction?	☐ Yes	☐ No
b	If "Yes," is the evidence written?	☐ Yes	☐ No

Part V　　**Other Expenses.**　List below business expenses not included on lines 8–26 or line 30.

AMORTIZATION	324.
Graphics Design Fees	395.
Printing	498.
Photo Costs	525.
Processing	314.
Internet Service	304.
Cell & Skype Service	315.
Museum Memberships	220.
See Line 48 Other Expenses	2,936.
48　**Total other expenses.** Enter here and on line 27a **48**	5,831.

SCHEDULE SE (Form 1040) Department of the Treasury Internal Revenue Service (99)	**Self-Employment Tax** ▶ Information about Schedule SE and its separate instructions is at *www.irs.gov/schedulese*. ▶ Attach to Form 1040 or Form 1040NR.	OMB No. 1545-0074 2015 Attachment Sequence No. **17**

Name of person with **self-employment** income (as shown on Form 1040 or Form 1040NR) Liz Brushstroke	Social security number of person with **self-employment** income ▶	333-44-5555

Before you begin: To determine if you must file Schedule SE, see the instructions.

May I Use Short Schedule SE or Must I Use Long Schedule SE?

Note. Use this flowchart **only if** you must file Schedule SE. If unsure, see *Who Must File Schedule SE* in the instructions.

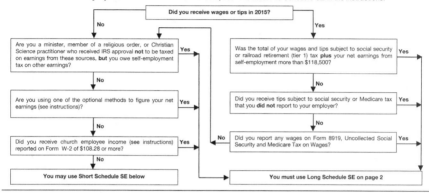

Section A—Short Schedule SE. Caution. Read above to see if you can use Short Schedule SE.

1a	Net farm profit or (loss) from Schedule F, line 34, and farm partnerships, Schedule K-1 (Form 1065), box 14, code A	**1a**		
b	If you received social security retirement or disability benefits, enter the amount of Conservation Reserve Program payments included on Schedule F, line 4b, or listed on Schedule K-1 (Form 1065), box 20, code Z	**1b**	(	)
2	Net profit or (loss) from Schedule C, line 31; Schedule C-EZ, line 3; Schedule K-1 (Form 1065), box 14, code A (other than farming); and Schedule K-1 (Form 1065-B), box 9, code J1. Ministers and members of religious orders, see instructions for types of income to report on this line. See instructions for other income to report	**2**		1,171.
3	Combine lines 1a, 1b, and 2	**3**		1,171.
4	Multiply line 3 by 92.35% (.9235). If less than $400, you do not owe self-employment tax; **do not** file this schedule unless you have an amount on line 1b . . . . ▶	**4**		1,081.
	Note. If line 4 is less than $400 due to Conservation Reserve Program payments on line 1b, see instructions.			
5	**Self-employment tax.** If the amount on line 4 is: • $118,500 or less, multiply line 4 by 15.3% (.153). Enter the result here and on **Form 1040, line 57,** or **Form 1040NR, line 55** • More than $118,500, multiply line 4 by 2.9% (.029). Then, add $14,694 to the result. Enter the total here and on **Form 1040, line 57,** or **Form 1040NR, line 55**	**5**		165.
6	**Deduction for one-half of self-employment tax.** Multiply line 5 by 50% (.50). Enter the result here and on **Form 1040, line 27,** or **Form 1040NR, line 27**	**6**	83.	

For Paperwork Reduction Act Notice, see your tax return instructions. **BAA**   REV 12/04/15 PRO   Schedule SE (Form 1040) 2015

Form **8829**	**Expenses for Business Use of Your Home**	OMB No. 1545-0074
Department of the Treasury Internal Revenue Service (99)	▶ File only with Schedule C (Form 1040). Use a separate Form 8829 for each home you used for business during the year. ▶ Information about Form 8829 and its separate instructions is at *www.irs.gov/form8829*.	**2015** Attachment Sequence No. **176**

Name(s) of proprietor(s)	Your social security number
Liz Brushstroke	333-44-5555

Part I Part of Your Home Used for Business   Visual Artist

1	Area used regularly and exclusively for business, regularly for daycare, or for storage of inventory or product samples (see instructions)	**1**	190
2	Total area of home	**2**	1,085
3	Divide line 1 by line 2. Enter the result as a percentage	**3**	17.51 %
	For daycare facilities not used exclusively for business, go to line 4. All others, go to line 7.		
4	Multiply days used for daycare during year by hours used per day	**4**	hr.
5	Total hours available for use during the year (365 days x 24 hours) (see instructions)	**5**	8,760 hr.
6	Divide line 4 by line 5. Enter the result as a decimal amount . . .	**6**	
7	Business percentage. For daycare facilities not used exclusively for business, multiply line 6 by line 3 (enter the result as a percentage). All others, enter the amount from line 3 . . . . . ▶	**7**	17.51 %

Part II Figure Your Allowable Deduction

			(a) Direct expenses	(b) Indirect expenses		
8	Enter the amount from Schedule C, line 29, **plus** any gain derived from the business use of your home, **minus** any loss from the trade or business not derived from the business use of your home (see instructions)				**8**	4,701.
	See instructions for columns (a) and (b) before completing lines 9–21.					
9	Casualty losses (see instructions).	**9**				
10	Deductible mortgage interest (see instructions)	**10**				
11	Real estate taxes (see instructions)	**11**				
12	Add lines 9, 10, and 11	**12**				
13	Multiply line 12, column (b) by line 7 .			13		
14	Add line 12, column (a) and line 13				**14**	
15	Subtract line 14 from line 8. If zero or less, enter -0-				**15**	4,701.
16	Excess mortgage interest (see instructions) .	**16**				
17	Insurance	**17**		308.		
18	Rent	**18**		19,850.		
19	Repairs and maintenance	**19**				
20	Utilities	**20**				
21	Other expenses (see instructions).	**21**				
22	Add lines 16 through 21	**22**		20,158.		
23	Multiply line 22, column (b) by line 7		23	3,530.		
24	Carryover of prior year operating expenses (see instructions) . .		24			
25	Add line 22, column (a), line 23, and line 24				**25**	3,530.
26	Allowable operating expenses. Enter the **smaller** of line 15 or line 25				**26**	3,530.
27	Limit on excess casualty losses and depreciation. Subtract line 26 from line 15				**27**	1,171.
28	Excess casualty losses (see instructions)	28				
29	Depreciation of your home from line 41 below	29				
30	Carryover of prior year excess casualty losses and depreciation (see instructions)	30				
31	Add lines 28 through 30				**31**	
32	Allowable excess casualty losses and depreciation. Enter the **smaller** of line 27 or line 31 . .				**32**	
33	Add lines 14, 26, and 32.				**33**	3,530.
34	Casualty loss portion, if any, from lines 14 and 32. Carry amount to **Form 4684** (see instructions)				**34**	
35	**Allowable expenses for business use of your home.** Subtract line 34 from line 33. Enter here and on Schedule C, line 30. If your home was used for more than one business, see instructions ▶				**35**	3,530.

Part III Depreciation of Your Home

36	Enter the **smaller** of your home's adjusted basis or its fair market value (see instructions) . .	**36**	
37	Value of land included on line 36	**37**	
38	Basis of building. Subtract line 37 from line 36	**38**	
39	Business basis of building. Multiply line 38 by line 7.	**39**	
40	Depreciation percentage (see instructions).	**40**	%
41	Depreciation allowable (see instructions). Multiply line 39 by line 40. Enter here and on line 29 above	**41**	

Part IV Carryover of Unallowed Expenses to 2016

42	Operating expenses. Subtract line 26 from line 25. If less than zero, enter -0-	**42**	0.
43	Excess casualty losses and depreciation. Subtract line 32 from line 31. If less than zero, enter -0-	**43**	

For Paperwork Reduction Act Notice, see your tax return instructions. **BAA**   REV 12/04/15 PRO   Form **8829** (2015)

Form **4562**	**Depreciation and Amortization**	OMB No. 1545-0172
Department of the Treasury Internal Revenue Service (99)	(Including Information on Listed Property) ▶ Attach to your tax return. ▶ Information about Form 4562 and its separate instructions is at *www.irs.gov/form4562*.	**2015** Attachment Sequence No. **179**

Name(s) shown on return	Business or activity to which this form relates	Identifying number
Liz Brushstroke	Sch C Visual Artist	333-44-5555

Part I Election To Expense Certain Property Under Section 179
  Note: If you have any listed property, complete Part V before you complete Part I.

1	Maximum amount (see instructions)	**1**	500,000.
2	Total cost of section 179 property placed in service (see instructions)	**2**	3,893.
3	Threshold cost of section 179 property before reduction in limitation (see instructions)	**3**	2,000,000.
4	Reduction in limitation. Subtract line 3 from line 2. If zero or less, enter -0-	**4**	0.
5	Dollar limitation for tax year. Subtract line 4 from line 1. If zero or less, enter -0-. If married filing separately, see instructions	**5**	500,000.

6	(a) Description of property	(b) Cost (business use only)	(c) Elected cost	
	Digital Camera	399.	399.	

7	Listed property. Enter the amount from line 29 . . . . [**7**]		
8	Total elected cost of section 179 property. Add amounts in column (c), lines 6 and 7	**8**	399.
9	Tentative deduction. Enter the **smaller** of line 5 or line 8	**9**	399.
10	Carryover of disallowed deduction from line 13 of your 2014 Form 4562	**10**	
11	Business income limitation. Enter the smaller of business income (not less than zero) or line 5 (see instructions)	**11**	54,781.
12	Section 179 expense deduction. Add lines 9 and 10, but do not enter more than line 11	**12**	399.
13	Carryover of disallowed deduction to 2016. Add lines 9 and 10, less line 12 ▶ [**13**]	0.	

Note: Do not use Part II or Part III below for listed property. Instead, use Part V.

Part II Special Depreciation Allowance and Other Depreciation (Do not include listed property.) (See instructions.)

14	Special depreciation allowance for qualified property (other than listed property) placed in service during the tax year (see instructions)	**14**	
15	Property subject to section 168(f)(1) election	**15**	
16	Other depreciation (including ACRS)	**16**	

Part III MACRS Depreciation (Do not include listed property.) (See instructions.)

Section A

17	MACRS deductions for assets placed in service in tax years beginning before 2015	**17**	189.
18	If you are electing to group any assets placed in service during the tax year into one or more general asset accounts, check here . . . . ▶ ☐		

Section B—Assets Placed in Service During 2015 Tax Year Using the General Depreciation System

(a) Classification of property	(b) Month and year placed in service	(c) Basis for depreciation (business/investment use only—see instructions)	(d) Recovery period	(e) Convention	(f) Method	(g) Depreciation deduction
19a 3-year property						
b 5-year property						
c 7-year property		3,494.	7.0	MQ	200 DB	257.
d 10-year property						
e 15-year property						
f 20-year property						
g 25-year property			25 yrs.		S/L	
h Residential rental property			27.5 yrs.	MM	S/L	
			27.5 yrs.	MM	S/L	
i Nonresidential real property			39 yrs.	MM	S/L	
				MM	S/L	

Section C—Assets Placed in Service During 2015 Tax Year Using the Alternative Depreciation System

20a Class life					S/L	
b 12-year			12 yrs.		S/L	
c 40-year			40 yrs.	MM	S/L	

Part IV Summary (See instructions.)

21	Listed property. Enter amount from line 28	**21**	
22	**Total.** Add amounts from line 12, lines 14 through 17, lines 19 and 20 in column (g), and line 21. Enter here and on the appropriate lines of your return. Partnerships and S corporations—see instructions	**22**	845.
23	For assets shown above and placed in service during the current year, enter the portion of the basis attributable to section 263A costs . . . . [**23**]		

For Paperwork Reduction Act Notice, see separate instructions. **BAA**   REV 12/27/15 PRO   Form **4562** (2015)

Form 4562 (2015)   Page **2**

Part V   **Listed Property** (Include automobiles, certain other vehicles, certain aircraft, certain computers, and property used for entertainment, recreation, or amusement.)

Note: For any vehicle for which you are using the standard mileage rate or deducting lease expense, complete **only** 24a, 24b, columns (a) through (c) of Section A, all of Section B, and Section C if applicable.

Section A—Depreciation and Other Information (Caution: See the instructions for limits for passenger automobiles.**)**

24a Do you have evidence to support the business/investment use claimed?   ☒ Yes ☐ No   **24b** If "Yes," is the evidence written? ☒ Yes ☐ No

(a) Type of property (list vehicles first)	(b) Date placed in service	(c) Business/ investment use percentage	(d) Cost or other basis	(e) Basis for depreciation (business/investment use only)	(f) Recovery period	(g) Method/ Convention	(h) Depreciation deduction	(i) Elected section 179 cost
25 Special depreciation allowance for qualified listed property placed in service during the tax year and used more than 50% in a qualified business use (see instructions) . **25**								
26 Property used more than 50% in a qualified business use:								
		%						
		%						
		%						
27 Property used 50% or less in a qualified business use:								
Auto	01/01/2010	25.57 %				S/L –		
		%				S/L –		
		%				S/L –		

28 Add amounts in column (h), lines 25 through 27. Enter here and on line 21, page 1 .   **28**

29 Add amounts in column (i), line 26. Enter here and on line 7, page 1 . . . .   **29**

Section B—Information on Use of Vehicles

Complete this section for vehicles used by a sole proprietor, partner, or other "more than 5% owner," or related person. If you provided vehicles to your employees, first answer the questions in Section C to see if you meet an exception to completing this section for those vehicles.

	(a) Vehicle 1		(b) Vehicle 2		(c) Vehicle 3		(d) Vehicle 4		(e) Vehicle 5		(f) Vehicle 6	
30 Total business/investment miles driven during the year (**do not** include commuting miles) .	4,137											
31 Total commuting miles driven during the year	2,650											
32 Total other personal (noncommuting) miles driven	9,391											
33 Total miles driven during the year. Add lines 30 through 32	16,178											
34 Was the vehicle available for personal use during off-duty hours?	Yes ☒	No	Yes	No	Yes	No	Yes	No	Yes	No	Yes	No
35 Was the vehicle used primarily by a more than 5% owner or related person? . .	☒											
36 Is another vehicle available for personal use?		☒										

Section C—Questions for Employers Who Provide Vehicles for Use by Their Employees

Answer these questions to determine if you meet an exception to completing Section B for vehicles used by employees who **are not** more than 5% owners or related persons (see instructions).

		Yes	No
37	Do you maintain a written policy statement that prohibits all personal use of vehicles, including commuting, by your employees?		
38	Do you maintain a written policy statement that prohibits personal use of vehicles, except commuting, by your employees? See the instructions for vehicles used by corporate officers, directors, or 1% or more owners . .		
39	Do you treat all use of vehicles by employees as personal use?		
40	Do you provide more than five vehicles to your employees, obtain information from your employees about the use of the vehicles, and retain the information received?		
41	Do you meet the requirements concerning qualified automobile demonstration use? (See instructions.) . . .		

Note: If your answer to 37, 38, 39, 40, or 41 is "Yes," do not complete Section B for the covered vehicles.

Part VI   **Amortization**

(a) Description of costs	(b) Date amortization begins	(c) Amortizable amount	(d) Code section	(e) Amortization period or percentage	(f) Amortization for this year
42 Amortization of costs that begins during your 2015 tax year (see instructions):					
Website Costs	07/01/2015	1,945.	A197	3.00 yrs	324.
43 Amortization of costs that began before your 2015 tax year **43**					
44 **Total.** Add amounts in column (f). See the instructions for where to report **44**					324.

REV 12/27/15 PRO   Form **4562** (2015)

Form 4562

Depreciation and Amortization Report

Tax Year 2015
▶ Keep for your records

2015

Liz Brushstroke
Sch C - Visual Artist

333-44-5555

Asset Description	*Code	Date In Service	Cost (Net of Land)	Land	Bus Use %	Section 179	Special Depreciation Allowance	Depreciable Basis	Life	Method/ Convention	Prior Depreciation	Current Depreciation
DEPRECIATION												
Studio Ventilation		07/01/15	1,844		100.00			1,844	7.0	200DB/MQ	0	198
Digital Camera		12/27/15	399		100.00	399		0	5.0	200DB/MQ	0	0
Flat Files		12/28/15	1,650		100.00			1,650	7.0	200DB/MQ	0	59
SUBTOTAL CURRENT YEAR			3,893	0		399	0	3,494			0	257
Auto	L	01/01/10			25.57							
Notebook Computer		07/01/11	1,644		100.00			1,644	5.0	200DB/HY	1,360	189
SUBTOTAL PRIOR YEAR			1,644	0		0	0	1,644			1,360	189
TOTALS			5,537	0		399	0	5,138			1,360	446
AMORTIZATION												
Website Costs		07/01/15	1,945		100.00			1,945	3.0		0	324
SUBTOTAL CURRENT YEAR			1,945			0	0	1,945			0	324
TOTALS			1,945				0	1,945			0	324

* Code: S = Sold, A = Auto, L = Listed, H = Home Office

Additional information from your 2015 Federal Tax Return

Schedule C (Visual Artist): Profit or Loss from Business
Line 39   **Itemization Statement**

Description	Amount
Printing	2,000.
Framing	6,000.
Total	**8,000.**

Schedule C (Visual Artist): Profit or Loss from Business
Line 48 Other Expenses   **Continuation Statement**

Description	Amount
Gallery Costs	89.
Shipping & Postage	1,341.
Publications	177.
Dues & Memberhips	215.
Show Entry Fees	195.
Art History Class (Ireland)	622.
Promotional Expense	297.
Total	**2,936.**

Liz Brushstroke   333-44-5555

Schedule C - Other Income

Juror Stipend	$100

Schedule C - Meals Detail Line 24B

Ireland	8	$126	$1,008
Phoenix	3	$59	$177
Lunch NYC			$42
NYC	2	$74	$148
Other professional meals			$401
			$1,776 (only 50% deductible)

Schedule C Travel Line 24A

Ireland - Airfare & Transportation	$1,952
Ireland Airbnb 8 days	$1,112
Phoenix - Airline	$348
Phoenix	$423
	$3,835

Schedule C - Other Costs of Goods Sold

Printing	$2,000
Framing	$6,000
	$8,000

7

For Writers

In this chapter I will look in detail at the activities of our good friend, Guy Focal, and the kind of income and deductions he had for the year.

First, let's walk through some of the expense items for writers specifically. I will note in parentheses the type of record keeping the IRS would require:

1. Union dues, professional societies, and organizations (invoices and payment verifications).

2. Professional fees for agents, attorneys, and accountants (invoices and payment verifications).

3. Agent commissions—this number is generally only found in the agent's year-end statement.

4. Classes, education, and seminars (bills, credit card receipts, and payment verifications).

5. Professional headshots, photographs, and résumés (bills, credit card receipts, and payment verifications).

6. Stationery and postage (bills, credit card receipts, and payment verifications).

7. Books on writing—these may need to be allocated between employment income and contract income (sales receipts, credit card receipts, and payment verifications).

8. Telephone, online communications (such as Skype), and cellular phone—actual business calls on your home phone are deductible, but the IRS does not allow the allocation of the base monthly rate. You can deduct only the actual long distance charges. The same rule is true with your cellular phone, data, and online service. If you get a second phone line strictly for business then it can be considered 100% deductible (bills and payment verifications).

9. Internet service—for research purposes, business e-mail, and e-mail while traveling. Be sure to allocate some of the costs for personal use (bills, payment verifications, invoices, and credit card receipts).

10. Purchasing books—be sure to allocate some book purchases to personal use. After all, you must sometimes be reading for personal enjoyment; it can't be all business. While the IRS typically hates this deduction, you can easily argue that the writer must read competitors' books to keep abreast of trends and dynamics within their profession. In an IRS audit you would need to explain specifically what the professional value was (bills, invoices, and payment verifications).

11. Viewing theatre and films (live and via DVD, streaming video, and cable)—this is for screen and play writers. I often call this expense line item "research"; others refer to it as "performance audit." Whatever you call it, like the purchase of books listed above make sure to not get "piggy." I often quote to clients the old Wall Street saying, "the pigs get fat and the hogs get slaughtered." As with the previous entry, the IRS dislikes the deduction, but you can easily argue that the stage and screenwriter must engage in these viewings to keep abreast of trends and dynamics within their profession. In an audit you would need to explain specifically what the professional value was (ticket stubs, receipts, and diary entries).

12. Office rent—you must be able to prove you need an outside office, you cannot maintain a tax-deductible home studio if you rent outside space (bills, invoices, and payment verifications).

13. Repair of equipment—computers, typewriters, etc. (bills, payment verifications, invoices, and credit card receipts).

14. Travel—hotels, airline, meals (per diem generally), Airbnb, Uber, train, bus, baggage fees, etc. (confirmation and payment verification). Very important: documentation proving the reason for the trip.

15. Tax preparation, bookkeeping and accounting fees (bills, invoices, and payment verifications).

16. Advertisement and listing in publications and on the Internet (bills, payment verifications, invoices, and credit card receipts).

17. Professional magazines (bills, payment verifications, invoices, and credit card receipts).

18. Insurance—this can include riders on your home policy that relate directly to your home office (bills, invoice, and payment verification).

19. Copyright fees (invoice and payment verification).

20. Equipment purchases—computers, tablets, smartphones, and office equipment (bills, payment verifications, invoices, and credit card receipts).

21. Office supplies and fixtures (bills, payment verifications, invoices, and credit card receipts).

Now let's see what kind of year our writer, Guy, had. Luckily for his Enrolled Agent, Guy downloaded our Excel spreadsheet for writers (found at www.artstaxinfo.com), loaded it on his computer at the beginning of the tax year, and carefully tracked his expenses all year!

We will now review Guy's 1040 income tax return in detail—and remember you can download the current year version from our website—www.artstaxinfo.com.

As you will remember, Guy has a primary job as a staff writer for a local magazine, *Swamp Life Living*, for which he receives a W-2 (this is found on Line 7 of his Form 1040).

In the winter, Guy attended an annual conference of the writer's organization PEN in New York City. Guy is a professional member of PEN and represented New Orleans writers at the conference. The trip gave him a chance to network with fellow writers and talk to some of the publishers that were present. The organization sponsors a series of educational events for the participants every day and Guy presented an article on post-Katrina wetlands issues that he had written for *Swamp Life Living*. Guy was at the conference for the entire 3 days he was gone. He made sure that he brought home the conference schedule and related literature and noted which events he attended. Guy can clearly show a business purpose as it relates to his primary employment; he will be able to deduct the entire trip on his Form 2106. His employer did not offer any reimbursement for this trip.

Over the summer Guy got a freelance assignment to write a travel article on Texas. Although he was familiar with Texas, he decided a visit would help in writing the article so he contacted the Texas Department of Tourism for help. He informed them that he only had a few days in which to travel in the state. They arranged a route that allowed him to hit the high spots (and the best BBQ joints!) in the least amount of time. He incurred the costs of travel, auto rental, meals, and hotel, because the magazine that hired him did not directly pick up any of the costs of the trip. He also bought a small "netbook" computer so that he could easily write while traveling. The trip had a clearly defined business purpose, so the costs were 100% deductible on his Schedule C against the income he received from the article.

The president of a national bookstore chain contacted Guy to ask if he would be interested in making some appearances at her stores. She liked Guy's children's books and felt his visit could help in promoting the chain's children's book departments. She wanted Guy to come to her stores in San Francisco, Cleveland, New York, and Boston to do a reading and sign books for the children at each one. The owner did not want to get involved in reimbursing expenses, so she offered Guy a straight fee for the appearances, from which he would cover all his expenses. All the costs associated with the travel, meals, etc. would be deductible against the income. Like the preceding example, the income from this activity would be reported on Guy's Schedule C.

Guy decided that he wanted a personal website where he could link to his popular blog, post his résumé, publish excerpts and reviews from his books and articles, etc. He would also use the website to directly sell signed copies of his children's books, which he promotes through social media. His illustrator agreed to let him post copies of some of the illustrations she did for his books. The costs of setting up the website, registering the domain name, and hosting the site are all deductible. Guy will be able to deduct the costs of having photos taken and transferred to digital images and of scanning the book illustrations for use on the site. The IRS stipulates that website development is written off (amortized) over 3 years. So all the costs of designing and setting up the site will be added up (capitalized) and expensed over 3 years.

In the fall, a well-known TV host asked Guy to appear on a panel on her show to discuss the current state of children's books in America. Guy was to be paid a small stipend and all his costs would be covered directly by the television network. To be on the show, Guy flew to California one day and came back the next, incurring absolutely no tax-deductible expenses on the trip.

In his home, Guy has a room set up as an office that he uses exclusively to write in. He uses Form 8829 to take a home office deduction for the office. This form allows him to take a portion of all his general home expenses as a deduction against his freelance writing income. If he makes alterations to the room specifically for the writing, he can take those expenses 100%. This year Guy had to upgrade his electrical system to power the office equipment he now has in the office; he also installed a wireless network and cable modem for Internet access. Guy's accountant will depreciate both of these items. In order to preserve the IRS rules regarding "exclusive use," Guy will have to be very careful about family use of the home office room.

An extensive children's book collection came on ebay in the fall; some of the books were very valuable and collectable, some were not. He called his tax advisor to ask if this purchase would be deductible. The advisor told him that it was not a clear-cut deduction; Guy would have to explain to the IRS how he was actually using the collection in his work as a children's author, otherwise the IRS would consider the books to be collectors' items and not deductible. If he could justify the deduction, it would be depreciated over 5 years on his Schedule C.

One of Guy's children's books was up for an award so he decided to take the trip to Los Angeles for the November ceremony with his wife. They flew to LA on Friday evening. They wanted to be in time for the related conference being held Saturday. They attended the award ceremony on Saturday evening, spent Sunday in LA, and returned home Sunday night. The airline ticket home Sunday would be deductible, as it was impractical for the couple to fly home late on Saturday night. All the costs of the trip will be deductible for Guy on his Schedule C; none of the costs will be deductible for his wife's travel. He will have to subtract the cost of her airline ticket and adjust for the extra cost of a double room at the hotel. He will also only be able to take the cost of *his* meals.

Over the course of the year Guy kept writing and submitting work to various magazines and publishers throughout the country. His accountant recommended that Guy send all submissions via registered mail with copies of the piece attached, and retain all responses from the editors and publishers. These could be very important if Guy is ever hit with a "hobby loss" audit. Of course all the postage, copies, etc., would be deductible against Guy's Schedule C income.

Guy had a significant collection of beautiful, atmospheric, black-and-white photos of the Louisiana swampland that he wanted to publish in conjunction with an anthology of his best articles on life on the bayous of Louisiana. He set up a crowdfunding project through Kickstarter to raise the money needed for printing the book. He estimated that he needed at least $50,000 to do a limited run of these books. He created a project on Kickstarter but was unable to raise the necessary cash and had to abandon the idea (for now). If he had succeeded, the $50,000 (less the 5% Kickstarter fee) would have been income for Guy on his Schedule C. Of course, the costs of printing the book would have been deductible as cost of goods sold to the extent that the books were sold, or sent to backers as rewards.

When Guy met with his accountant at year-end to do some tax planning and to check on his estimated tax payments for the year, he had more income than he had anticipated. Guy had royalty income from his books, as well as income from magazine articles, the book tour, and the stipend from his TV appearance. His accountant asked if there were some expenses that he could accelerate into the current year; that way he would get the tax benefit of the deductions in the current year. Guy had been thinking about buying a new iMac computer. He decided to purchase the new computer before December 31st. By purchasing before year-end, he was able to use the Section 179 election and write it off 100% in the current year. He can do this, even if he charges the computer on his credit card and pays it off in the next year, as long as the computer is "in use" before December 31st.

For some work on one of his books, Guy had paid one of his illustrators $1,450 during the year. His accountant told him that he needed to issue the illustrator a 1099-MISC, because the amount was in excess of $600. Guy called the illustrator, verified her name and address, and got her Social Security number so that the accountant could prepare the form and mail it to her by the January 31st deadline.

Writers

Professional Fees & Dues

Association & Union Dues	
Credentials	
License	
Professional Associations	
Union Dues	
Other: _____	

Continuing Education

Correspondence Course Fees	
College Courses	
Courses Registration	
Materials & Supplies	
Photocopy Expense	
Reference Material	
Books Purchased for Research	
Seminar Fees	
Textbooks	
Other: _____	

Supplies & Other Expenses

Briefcase, Computer, or Tablet Case	
Business Meals (enter 100% of expenses)	
Business Cards	
Clerical Service	
Computer Software	
Computer Supplies	
Customer Lists	
Entertainment (enter 100% of expense)	
Equipment Repair	
FAX Supplies	
Gifts & Greeting Cards	
Online Charges	

Legal & Professional Services

Office Expenses

Photocopying

Postage & Shipping

DVDs, Films, & Streaming Videos for Research

Stationery

Website Development & Hosting

Other: _____

Auto Travel (in miles)

Between Jobs or Locations

Client & Publisher Meetings

Continuing Education

Job Seeking

Out-of-Town Business Trips

Purchasing Job Supplies & Materials

Professional Society Meetings

Parking Fees & Tolls

Other: _____

Travel—Out of Town

Airfare

Car Rental, Taxi, Bus, Train, & Subway

Parking & Tolls

Lodging & Housing (do not combine with meals)

Meals (do not combine with lodging)

Porter, Bell Captain, & Laundry

Telephone Calls (including home)

Other: _____

Communications Costs

Land Line

Internet Service or Skype

Cellular or Wireless Data Service

Other: _____

Equipment Purchases

Smart Phone	
FAX Machine, Calculator, & Copier	
Pager, Recorder, & Tablet	
Computers & Printers	
Technology	
Other: _____	

Miscellaneous Expenses

Liability Insurance—Business	
Subscriptions	
Resume	

Form **1040**	Department of the Treasury—Internal Revenue Service (99) **U.S. Individual Income Tax Return**	20**15**	OMB No. 1545-0074	IRS Use Only—Do not write or staple in this space.

For the year Jan. 1–Dec. 31, 2015, or other tax year beginning , 2015, ending , 20

Your first name and initial	Last name	Your social security number
Guy	Focal	444–55–6666

If a joint return, spouse's first name and initial	Last name	Spouse's social security number
Mary	Focal	555–66–7777

Home address (number and street). If you have a P.O. box, see instructions. | Apt. no.

Camp Place

▲ Make sure the SSN(s) above and on line 6c are correct.

City, town or post office, state, and ZIP code. If you have a foreign address, also complete spaces below (see instructions).

New Orleans LA 70130

Presidential Election Campaign

Foreign country name | Foreign province/state/county | Foreign postal code

Check here if you, or your spouse if filing jointly, want $3 to go to this fund. Checking a box below will not change your tax or refund. ☐ You ☐ Spouse

Filing Status

Check only one box.

1 ☐ Single
2 ☒ Married filing jointly (even if only one had income)
3 ☐ Married filing separately. Enter spouse's SSN above and full name here. ▶
4 ☐ Head of household (with qualifying person). (See instructions.) If the qualifying person is a child but not your dependent, enter this child's name here. ▶
5 ☐ Qualifying widow(er) with dependent child

Exemptions

6a ☒ **Yourself.** If someone can claim you as a dependent, **do not** check box 6a . . . . .
b ☒ **Spouse** . . . .

	Boxes checked on 6a and 6b	2

c **Dependents:**

(1) First name Last name	(2) Dependent's social security number	(3) Dependent's relationship to you	(4) ✓ if child under age 17 qualifying for child tax credit (see instructions)
			☐
			☐
			☐
			☐

If more than four dependents, see instructions and check here ▶ ☐

No. of children on 6c who:
• lived with you
• did not live with you due to divorce or separation (see instructions)

Dependents on 6c not entered above

Add numbers on lines above ▶

d Total number of exemptions claimed . . . .

Income

Attach Form(s) W-2 here. Also attach Forms W-2G and 1099-R if tax was withheld.

If you did not get a W-2, see instructions.

7	Wages, salaries, tips, etc. Attach Form(s) W-2	7	89,632.
8a	**Taxable interest.** Attach Schedule B if required	8a	147.
b	Tax-exempt interest. **Do not** include on line 8a . . .	8b		
9a	Ordinary dividends. Attach Schedule B if required	9a	89.
b	Qualified dividends	9b	71.	
10	Taxable refunds, credits, or offsets of state and local income taxes	10	
11	Alimony received	11	
12	Business income or (loss). Attach Schedule C or C-EZ	12	2,379.
13	Capital gain or (loss). Attach Schedule D if required. If not required, check here ▶ ☒	13	44.
14	Other gains or (losses). Attach Form 4797	14	
15a	IRA distributions .	15a		b Taxable amount . . .	15b	
16a	Pensions and annuities	16a		b Taxable amount . . .	16b	
17	Rental real estate, royalties, partnerships, S corporations, trusts, etc. Attach Schedule E	17	
18	Farm income or (loss). Attach Schedule F	18	
19	Unemployment compensation	19	
20a	Social security benefits	20a		b Taxable amount . . .	20b	
21	Other income. List type and amount	21	
22	Combine the amounts in the far right column for lines 7 through 21. This is your **total income** ▶	22	92,291.

Adjusted Gross Income

23	Educator expenses . . .	23	250.		
24	Certain business expenses of reservists, performing artists, and fee-basis government officials. Attach Form 2106 or 2106-EZ	24			
25	Health savings account deduction. Attach Form 8889 .	25			
26	Moving expenses. Attach Form 3903	26			
27	Deductible part of self-employment tax. Attach Schedule SE .	27	168.		
28	Self-employed SEP, SIMPLE, and qualified plans . .	28			
29	Self-employed health insurance deduction	29			
30	Penalty on early withdrawal of savings	30			
31a	Alimony paid b Recipient's SSN ▶	31a			
32	IRA deduction	32			
33	Student loan interest deduction	33			
34	Tuition and fees. Attach Form 8917	34			
35	Domestic production activities deduction. Attach Form 8903	35			
36	Add lines 23 through 35	36		418.
37	Subtract line 36 from line 22. This is your **adjusted gross income** . . . . . ▶	37		91,873.

For Disclosure, Privacy Act, and Paperwork Reduction Act Notice, see separate instructions. **BAA**   REV 12/30/15 PRO   Form **1040** (2015)

Form 1040 (2015)   Page **2**

Tax and Credits	38	Amount from line 37 (adjusted gross income)		38	91,873.
	39a	Check if: ☐ **You** were born before January 2, 1951, ☐ Blind. ☐ **Spouse** was born before January 2, 1951, ☐ Blind. } **Total boxes checked ▶** 39a			
	b	If your spouse itemizes on a separate return or you were a dual-status alien, check here ▶ 39b ☐			
Standard Deduction for— • People who check any box on line 39a or 39b or who can be claimed as a dependent, see instructions. • All others: Single or Married filing separately, $6,300 Married filing jointly or Qualifying widow(er), $12,600 Head of household, $9,250	40	**Itemized deductions** (from Schedule A) **or** your **standard deduction** (see left margin)		40	13,604.
	41	Subtract line 40 from line 38		41	78,269.
	42	**Exemptions.** If line 38 is $154,950 or less, multiply $4,000 by the number on line 6d. Otherwise, see instructions		42	8,000.
	43	**Taxable income.** Subtract line 42 from line 41. If line 42 is more than line 41, enter -0-		43	70,269.
	44	**Tax** (see instructions). Check if any from: **a** ☐ Form(s) 8814 **b** ☐ Form 4972 **c** ☐		44	9,604.
	45	**Alternative minimum tax** (see instructions). Attach Form 6251		45	
	46	Excess advance premium tax credit repayment. Attach Form 8962		46	
	47	Add lines 44, 45, and 46 ▶		47	9,604.
	48	Foreign tax credit. Attach Form 1116 if required	48		
	49	Credit for child and dependent care expenses. Attach Form 2441	49		
	50	Education credits from Form 8863, line 19	50		
	51	Retirement savings contributions credit. Attach Form 8880	51		
	52	Child tax credit. Attach Schedule 8812, if required.	52		
	53	Residential energy credits. Attach Form 5695	53		
	54	Other credits from Form: **a** ☐ 3800 **b** ☐ 8801 **c** ☐	54		
	55	Add lines 48 through 54. These are your **total credits**		55	
	56	Subtract line 55 from line 47. If line 55 is more than line 47, enter -0- ▶		56	9,604.
Other Taxes	57	Self-employment tax. Attach Schedule SE		57	336.
	58	Unreported social security and Medicare tax from Form: **a** ☐ 4137 **b** ☐ 8919		58	
	59	Additional tax on IRAs, other qualified retirement plans, etc. Attach Form 5329 if required		59	
	60a	Household employment taxes from Schedule H		60a	
	b	First-time homebuyer credit repayment. Attach Form 5405 if required		60b	
	61	Health care: individual responsibility (see instructions) Full-year coverage ☒		61	
	62	Taxes from: **a** ☐ Form 8959 **b** ☐ Form 8960 **c** ☐ Instructions; enter code(s)		62	
	63	Add lines 56 through 62. This is your **total tax** ▶		63	9,940.
Payments If you have a qualifying child, attach Schedule EIC.	64	Federal income tax withheld from Forms W-2 and 1099	64	12,310.	
	65	2015 estimated tax payments and amount applied from 2014 return	65		
	66a	**Earned income credit (EIC)** No	66a		
	b	Nontaxable combat pay election	66b		
	67	Additional child tax credit. Attach Schedule 8812	67		
	68	American opportunity credit from Form 8863, line 8	68		
	69	Net premium tax credit. Attach Form 8962	69		
	70	Amount paid with request for extension to file	70		
	71	Excess social security and tier 1 RRTA tax withheld	71		
	72	Credit for federal tax on fuels. Attach Form 4136	72		
	73	Credits from Form: **a** ☐ 2439 **b** ☐ Reserved **c** ☐ 8885 **d** ☐	73		
	74	Add lines 64, 65, 66a, and 67 through 73. These are your **total payments** ▶		74	12,310.
Refund Direct deposit? ▶ See instructions.	75	If line 74 is more than line 63, subtract line 63 from line 74. This is the amount you **overpaid**		75	2,370.
	76a	Amount of line 75 you want **refunded to you.** If Form 8888 is attached, check here ▶ ☐		76a	2,370.
	▶ b	Routing number X X X X X X X X X ▶ c Type: ☐ Checking ☐ Savings			
	▶ d	Account number X X X X X X X X X X X X X X X X X			
	77	Amount of line 75 you want **applied to your 2016 estimated tax ▶** 77			
Amount You Owe	78	**Amount you owe.** Subtract line 74 from line 63. For details on how to pay, see instructions ▶		78	
	79	Estimated tax penalty (see instructions)	79		

Third Party Designee
Do you want to allow another person to discuss this return with the IRS (see instructions)? ☐ **Yes.** Complete below. ☒ **No**

Designee's name ▶	Phone no. ▶	Personal identification number (PIN) ▶

Sign Here
Joint return? See instructions.
Keep a copy for your records.

Under penalties of perjury, I declare that I have examined this return and accompanying schedules and statements, and to the best of my knowledge and belief, they are true, correct, and complete. Declaration of preparer (other than taxpayer) is based on all information of which preparer has any knowledge.

Your signature	Date	Your occupation	Daytime phone number
		Writer	
Spouse's signature. If a joint return, **both** must sign.	Date	Spouse's occupation	If the IRS sent you an Identity Protection PIN, enter it here (see inst.)
		Teacher	

Paid Preparer Use Only

Print/Type preparer's name	Preparer's signature	Date	Check ☐ if self-employed	PTIN
Peter Jason Riley CPA	Peter Jason Riley CPA	01/24/2016		P00413102
Firm's name ▶ RILEY & ASSOCIATES, P.C.			Firm's EIN ▶	04-3577120
Firm's address ▶ 5 PERRY WAY – P O BOX 157 NEWBURYPORT MA 01950			Phone no.	(978)463-9350

www.irs.gov/form1040   REV 12/30/15 PRO   Form **1040** (2015)

SCHEDULE A (Form 1040)	**Itemized Deductions**	OMB No. 1545-0074

SCHEDULE A (Form 1040) — Department of the Treasury, Internal Revenue Service (99)

Itemized Deductions

► Information about Schedule A and its separate instructions is at *www.irs.gov/schedulea*.
► Attach to Form 1040.

OMB No. 1545-0074
20**15**
Attachment Sequence No. **07**

Name(s) shown on Form 1040: **Guy & Mary Focal**

Your social security number: **444-55-6666**

Caution: Do not include expenses reimbursed or paid by others.

Medical and Dental Expenses

1	Medical and dental expenses (see instructions)	**1**	
2	Enter amount from Form 1040, line 38 **2**		
3	Multiply line 2 by 10% (.10). But if either you or your spouse was born before January 2, 1951, multiply line 2 by 7.5% (.075) instead	**3**	
4	Subtract line 3 from line 1. If line 3 is more than line 1, enter -0-		**4**	

Taxes You Paid

5	State and local (check only one box):		
	a ☒ Income taxes, or	**5**	4,422.
	b ☐ General sales taxes		
6	Real estate taxes (see instructions)	**6**	2,704.
7	Personal property taxes	**7**	
8	Other taxes. List type and amount ► _____	**8**	
9	Add lines 5 through 8	**9**	7,126.

Interest You Paid

Note: Your mortgage interest deduction may be limited (see instructions).

10	Home mortgage interest and points reported to you on Form 1098	**10**	5,515.
11	Home mortgage interest not reported to you on Form 1098. If paid to the person from whom you bought the home, see instructions and show that person's name, identifying no., and address ► _____	**11**	
12	Points not reported to you on Form 1098. See instructions for special rules	**12**	
13	Mortgage insurance premiums (see instructions)	**13**	
14	Investment interest. Attach Form 4952 if required. (See instructions.)	**14**	
15	Add lines 10 through 14	**15**	5,515.

Gifts to Charity

If you made a gift and got a benefit for it, see instructions.

16	Gifts by cash or check. If you made any gift of $250 or more, see instructions	**16**	580.
17	Other than by cash or check. If any gift of $250 or more, see instructions. You **must** attach Form 8283 if over $500	**17**	250.
18	Carryover from prior year	**18**	
19	Add lines 16 through 18	**19**	830.

Casualty and Theft Losses

20	Casualty or theft loss(es). Attach Form 4684. (See instructions.)	**20**	

Job Expenses and Certain Miscellaneous Deductions

21	Unreimbursed employee expenses—job travel, union dues, job education, etc. Attach Form 2106 or 2106-EZ if required. (See instructions.) ► See Schedule A, Line 21 Statement	**21**	1,970.
22	Tax preparation fees	**22**	
23	Other expenses—investment, safe deposit box, etc. List type and amount ► _____	**23**	
24	Add lines 21 through 23	**24**	1,970.
25	Enter amount from Form 1040, line 38 **25** 91,873.		
26	Multiply line 25 by 2% (.02)	**26**	1,837.
27	Subtract line 26 from line 24. If line 26 is more than line 24, enter -0-	**27**	133.

Other Miscellaneous Deductions

28	Other—from list in instructions. List type and amount ► _____	**28**	

Total Itemized Deductions

29	Is Form 1040, line 38, over $154,950?		
	☒ **No.** Your deduction is not limited. Add the amounts in the far right column for lines 4 through 28. Also, enter this amount on Form 1040, line 40.	**29**	13,604.
	☐ **Yes.** Your deduction may be limited. See the Itemized Deductions Worksheet in the instructions to figure the amount to enter.		
30	If you elect to itemize deductions even though they are less than your standard deduction, check here ► ☐		

For Paperwork Reduction Act Notice, see Form 1040 instructions. **BAA**   REV 12/30/15 PRO   Schedule A (Form 1040) 2015

SCHEDULE C
(Form 1040)

Department of the Treasury
Internal Revenue Service (99)

Profit or Loss From Business
(Sole Proprietorship)

▶ Information about Schedule C and its separate instructions is at *www.irs.gov/schedulec*.
▶ Attach to Form 1040, 1040NR, or 1041; partnerships generally must file Form 1065.

OMB No. 1545-0074

2015

Attachment
Sequence No. **09**

Name of proprietor	Social security number (SSN)
Guy Focal	444-55-6666

A Principal business or profession, including product or service (see instructions)
Writer

B Enter code from instructions
▶ | 7 | 1 | 1 | 5 | 1 | 0 |

C Business name. If no separate business name, leave blank.

D Employer ID number (EIN), (see instr.)

E Business address (including suite or room no.) ▶ Camp Place
City, town or post office, state, and ZIP code   New Orleans, LA 70130

F Accounting method: (1) ☒ Cash   (2) ☐ Accrual   (3) ☐ Other (specify) ▶

G Did you "materially participate" in the operation of this business during 2015? If "No," see instructions for limit on losses . ☒ Yes ☐ No

H If you started or acquired this business during 2015, check here . . . . ▶ ☐

I Did you make any payments in 2015 that would require you to file Form(s) 1099? (see instructions) . . . . ☒ Yes ☐ No

J If "Yes," did you or will you file required Forms 1099? . . . . ☒ Yes ☐ No

Part I   Income

1	Gross receipts or sales. See instructions for line 1 and check the box if this income was reported to you on Form W-2 and the "Statutory employee" box on that form was checked . . . . . . ▶ ☐	1	22,744.
2	Returns and allowances	2	
3	Subtract line 2 from line 1	3	22,744.
4	Cost of goods sold (from line 42)	4	2,757.
5	**Gross profit.** Subtract line 4 from line 3	5	19,987.
6	Other income, including federal and state gasoline or fuel tax credit or refund (see instructions)	6	350.
7	**Gross income.** Add lines 5 and 6 . . . . ▶	7	20,337.

Part II   Expenses. Enter expenses for business use of your home **only** on line 30.

8	Advertising	8		18	Office expense (see instructions)	18	187.
9	Car and truck expenses (see instructions)	9	1,191.	19	Pension and profit-sharing plans .	19	
				20	Rent or lease (see instructions):		
10	Commissions and fees .	10		a	Vehicles, machinery, and equipment	20a	
11	Contract labor (see instructions)	11	1,520.	b	Other business property . . .	20b	
12	Depletion	12		21	Repairs and maintenance . . .	21	120.
13	Depreciation and section 179 expense deduction (not included in Part III) (see instructions)	13	3,462.	22	Supplies (not included in Part III) .	22	288.
				23	Taxes and licenses	23	
				24	Travel, meals, and entertainment:		
14	Employee benefit programs (other than on line 19) . .	14		a	Travel	24a	3,940.
15	Insurance (other than health)	15		b	Deductible meals and entertainment (see instructions) .	24b	421.
16	Interest:			25	Utilities	25	
a	Mortgage (paid to banks, etc.)	16a		26	Wages (less employment credits) .	26	
b	Other	16b		27a	Other expenses (from line 48) . .	27a	3,106.
17	Legal and professional services	17	300.	b	Reserved for future use . . .	27b	

28	**Total expenses** before expenses for business use of home. Add lines 8 through 27a . . . . . ▶	28	14,535.
29	Tentative profit or (loss). Subtract line 28 from line 7	29	5,802.
30	Expenses for business use of your home. Do not report these expenses elsewhere. Attach Form 8829 unless using the simplified method (see instructions). **Simplified method filers only:** enter the total square footage of: (a) your home: _____ and (b) the part of your home used for business: _____ . Use the Simplified Method Worksheet in the instructions to figure the amount to enter on line 30	30	3,423.
31	**Net profit or (loss).** Subtract line 30 from line 29. • If a profit, enter on both **Form 1040, line 12** (or **Form 1040NR, line 13**) and on **Schedule SE, line 2.** (If you checked the box on line 1, see instructions). Estates and trusts, enter on **Form 1041, line 3.** • If a loss, you **must** go to line 32.	31	2,379.
32	If you have a loss, check the box that describes your investment in this activity (see instructions). • If you checked 32a, enter the loss on both **Form 1040, line 12,** (or **Form 1040NR, line 13**) and on **Schedule SE, line 2.** (If you checked the box on line 1, see the line 31 instructions). Estates and trusts, enter on **Form 1041, line 3.** • If you checked 32b, you **must** attach Form 6198. Your loss may be limited.	32a ☒ All investment is at risk. 32b ☐ Some investment is not at risk.	

For Paperwork Reduction Act Notice, see the separate instructions.   **BAA**   REV 12/07/15 PRO   Schedule C (Form 1040) 2015

Schedule C (Form 1040) 2015 | Page **2**

Part III Cost of Goods Sold (see instructions)

33 Method(s) used to value closing inventory: **a** ☐ Cost **b** ☐ Lower of cost or market **c** ☐ Other (attach explanation)

34 Was there any change in determining quantities, costs, or valuations between opening and closing inventory?
If "Yes," attach explanation . . . . ☐ Yes ☐ No

35 Inventory at beginning of year. If different from last year's closing inventory, attach explanation . . .	**35**	
36 Purchases less cost of items withdrawn for personal use	**36**	1,307.
37 Cost of labor. Do not include any amounts paid to yourself	**37**	1,450.
38 Materials and supplies	**38**	
39 Other costs	**39**	
40 Add lines 35 through 39	**40**	2,757.
41 Inventory at end of year	**41**	
42 **Cost of goods sold.** Subtract line 41 from line 40. Enter the result here and on line 4	**42**	2,757.

Part IV Information on Your Vehicle. Complete this part **only** if you are claiming car or truck expenses on line 9 and are not required to file Form 4562 for this business. See the instructions for line 13 to find out if you must file Form 4562.

43 When did you place your vehicle in service for business purposes? (month, day, year) ▶ _____

44 Of the total number of miles you drove your vehicle during 2015, enter the number of miles you used your vehicle for:

a Business _____ **b** Commuting (see instructions) _____ **c** Other _____

45 Was your vehicle available for personal use during off-duty hours? . . . . ☐ Yes ☐ No

46 Do you (or your spouse) have another vehicle available for personal use? . . . . ☐ Yes ☐ No

47a Do you have evidence to support your deduction? . . . . ☐ Yes ☐ No

b If "Yes," is the evidence written? . . . . ☐ Yes ☐ No

Part V Other Expenses. List below business expenses not included on lines 8–26 or line 30.

AMORTIZATION	308.
Merchant/PayPal Fees	143.
Image Scanning	395.
ISP	205.
Publications	877.
Research - Streaming Video/DVD	204.
Dues and Subscriptions	305.
Communications	287.
Postage	382.
48 Total other expenses. Enter here and on line 27a **48**	3,106.

REV 12/07/15 PRO Schedule C (Form 1040) 2015

SCHEDULE SE (Form 1040) Department of the Treasury Internal Revenue Service (99)	**Self-Employment Tax** ► Information about Schedule SE and its separate instructions is at *www.irs.gov/schedulese.* ►**Attach to Form 1040 or Form 1040NR.**	OMB No. 1545-0074 20**15** Attachment Sequence No. **17**

Name of person with **self-employment** income (as shown on Form 1040 or Form 1040NR) Guy Focal	Social security number of person with **self-employment** income ►	444-55-6666

Before you begin: To determine if you must file Schedule SE, see the instructions.

May I Use Short Schedule SE or Must I Use Long Schedule SE?

Note. Use this flowchart **only if** you must file Schedule SE. If unsure, see *Who Must File Schedule SE* in the instructions.

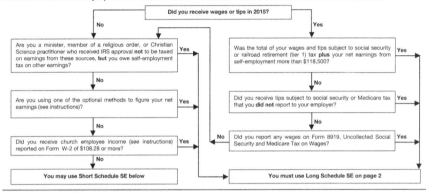

Section A—Short Schedule SE. **Caution.** Read above to see if you can use Short Schedule SE.

1a	Net farm profit or (loss) from Schedule F, line 34, and farm partnerships, Schedule K-1 (Form 1065), box 14, code A	**1a**	
b	If you received social security retirement or disability benefits, enter the amount of Conservation Reserve Program payments included on Schedule F, line 4b, or listed on Schedule K-1 (Form 1065), box 20, code Z	**1b** (	)
2	Net profit or (loss) from Schedule C, line 31; Schedule C-EZ, line 3; Schedule K-1 (Form 1065), box 14, code A (other than farming); and Schedule K-1 (Form 1065-B), box 9, code J1. Ministers and members of religious orders, see instructions for types of income to report on this line. See instructions for other income to report	**2**	2,379.
3	Combine lines 1a, 1b, and 2	**3**	2,379.
4	Multiply line 3 by 92.35% (.9235). If less than $400, you do not owe self-employment tax; **do not** file this schedule unless you have an amount on line 1b . . . . ►	**4**	2,197.
	Note. If line 4 is less than $400 due to Conservation Reserve Program payments on line 1b, see instructions.		
5	**Self-employment tax.** If the amount on line 4 is: • $118,500 or less, multiply line 4 by 15.3% (.153). Enter the result here and on **Form 1040, line 57,** or **Form 1040NR, line 55** • More than $118,500, multiply line 4 by 2.9% (.029). Then, add $14,694 to the result. Enter the total here and on **Form 1040, line 57,** or **Form 1040NR, line 55**	**5**	336.
6	**Deduction for one-half of self-employment tax.** Multiply line 5 by 50% (.50). Enter the result here and on **Form 1040, line 27, or Form 1040NR, line 27**	**6**	168.	

For Paperwork Reduction Act Notice, see your tax return instructions. **BAA**   REV 12/04/15 PRO   Schedule SE (Form 1040) 2015

Form **2106-EZ**	**Unreimbursed Employee Business Expenses**	OMB No. 1545-0074

▶ Attach to Form 1040 or Form 1040NR.

Department of the Treasury
Internal Revenue Service (99)　▶ Information about Form 2106 and its separate instructions is available at *www.irs.gov/form2106*.

20**15**

Attachment
Sequence No. **129A**

Your name	Occupation in which you incurred expenses	Social security number
Guy Focal	Staff Writer	444-55-6666

You Can Use This Form Only if All of the Following Apply.

- You are an employee deducting ordinary and necessary expenses attributable to your job. An ordinary expense is one that is common and accepted in your field of trade, business, or profession. A necessary expense is one that is helpful and appropriate for your business. An expense does not have to be required to be considered necessary.

- You **do not** get reimbursed by your employer for any expenses (amounts your employer included in box 1 of your Form W-2 are not considered reimbursements for this purpose).

- If you are claiming vehicle expense, you are using the standard mileage rate for 2015.

Caution: *You can use the standard mileage rate for 2015 **only if: (a)** you owned the vehicle and used the standard mileage rate for the first year you placed the vehicle in service, **or (b)** you leased the vehicle and used the standard mileage rate for the portion of the lease period after 1997.*

Part I　**Figure Your Expenses**

1	Complete Part II. Multiply line 8a by 57.5¢ (.575). Enter the result here	**1**	
2	Parking fees, tolls, and transportation, including train, bus, etc., that **did not** involve overnight travel or commuting to and from work	**2**	386.
3	Travel expense while away from home overnight, including lodging, airplane, car rental, etc. **Do not** include meals and entertainment . . . . , , .	**3**	1,178.
4	Business expenses not included on lines 1 through 3. **Do not** include meals and entertainment	**4**	295.
5	Meals and entertainment expenses:　$ ___222.___ × 50% (.50). (Employees subject to Department of Transportation (DOT) hours of service limits: Multiply meal expenses incurred while away from home on business by 80% (.80) instead of 50%. For details, see instructions.)	**5**	111.
6	**Total expenses.** Add lines 1 through 5. Enter here and on **Schedule A (Form 1040), line 21** (or on **Schedule A (Form 1040NR), line 7**). (Armed Forces reservists, fee-basis state or local government officials, qualified performing artists, and individuals with disabilities: See the instructions for special rules on where to enter this amount.)	**6**	1,970.

Part II　**Information on Your Vehicle.** Complete this part **only** if you are claiming vehicle expense on line 1.

7　When did you place your vehicle in service for business use? (month, day, year) ▶ _____

8　Of the total number of miles you drove your vehicle during 2015, enter the number of miles you used your vehicle for:

a　Business _____　b　Commuting (see instructions) _____　c　Other _____

9　Was your vehicle available for personal use during off-duty hours? . . . . ☐ Yes ☐ No

10　Do you (or your spouse) have another vehicle available for personal use? . . . . ☐ Yes ☐ No

11a　Do you have evidence to support your deduction? . . . . ☐ Yes ☐ No

b　If "Yes," is the evidence written? . . . . ☐ Yes ☐ No

For Paperwork Reduction Act Notice, see your tax return instructions. BAA　REV 01/07/16 PRO　Form **2106-EZ** (2015)

Form 8829

Department of the Treasury
Internal Revenue Service (99)

Expenses for Business Use of Your Home

► File only with Schedule C (Form 1040). Use a separate Form 8829 for each home you used for business during the year.
► Information about Form 8829 and its separate instructions is at *www.irs.gov/form8829*.

OMB No. 1545-0074

2015

Attachment
Sequence No. **176**

Name(s) of proprietor(s)
Guy Focal

Your social security number
444-55-6666

Part I   Part of Your Home Used for Business   Writer

1	Area used regularly and exclusively for business, regularly for daycare, or for storage of inventory or product samples (see instructions)	**1**	236
2	Total area of home	**2**	1,688
3	Divide line 1 by line 2. Enter the result as a percentage	**3**	13.98 %

For daycare facilities not used exclusively for business, go to line 4. All others, go to line 7.

4	Multiply days used for daycare during year by hours used per day	**4**		hr.
5	Total hours available for use during the year (365 days x 24 hours) (see instructions)	**5**	8,760	hr.
6	Divide line 4 by line 5. Enter the result as a decimal amount	**6**		
7	Business percentage. For daycare facilities not used exclusively for business, multiply line 6 by line 3 (enter the result as a percentage). All others, enter the amount from line 3 ►	**7**	13.98 %	

Part II   Figure Your Allowable Deduction

8	Enter the amount from Schedule C, line 29, **plus** any gain derived from the business use of your home, **minus** any loss from the trade or business not derived from the business use of your home (see instructions)		**8**	5,802.

See instructions for columns **(a)** and **(b)** before completing lines 9–21.

		(a) Direct expenses	**(b)** Indirect expenses		
9	Casualty losses (see instructions)	**9**			
10	Deductible mortgage interest (see instructions)	**10**		6,411.	
11	Real estate taxes (see instructions)	**11**		3,144.	
12	Add lines 9, 10, and 11	**12**		9,555.	
13	Multiply line 12, column (b) by line 7		**13**	1,336.	
14	Add line 12, column (a) and line 13			**14**	1,336.
15	Subtract line 14 from line 8. If zero or less, enter -0-			**15**	4,466.
16	Excess mortgage interest (see instructions)	**16**			
17	Insurance	**17**		2,966.	
18	Rent	**18**			
19	Repairs and maintenance	**19**		841.	
20	Utilities	**20**		3,188.	
21	Other expenses (see instructions)	**21**			
22	Add lines 16 through 21	**22**		6,995.	
23	Multiply line 22, column (b) by line 7		**23**	978.	
24	Carryover of prior year operating expenses (see instructions)		**24**		
25	Add line 22, column (a), line 23, and line 24			**25**	978.
26	Allowable operating expenses. Enter the **smaller** of line 15 or line 25			**26**	978.
27	Limit on excess casualty losses and depreciation. Subtract line 26 from line 15			**27**	3,488.
28	Excess casualty losses (see instructions)		**28**		
29	Depreciation of your home from line 41 below		**29**	1,109.	
30	Carryover of prior year excess casualty losses and depreciation (see instructions)		**30**		
31	Add lines 28 through 30			**31**	1,109.
32	Allowable excess casualty losses and depreciation. Enter the **smaller** of line 27 or line 31			**32**	1,109.
33	Add lines 14, 26, and 32			**33**	3,423.
34	Casualty loss portion, if any, from lines 14 and 32. Carry amount to **Form 4684** (see instructions)			**34**	
35	**Allowable expenses for business use of your home.** Subtract line 34 from line 33. Enter here and on Schedule C, line 30. If your home was used for more than one business, see instructions ►			**35**	3,423.

Part III   Depreciation of Your Home

36	Enter the **smaller** of your home's adjusted basis or its fair market value (see instructions)	**36**	370,000.
37	Value of land included on line 36	**37**	65,000.
38	Basis of building. Subtract line 37 from line 36	**38**	305,000.
39	Business basis of building. Multiply line 38 by line 7	**39**	42,639.
40	Depreciation percentage (see instructions)	**40**	2.5641 %
41	Depreciation allowable (see instructions). Multiply line 39 by line 40. Enter here and on line 29 above	**41**	1,109.

Part IV   Carryover of Unallowed Expenses to 2016

42	Operating expenses. Subtract line 26 from line 25. If less than zero, enter -0-	**42**	0.
43	Excess casualty losses and depreciation. Subtract line 32 from line 31. If less than zero, enter -0-	**43**	0.

For Paperwork Reduction Act Notice, see your tax return instructions.   **BAA**   REV 12/04/15 PRO   Form **8829** (2015)

Form **4562**	**Depreciation and Amortization**	OMB No. 1545-0172
Department of the Treasury Internal Revenue Service (99)	(Including Information on Listed Property) ▶ Attach to your tax return. ▶ Information about Form 4562 and its separate instructions is at *www.irs.gov/form4562*.	**2015** Attachment Sequence No. **179**

Name(s) shown on return	Business or activity to which this form relates	Identifying number
Guy & Mary Focal	Sch C Writer	444-55-6666

Part I Election To Expense Certain Property Under Section 179
Note: If you have any listed property, complete Part V before you complete Part I.

1	Maximum amount (see instructions)	**1**	500,000.
2	Total cost of section 179 property placed in service (see instructions)	**2**	11,625.
3	Threshold cost of section 179 property before reduction in limitation (see instructions)	**3**	2,000,000.
4	Reduction in limitation. Subtract line 3 from line 2. If zero or less, enter -0-	**4**	0.
5	Dollar limitation for tax year. Subtract line 4 from line 1. If zero or less, enter -0-. If married filing separately, see instructions	**5**	500,000.

6	(a) Description of property	(b) Cost (business use only)	(c) Elected cost
	iMac	1,699.	1,699.

7	Listed property. Enter the amount from line 29	**7**	
8	Total elected cost of section 179 property. Add amounts in column (c), lines 6 and 7	**8**	1,699.
9	Tentative deduction. Enter the **smaller** of line 5 or line 8	**9**	1,699.
10	Carryover of disallowed deduction from line 13 of your 2014 Form 4562	**10**	
11	Business income limitation. Enter the smaller of business income (not less than zero) or line 5 (see instructions)	**11**	93,710.
12	Section 179 expense deduction. Add lines 9 and 10, but do not enter more than line 11	**12**	1,699.
13	Carryover of disallowed deduction to 2016. Add lines 9 and 10, less line 12 ▶	**13**	0.

Note: Do not use Part II or Part III below for listed property. Instead, use Part V.

Part II Special Depreciation Allowance and Other Depreciation (Do not include listed property.) (See instructions.)

14	Special depreciation allowance for qualified property (other than listed property) placed in service during the tax year (see instructions)	**14**	
15	Property subject to section 168(f)(1) election	**15**	
16	Other depreciation (including ACRS)	**16**	

Part III MACRS Depreciation (Do not include listed property.) (See instructions.)

Section A

17	MACRS deductions for assets placed in service in tax years beginning before 2015	**17**	1,534.
18	If you are electing to group any assets placed in service during the tax year into one or more general asset accounts, check here ▶ ☐		

Section B—Assets Placed in Service During 2015 Tax Year Using the General Depreciation System

(a) Classification of property	(b) Month and year placed in service	(c) Basis for depreciation (business/investment use only—see instructions)	(d) Recovery period	(e) Convention	(f) Method	(g) Depreciation deduction
19a 3-year property						
b 5-year property		9,926.	5.0	HY	Various	1,338.
c 7-year property						
d 10-year property						
e 15-year property						
f 20-year property						
g 25-year property			25 yrs.		S/L	
h Residential rental property			27.5 yrs.	MM	S/L	
			27.5 yrs.	MM	S/L	
i Nonresidential real property			39 yrs.	MM	S/L	
				MM	S/L	

Section C—Assets Placed in Service During 2015 Tax Year Using the Alternative Depreciation System

20a Class life					S/L	
b 12-year			12 yrs.		S/L	
c 40-year			40 yrs.	MM	S/L	

Part IV Summary (See instructions.)

21	Listed property. Enter amount from line 28	**21**	
22	**Total.** Add amounts from line 12, lines 14 through 17, lines 19 and 20 in column (g), and line 21. Enter here and on the appropriate lines of your return. Partnerships and S corporations—see instructions	**22**	4,571.
23	For assets shown above and placed in service during the current year, enter the portion of the basis attributable to section 263A costs	**23**	

For Paperwork Reduction Act Notice, see separate instructions. **BAA**   REV 12/27/15 PRO   Form **4562** (2015)

Form 4562 (2015)   Page **2**

Part V **Listed Property** (Include automobiles, certain other vehicles, certain aircraft, certain computers, and property used for entertainment, recreation, or amusement.)

Note: For any vehicle for which you are using the standard mileage rate or deducting lease expense, complete **only** 24a, 24b, columns (a) through (c) of Section A, all of Section B, and Section C if applicable.

Section A—Depreciation and Other Information (Caution: See the instructions for limits for passenger automobiles.**)**

24a Do you have evidence to support the business/investment use claimed? ☒ **Yes** ☐ **No**   24b If "Yes," is the evidence written? ☒ **Yes** ☐ **No**

(a) Type of property (list vehicles first)	(b) Date placed in service	(c) Business/ investment use percentage	(d) Cost or other basis	(e) Basis for depreciation (business/investment use only)	(f) Recovery period	(g) Method/ Convention	(h) Depreciation deduction	(i) Elected section 179 cost
25 Special depreciation allowance for qualified listed property placed in service during the tax year and used more than 50% in a qualified business use (see instructions) . **25**								
26 Property used more than 50% in a qualified business use:								
		%						
		%						
		%						
27 Property used 50% or less in a qualified business use:								
Vehicle	01/01/2011	17.54 %				S/L –		
		%				S/L –		
		%				S/L –		

28 Add amounts in column (h), lines 25 through 27. Enter here and on line 21, page 1 . **28**
29 Add amounts in column (i), line 26. Enter here and on line 7, page 1 . . . . **29**

Section B—Information on Use of Vehicles

Complete this section for vehicles used by a sole proprietor, partner, or other "more than 5% owner," or related person. If you provided vehicles to your employees, first answer the questions in Section C to see if you meet an exception to completing this section for those vehicles.

	(a) Vehicle 1		(b) Vehicle 2		(c) Vehicle 3		(d) Vehicle 4		(e) Vehicle 5		(f) Vehicle 6	
30 Total business/investment miles driven during the year (**do not** include commuting miles) .	2,072											
31 Total commuting miles driven during the year	3,500											
32 Total other personal (noncommuting) miles driven	6,241											
33 Total miles driven during the year. Add lines 30 through 32	11,813											
34 Was the vehicle available for personal use during off-duty hours?	Yes	No	Yes	No	Yes	No	Yes	No	Yes	No	Yes	No
	X											
35 Was the vehicle used primarily by a more than 5% owner or related person? . .	X											
36 Is another vehicle available for personal use?	X											

Section C—Questions for Employers Who Provide Vehicles for Use by Their Employees

Answer these questions to determine if you meet an exception to completing Section B for vehicles used by employees who **are not** more than 5% owners or related persons (see instructions).

	Yes	No
37 Do you maintain a written policy statement that prohibits all personal use of vehicles, including commuting, by your employees?		
38 Do you maintain a written policy statement that prohibits personal use of vehicles, except commuting, by your employees? See the instructions for vehicles used by corporate officers, directors, or 1% or more owners . .		
39 Do you treat all use of vehicles by employees as personal use?		
40 Do you provide more than five vehicles to your employees, obtain information from your employees about the use of the vehicles, and retain the information received?		
41 Do you meet the requirements concerning qualified automobile demonstration use? (See instructions.) . . .		

Note: If your answer to 37, 38, 39, 40, or 41 is "Yes," do not complete Section B for the covered vehicles.

Part VI **Amortization**

(a) Description of costs	(b) Date amortization begins	(c) Amortizable amount	(d) Code section	(e) Amortization period or percentage	(f) Amortization for this year
42 Amortization of costs that begins during your 2015 tax year (see instructions):					
Website Costs	07/01/2015	1,850.	197	3.00 yrs	308.
43 Amortization of costs that began before your 2015 tax year **43**					
44 **Total.** Add amounts in column (f). See the instructions for where to report **44**					308.

REV 12/27/15 PRO   Form **4562** (2015)

Form 4562

Depreciation and Amortization Report

2015

Tax Year 2015
► Keep for your records

444-55-6666

Guy & Mary Focal
Sch C - Writer

Asset Description	*Code	Date In Service	Cost (Net of Land)	Land	Bus Use %	Section 179	Special Depreciation Allowance	Depreciable Basis	Life	Method/ Convention	Prior Depreciation	Current Depreciation
DEPRECIATION												
Cable Modem		07/01/15	129		100.00			129	5.0	200DB/HY		26
Netbook Computer		07/01/15	1,249		100.00			1,249	5.0	200DB/HY		250
Library (historical books)		07/01/15	6,480		100.00			6,480	5.0	SL/HY		648
iPad		07/01/15	544		100.00			544	5.0	200DB/HY		109
Galaxy S7 phone		07/01/15	299		100.00			299	5.0	200DB/HY		60
Wireless Network Hardware		07/01/15	481		100.00			481	5.0	200DB/HY		96
Office Electrical Upgrade		07/01/15	744		100.00			744	5.0	200DB/HY	0	149
iMac		12/27/15	1,699		100.00	1,699		0	5.0	200DB/HY	0	0
SUBTOTAL CURRENT YEAR			11,625	0		1,699	0	9,926			0	1,338
Home	H	01/01/11	305,000	65,000	13.98			42,639	39.0	SL/MM	3,795	1,109
Vehicle	L	01/01/11			17.54							
Technology		07/01/11	3,941		100.00			3,941	5.0	200DB/HY	3,303	425
SUBTOTAL PRIOR YEAR			308,941	65,000		0	0	46,580			7,098	1,534
TOTALS			320,566	65,000		1,699	0	56,506			7,098	2,872
AMORTIZATION												
Website Costs		07/01/15	1,850		100.00			1,850	3.0		0	308
SUBTOTAL CURRENT YEAR			1,850			0	0	1,850			0	308
TOTALS			1,850			0	0	1,850			0	308

* Code: S = Sold, A = Auto, L = Listed, H = Home Office

Guy & Mary Focal   444-55-6666   1

Additional information from your 2015 Federal Tax Return

Schedule A: Itemized Deductions

Line 21 - Employee Business Expenses Subject to 2% Limitation   **Continuation Statement**

Description	Amount
Deductible expenses from Form 2106	1,970.
Excess Educator Expenses	0.
Total	1,970.

Guy & Mary Focal   444-55-6666

Schedule C - Other Income	
Stipend	$350

Schedule C - Other Costs of Goods Sold	
Illustrator	$1,450

Books Sold	$1,307

Travel Detail - Form 2106 - line 3	
NYC Airfare	$489
NYC Hotel	$689
	$1,178

Other Business Expenses Form 2106 Line 4	
Conference Fee	$195
PEN Membership	$100
	$295

Meals Detail - Form 2106 - line 5			
NYC - 3 days @ $71	3	$74	$222

Schedule C - Meals			
Texas	4	$51	$204
Book Tour	10	$51	$510
LA	2	$64	$128
			$842

Schedule C - Travel	
Texas Hotel	$389
Texas Auto Rental	$377
Book Tour Lodging	$874
Book Tour Airfare	$1,504
LA - Lodging	$388
LA - Airfare (Guy only)	$408
	$3,940

8

Setting Up a Business Entity

I think of this as the "should I incorporate?" discussion because that invariably seems to be the opening volley on this topic. The artist will generally have talked to a colleague or family member who has told them that *they must incorporate immediately* for whatever purpose, most frequently for the extensive tax benefits offered. So let's look at the choices the artist has for setting up a business entity: sole proprietorship, partnership, corporation, and limited liability company.

The Sole Proprietorship

So far I have focused on the sole proprietorship, which is how most artists operate. Until the artist sets up a formal entity, he or she is, by default, a sole proprietor. The sole proprietor simply means one owner (a husband–wife team can function as joint proprietors). You will be automatically set up as a sole proprietorship if you do nothing else. The main feature of this form is that it is identified and intertwined with you, which gives it both strengths and weaknesses. If the business makes a profit, it is automatically income for you. If the business incurs a debt, it is your personal debt. If the business gets sued, you will be sued personally as well. It gives you complete flexibility, which enables you to instantly shift the direction, policies, and focus of your company. But if there is a problem, any damage can potentially extend into your personal life. To limit this potential liability, you may choose to set up a "single-member" LLC (limited liability company). The "single-member" LLC customarily operates as a sole proprietor and might offer some liability protection (ask your attorney about this before moving forward).

The Partnership

When talking to clients, I describe the partnership as a multiperson sole proprietorship because these two entities are taxed in a very similar manner. The sole proprietorship files its taxes as part of the owner's Form 1040, whereas the partnership files its own separate income tax return (on federal Form 1065), which reports the total income and expenses of the business. The partnership then passes the net "bottom-line" income or losses directly to the personal income tax returns of the partners via the federal Form K-1. This means that the partnership itself almost never pays any income tax directly, but passes the income or loss directly to the partners to be dealt with on their personal returns. You can see why partnerships are often referred to as "flow-through" entities: the income or loss "flows through" the partnership onto the partners' personal income tax returns. The partnership does have the unique and critical tax advantage of "special allocations." Simply put, special allocations allow the partnership to customize the distribution of income and loss by mutual consent, through the use of the partnership agreement. For instance, two partners may own the business 50%–50%, but choose to split any losses 75%–25% if that yields a better tax result for them. Partnerships can also, if properly structured, have tax advantages relating to film and sound-recording activities.

Although easily formed on a handshake, a partnership is rarely as easy to dissolve. It pays to be very careful when forming a partnership. You will get to know all the good and all the bad things about your partner. Bad partnerships can destroy friendships. Most importantly, you are completely and personally liable for whatever your partner does (we are speaking here of the common general partnership; the exception to this is the limited partnership, in which a limited partner has some liability protection). For instance, in a common general partnership, if our musician Sonny Phunky takes a partner and the partner signs him up to play a series of engagements with his band, then skips town with all the money in the partnership bank account, not only will Sonny be out the money, he will also be liable for playing all the gigs!

Partnerships can certainly work when there is a clear division of responsibilities and abilities. If you are an actor, musician, visual artist, or writer, but you lack management or promotional skills and your paperwork is usually a shambles, a potential partner who is a good agent, meticulous and detail oriented, but does not have your artistic abilities, may be natural match.

Partnerships are beneficial when you need to raise more capital. A partner's contribution may help to launch your business venture or project. Because of the sums of money involved, many major films are produced within the limited partnership (and limited liability company, or LLC) form of entity. In this case the partnership/LLC is a natural way to raise the money for a specific project like a movie, book, or other artistic endeavor and then split the profits from it. When the project is completed the partnership will typically dissolve.

If you do contemplate a partnership, have an attorney draw up a clearly defined partnership agreement. The agreement should address issues of operation and specify procedures for termination of one of the partners. What if one of the partners dies? Who will do what jobs within the operation of the partnership? How will decisions be made? What happens if you can't agree? Who will pay for what? Settle all these points in advance, before they have a chance to cause disruption in the business. Nothing kills a business faster than feuding partners.

The Corporation

The third form of business is the corporation. Incorporation gives two main advantages:

1. You can have people invest in your company to raise money.

2. Because a corporation exists legally as a separate entity, it provides a liability shield between you and your personal assets and the business. If the company gets sued, you have some protection (albeit not ironclad). Company debts are separate from your personal financial situation.

For tax purposes, there are two main types of corporations: the subchapter "C" and the subchapter "S" (the letters refer to subchapters of the tax code). Both are corporations in the legal sense, but the taxation of income and losses is handled differently.

The "C" corporation is the standard. All companies listed on the stock exchange are "C" corporations. These corporations can have unlimited shareholders (investors). If one sells one hundred thousand shares at $10 each, it has a million dollars in capital available. The investors can be individuals, mutual funds, companies, etc. "C" corporations pay income tax directly on their profits, which highlights the disadvantage of the "C" corporation: double taxation. For example, if your business earns $100,000 in profit, a corporate tax has to be paid first. Then if you draw a salary (since in a corporation you are, in fact, an employee), you must declare that salary and pay personal income tax. So, the same money gets taxed twice before you get to spend any of it. Recognizing that this was unfair to the small business, the "S" corporation was created.

The "S" corporation is a "flow-through" entity, much like a partnership. Unlike the "C" corporation, an "S" corporation will not pay income tax directly on its profit. Its net income or loss is simply transferred onto the personal income tax returns of the shareholders via the federal Form K-1 (same as the partnership), and the shareholders will pay the income taxes on their share of the profits of the corporation. Be aware that the "S" corporation does not allow the "special allocations" of the partnership. If two shareholders own the corporation 50%–50%, the profits or losses have to be split 50%–50% as well.

The standard "C" corporation files federal Form 1120 annually; the "S" corporation files federal Form 1120S annually.

The Limited Liability Company

Because it provides the liability shielding of a corporation and the flexibility of a partnership, this relatively new form of business entity, the limited liability company (LLC) is quickly becoming predominant in the creative world. The Internal Revenue Service does not have any "LLC" tax forms, so the individuals decide how they wish to be taxed when they create the LLC. Probably the most common tax entity chosen for LLCs is the partnership, but they can also be S corporations or a sole proprietorship. If you are considering setting up your business as a partnership, look long and hard at the LLC. It is generally preferable to the standard partnership. The LLC combines many of the features of a partnership with those of an "S" corporation, without the restrictions that are applied to "S" corporations. It allows the reporting of income or loss directly on the personal income tax returns of the "partners" (or "members" in the parlance of an LLC), but provides some of the liability protection of a corporation. The LLC is also a "flow-through" entity that generally files the same federal income tax forms as a partnership (Form 1065), and it does allow for the use of the "special allocations" we discussed in the section on partnerships. As with a standard partnership, you do need two individuals to set up an LLC, although a "single-person" LLC can be established for a sole proprietorship.

When and Which Entity Would the Artist Set Up?

In essence, artists have three choices of business entity: the sole proprietorship, the partnership/LLC, and the corporation. First the artist decides whether he or she even needs to set up a separate business entity. Having decided, he or she must determine the type of entity to create. Deliberations should involve both an attorney and a tax professional. I would generally advise the artist never to set up a business entity without obtaining separate legal and financial/tax advice. Your attorney will explain the legal benefits of setting up a business entity, as well as actually creating the entity in the legal sense.

Your accountant and tax advisor will clarify what new expenses, responsibilities, and functions will be entailed in your new business entity. Commonly, the attorney and tax professional will need to confer on behalf of their client, because the legal and financial matters are interrelated.

What prompts consideration of establishing a business entity is that the artist has an issue or problem that *cannot be solved any other way*. Unless there is a clear need or reason to set up an entity, don't consider it. They are costly to set up and maintain unless they can serve a clear and identifiable purpose. Furthermore, they complicate the operation of your business. Accounting and tax filings (as well as the associated fees) increase. With the help of an attorney and an accountant, the artist needs to do a careful cost–benefit analysis to help him or her decide whether it is worth setting up the business entity (a cost–benefit analysis is where you weigh the cost incurred versus the benefit received). It might be that personal liability is an issue for the artist. A cost–benefit analysis may find that insurance is a more effective solution. An artist desiring to bring someone into the business might be better served by simply hiring an employee.

So, what are some of the situations or needs that might finally lead the artist to set up a separate business entity?

- Need for the liability protection provided by a corporation or LLC.
- Need for more than one owner in the business.
- To isolate some specific business venture or project, like a film, book, or musical.
- To separate ownership and control of business operations.
- To shift income to other family members, associates, or friends to take advantage of those individuals' lower income tax rates.
- To raise capital for a specific venture or project by bringing in investors.
- IRS audit concerns. For many years sole proprietorships have been, and will probably continue to be, #1 on the IRS audit hit list. Other formal business entities are less likely to be audit targets.
- Tax savings available in particular entities, such as potential payroll tax savings available in "S" corporations.
- Working in a multistate environment: corporations are probably the most portable and practical entity for artists working across state lines.

Taking our four artists, let's look at when and why an artist might chose to set up a separate business entity.

Example One

Actor Ima Starr is beginning to hit it big and make some serious money. She decides to set up a corporation for her acting business (sometimes referred to as "loan-out" corporations). With this setup, the film companies would pay her corporation for her services and she would, in turn, be an employee of her own corporation. The benefits to Ima could be that (1) she is able to shift income to later tax years and allow her to delay payment of income taxes, (2) she might save payroll (FICA) taxes by operating as an "S" corporation, and (3) she may use the corporation to shift income to other members of her family or household (and into lower tax brackets). The corporation would help her limit her personal liability and at the same time potentially lower her statistical chances of being audited. It would isolate her business activity from the rest of her life. The IRS frequently zeros in on "loan-out" corporations, so they have to be structured with great care in order to sidestep punitive personal holding company (PHC) rules.

Ima is also considering an LLC to produce her own film, book, or other project. The project would be produced inside the LLC; when the project is sold, the LLC would distribute the profits to the investors/members and perhaps dissolve. If Ima already has the corporation, why would she set up a separate LLC for her film project? She would do this to isolate this one project from the rest of her business activities. From both a legal and financial point of view, she would want to do this in order to avoid involving the individuals who are members of the LLC in the primary operations inside her corporation. Also, because the LLC operates (for tax purposes) as a partnership, she may have some advantages in writing off the costs of the film.

Example Two

Musician Sonny Phunky needs some investor money in order to make a new recording with a big band. He could set up an LLC, much the way Ima did, to attract investors and isolate that activity, and later to channel the profits (or losses) directly to the investors.

As we discussed in Chapter 5, Sonny's band, The Over the Hill Gang, set up an LLC for a showcase U.S. tour. The band subsequently had a song picked up as a theme for a hit cable TV show and had royalty income of over $100,000. Having been discovered, a major tour is being planned and Sonny is worried about touring liabilities concerning his band and crew. His lawyer advises him that he could set up all the band members as "single-member" LLCs and these in turn would be the members of the primary band LLC, "The Lido Shuffle." Income from the tour would be paid into the band

LLC, the crew would be employees, and the band members would all be paid distributions directly to their own "single-member" LLCs. This would help limit Sonny's (and the band's) personal liability in case of accidents and other unforeseen problems.

His tax advisor also discussed setting up a music equipment leasing company that would own all the equipment used by the band on the tour. Sonny's LLC would then lease (pay rent) to the leasing company for the use of the sound and lighting equipment. If the leasing company were an LLC, it would give Sonny an additional layer of liability protection. The leasing company can be set up by Sonny and his attorney using a generic name. A generic name gives Sonny some privacy, in that people need not know that Sonny owns the leasing company. Such a move can be very tax efficient, as it gives Sonny another means of receiving profits from the band's activities.

Should Sonny's songwriting continue to grow (as it seems to be now), he is considering setting up a second publishing LLC (or other business entity) to control his songwriting activities and royalties.

Example Three

Suppose our painter, Liz Brushstroke, befriends an individual who becomes her business manager and agent, and as such is a vital and essential part of her artistic activities. Liz decides to make this person a legal part of her business by setting up a corporation or LLC (either one would probably work, but the LLC would be more flexible and user-friendly), giving him or her a real equity stake in her artistic life. By making this individual a shareholder or member of her business, Liz legally recognizes this person's importance in her business life and will be able, depending on how the entity is structured, to give him or her a share of the profits. Liz's advisors told her that she could simply hire her friend as an employee, but Liz prefers setting up the business entity.

Liz has an investor interested in funding the publication of a limited-edition book of her works, and for this her attorney and tax advisor both recommended an LLC. The LLC will be structured to receive cash from the investor. In turn, it will receive all the income from book sales, pay all the expenses of the publication, then distribute the net profits (or loss) to Liz and the investor according to their LLC agreement. After all the books are sold, the final profits will be distributed. The LLC will then file a final income tax return and fold.

Example Four

Guy Focal has his first big year as a writer when one of his books is sold for a major film adaptation. He decides to incorporate his writing activities and sets up an "S" corporation. His agent or publisher will pay his royalties directly into the corporation from now on. The corporation will allow him to put some family members (who are helping him with his correspondence and research) on his payroll, thus diversifying his income into their lower tax brackets. The corporation will also give Guy some liability protection.

With knowledge gained from this recent film experience, Guy decides to try to adapt and make a film of another of his books. He finds some investors and sets up an LLC to act as a production company for the film project, because he does not want the investors to be a part of his "S" corporation. If the project doesn't succeed, the LLC investors/members will most likely be able to use the losses on their personal income tax returns. If it succeeds and sells, the income from the film will become income on the members' income taxes.

In Closing

It may appear to some readers that this is the first matter we should discuss. At the beginning of their careers, very few artists would have any need to set up a formal business structure. Even many successful artists never set up any formal business entity. At the early stage of an artist's career it would rarely be cost effective and, more importantly, the direction and scope of the artist's ultimate activity would be insufficiently developed to allow effective decisions regarding business structures.

By the way, most of what we have talked about in the book regarding rules relating to income and expenses still applies to any structure within which you may happen to operate. While the mechanics may change, in general, the IRS view of taxable income and what it considers a justifiable expense does not alter much across the spectrum of different business entities.

Please keep in mind that we have barely scratched the surface of this very complex topic. You can see that this whole subject is a balancing act among financial, legal, estate, and income tax concerns. Any decisions are subjective and relate directly to personal financial goals, so what works for the colleague you spoke to at a party may not work at all for you. Be *very* careful of anything that sounds like a boilerplate solution. I feel that most financial decisions are far more personal than most people realize, and business structure is very much in that camp. Make any decisions in this area after careful discussions of your personal desires, goals, and concerns, which would involve strategic issues such as estate planning.

9

The Audit Process, Record Keeping, and Your Taxpayer Rights

An important fact to keep firmly in mind as you approach your record keeping and documentation is that IRS audits occur typically 12 to 18 months *after* the end of the tax year being audited. You can very easily be in the position of having an IRS agent ask you detailed questions about a business meal, travel expense, or other deduction that happened more than 2 years ago!

Simple mistakes can cause a return to be questioned. These mistakes and oversights can include:

- ✓ Mathematical errors—simple: you didn't add or subtract correctly!
- ✓ Not attaching required forms such as W-2s and 1099s with withholding tax.
- ✓ Income that was independently reported to the IRS that its computers couldn't find on your tax return. These can be 1099s and W-2s that the IRS computer scans and cannot match on your return. Sometimes the IRS is correct; sometimes it is not.
- ✓ Social Security number and name do not match—the IRS now matches the first three characters of all last names against the individual's Social Security number using the Social Security Administration's database. If there isn't a match between the name and Social Security number, you are sent a letter.

How is a tax return typically selected for audit? The IRS subjects all personal income tax returns to a computerized analysis based on a mathematical technique known as "discriminant function" (DIF), which identifies income tax returns with a high probability of error and a chance of significant tax change. The DIF program evolved from a concern during the 1960s that too many "no change" audits were occurring, and that IRS audits should focus on returns likely to have errors. Under the DIF procedure, returns with high DIF scores or other special features are manually inspected to select some for audit. Thus, the DIF score acts as a red flag for IRS audits. The DIF formula is secret, known to only a very few senior IRS officials. Experience indicates that certain factors are likely to increase the DIF score and the possibility of an audit. Among these factors are high salaries or other compensation, high expenses relative to income, and the presence of certain types of deductions such as charitable contributions and medical expenses. DIF formula data is developed from a range of sources, including IRS audit experience. Unfortunately for many of the readers of this book, self-employed individuals are usually at the top of the IRS's "most audited" list.

Your business code can also subject you to audit. As you can see on our sample returns, there is a box for an industry code on your Schedule C (Box B at the top of the form). This code identifies to the IRS the type of business you are in. Some IRS auditing is being done based on this code rather than on the actual numbers in the return. In other words, the IRS in your district may be looking into "independent artists, writers, and performers" code 711510, and your return could be chosen for a full-blown audit regardless of your DIF score.

Your audit might be the result of having the wrong preparer. If, in the course of doing audits, the Internal Revenue Service notices certain patterns of abuse or incompetence by a tax preparer, then they might decide to target taxpayers who used that particular preparer. See Chapter 11 for guidance in choosing a tax preparer.

The DIF score is just the first stage of the potential audit process. Once the return is flagged, an IRS examiner will review it to see if he or she thinks it is worth auditing, and if they have the time to perform the audit. This same IRS agent is generally the one who decides if your return will actually be audited. If the amounts "flagged" on your return concern just one or two line items, it may be subjected to a "desk audit," which causes you to get a letter asking for substantiation or detail on a particular line item on the return. This type of audit is all done via mail. The taxpayer sends in the supporting documentation, the agent reviews it, and if there are no further questions, the agent lets you know the result.

The second type of audit is the live and in-person kind. Usually the IRS will ask you to come into their office bringing all your supporting documentation. In some instances, if the audit is big enough, they may choose to visit your place of business (virtually all LLC, partnership, or corporate audits are done in person). The audit notification will tell you in advance exactly what type of documentation is wanted and what line items on the return are being examined. The IRS does not allow the auditor to turn the audit into what we call a "fishing expedition."

The audit can be conducted with the taxpayer and/or with an authorized representative such as a CPA, attorney, or enrolled agent. The taxpayer may bring a professional with him or her.

Audits are very time consuming to prepare for, but usually fairly straightforward affairs once they begin. They start with a detailed interview. The interview helps to develop a profile of you, your business, and the manner in which you operate your business. You will also be asked questions about your finances as they relate to your tax return.

The audit process in some ways is fairly simple: the auditor points to a line on the tax return and asks for all the substantiating documents for that number. For instance, if you are self-employed, the agent might ask you for copies of all your bank statements. The agent will add up all your bank deposits for the year and compare them to your total gross income on your Schedule C form. If your Schedule C form says that your gross income was $50,000 and you in fact deposited $75,000 in your bank accounts during the year, you'd better be ready to do some explaining!

If you accept credit cards or online payments with services such as PayPal, the agent will ask for independent reports of that activity. In 2011, the IRS implemented the new Form 1099-K for reporting payments made to you by credit and debit cards. Banks and other payment settlement services must report gross annual receipts on Form 1099-K (the 1099-K will not be required if your receipts are less than $20,000, or the total number of transactions is less than 200). Since 2011, 1099-Ks have become important data the Internal Revenue Service uses to target audits.

Substantiation for expenses and deductions means producing two documents: the actual receipts *and* proof of payment in the form of a cancelled check, debit from your bank account, or credit card statement.

When I say "actual receipt," what do I mean? I mean a piece of paper from the vendor that states what I purchased and when. For online sales this might be an electronic confirmation, but generally when you purchase something tangible there will be a receipt of some kind. You can print it or keep it digitally, take a picture on your phone to store it in an app or scan it, but whatever you do you *have* to be able to print it out if the Internal Revenue Service comes to call—even if that call comes 2 or 3 years after the purchase.

The IRS does not as a rule accept canceled checks or credit card statements as receipts in and of themselves (though some auditors will in practice, especially when the taxpayer has noted the specifics of the expense on the memo section of the check or on the credit card receipt). The other hurdle is that you will be asked to explain the nature of the expense or deduction. In other words, how and why is that deduction an "ordinary and necessary" expense of your profession?

On a recent Internal Revenue Service audit, I had a well-known writer who had to explain a research-related travel deduction for her latest book. In this case, she had all the receipts and printed e-mails for the tour operator, but she then had to open her book and discuss with the agent the relationship between specific passages in her book and the trip in question. This is always an interesting dialogue because the agents rarely have much experience in auditing folks in the arts, so there is always a process of educating the agent about your professional life (except if you are in the New England district where the agents use my book as audit preparation!). The artist who gets audited will always have some conversation helping the agent to understand the artist's business in conjunction with justifying and proving the specific deductions.

Let's take some examples of the more contentious and difficult areas and see how they might play out during an audit:

1. Meals and entertainment expense: while we know that meals and entertainment are only 50% deductible, they are still a real audit target for the IRS. First the agent will want to see a list of all the meals for the year by amount. This list must equal the total amount of meals that has been put on the tax return and must include the "who, what, and where" detail. You should bring your schedule book/diary with your notations for each meal to the audit, so when the agent wants substantiation you can show him or her your entry and explain the reason for the deduction. If the situation was travel related and you used the government per diem rates, the agent will ask you about the trip itself. Be ready to talk to the agent about your profession to help justify this deduction, to show why this trip and/or this meal was "ordinary and necessary." If the trip is deductible, the meals are as well. The agent might ask to look at contracts for specific jobs to make sure that the producer or employer was not reimbursing you for your meals expense.

2. Travel: the agent will want to know what the business purpose was. The less defined and flabbier your argument, the more

likely the agent is to disallow the deduction. Some play-acting on this one might help. You may remember that actor Ima Starr and musician Sonny Phunky both took business trips to Los Angeles. Ima did her homework in advance and set up appointments, attended some auditions, and kept a good schedule and diary of events. Sonny just showed up in LA, hung out, talked to some folks, then came home. Against the advice of his accountant, Sonny decided to deduct the full trip. His interview with the agent might go like this:

Agent: Sonny, what about this trip to LA?

Sonny: Yeah, there is a great music scene out there and I wanted to check it out.

Agent: Can I see your schedule of the trip? Did you plan the trip in advance?

Sonny: Well, I didn't have anything scheduled in advance. I just made some calls when I got there.

Agent: Did you have business activity every day?

Sonny: Most days I did something, like I had lunch with Sam Smith; he owns a recording studio out there and I talked to him about getting studio work.

Agent: Do you have any evidence of this meeting? Did you save his business card?

Sonny: I'm not sure if I still have it.

And Ima's interview might go this way:

Agent: Ima, what about this trip to LA?

Ima: I had recently worked on a film with Mel Funn and I made some connections in LA that I wanted to explore further.

Agent: Can I see your schedule of the trip?

Ima: Yes, I have outlined it on this calendar. Most of my appointments and lunch engagements were made in advance. I have business cards, copies of e-mails and thank you letters I wrote to the participants and copies of their replies, if I received any.

Agent: Did you have business activity every day?

> Ima: Yes, I had a meeting and/or audition every day. I also spent some of the time in LA making phone calls, which I have recorded in my schedule as well.
>
> Agent: Did you do anything after you called to follow up?
>
> Ima: I had brought along some sample videos on DVD and USB drives, my résumé and a copy of my CD. These all had my website listed on them. If the phone call was positive, I dropped off my package right away and called back the next day to see if I could get an appointment before I left LA.

I think it is clear which trip the agent is likely to allow! Ima did her homework and focused on the trip in such a way that it would be difficult for the agent to disallow the deduction of her trip.

1. Mileage: the agent will want to see a listing of total mileage for business use for the year, which includes a line item for each trip, an estimate of miles driven, and a note about the business purpose of the trip. Though the IRS likes odometer readings, it does not require them. It is my experience that a reasonable round-trip estimate will usually suffice. It is the business purpose that is most important. Most items on your list will probably be straightforward, such as trips to your agent's office or to a gig or performance, but the agent might select a few to ask you about specifically. Obviously, the more business miles you write off the more likely it is that the agent will question trips.

2. Research and performance audit: much of what the IRS is looking for when it audits the artist is the personal expense masquerading as business deductions. The agent will questions such things as:

   ✓ Writers buying books
   ✓ Actors and other show biz folks buying cable TV service; Netflix, Hulu, and Amazon accounts; and tickets to movies, plays, and shows
   ✓ Musicians purchasing CDs, downloading or streaming music, and tickets to concerts
   ✓ Visual artists going to museums and galleries

If the agent has an issue with these allowable expenses, he or she might ask for a logbook or diary entry where you listed the exact business purpose of the particular item. A good example of deductible "research" might be when Ima Starr purchased Mel Funn's movies in anticipation of performing in his movie, or when Sonny Phunky purchased some CDs and downloaded some tunes from iTunes to learn songs for his gig with the Butterball Kings. Similarly, our writer, Guy, purchased children's books that allowed him to monitor his competition and Liz Brushstroke visited galleries for the same reason. Keep in mind that the agent *can* ask for very specific documentation regarding, say, the rental of a DVD or the attendance to a play or museum, i.e., *specifically* what business purpose was served? Again, educating the auditor on the nature of your business goes a long way in the audit; if the agent understands your profession he or she will be better able to grasp the nature and necessity of your expenses.

Unfortunately, what tends to happen in real life is that people simply take a percentage of these costs as "business," such as the actor sitting with his or her accountant and saying something like, "My total cable bill was $545 and I'd say 40% was business." For an audit, you may be able to prove something close to the chosen number, or the agent may feel that the amount appears reasonable and not even question it. The agent may in fact be thrilled that you did not get piggy and try to take the whole $545! But beware: the agent can get really specific on these deductions and make your life miserable.

MSSP—The IRS Audit Training Manuals

It surprises many folks to learn that the IRS actually publishes its training manuals concerning audits, part of its "Market Segment Specialization Program" (MSSP). These manuals can be downloaded from our website (www.artstaxinfo.com) and are absolutely indispensable guides. Many industries are covered by the manuals, but only three directly concern us:

1. Entertainment Industry

We learn that the IRS is fully cognizant that reimbursements are a common part of the industry. The guide talks at length about SAG, the Directors Guild of America (DGA), and Actors' Equity, and tells the agent how reimbursements are handled and what types of things are reimbursed. It instructs the agent to review all employment contracts, including those for product endorsements, to look for reimbursements and "perks," such as free products.

Another interesting audit target is the issue of the "tax home." In recent audits, the IRS has been attempting to declare some folks in the entertainment industry "itinerant." If the IRS can declare you an itinerant, then all your travel, mileage, and meals expenses are blown off the return. After all, how can someone with no home deduct expenses for travel while away from home? The tax home issue can sneak up on you in an audit. While you are busy lining up your substantiation and getting worksheets for your expenses, the agent may be deciding to go for a bigger issue and eliminate the travel expense outright! I discuss the "tax home" in greater detail in Chapter 10.

Because gift giving is so prevalent in the industry, the guide reminds the agent that business gifts are limited to $25 per person per year. On top of that you will still need a receipt and a diary entry describing the "why" of the gift.

Other deductions that the IRS is specifically targeting in its audit guide:

- ✓ Hairstyles
- ✓ Clothing and wardrobe, unless "period" clothing
- ✓ Laundry expense, unless used for deductible clothing
- ✓ Security, bodyguards, and limousines, except when needed for protection at public appearances
- ✓ Makeup, unless stage makeup unsuitable for any other use
- ✓ Physical fitness, except for the duration of employment requiring physical conditioning or if the actors' roles require the maintenance of body building and/or weight-lifting skills
- ✓ Payments to business managers to the extent that the manager is engaged in personal bills and affairs
- ✓ Legal expenses if the claim is personal
- ✓ A coach, personal trainer, or personal guru
- ✓ Toupees, false teeth, hearing aids, etc.
- ✓ Cosmetic surgery

2. Music Industry

This guide covers songwriters, publishers, managers, producers, music video production, and musicians. The music industry guide has two of my favorite quotes in all IRS literature:

1. *The performing artist is usually a very creative person as far as talent goes, but may lack knowledge in understanding bookkeeping, taxes, and cash flow.*

2. *Musicians who have not reached an income level sufficient to hire business managers often have a poor record-keeping system. This doesn't appear to be due to an intent to cheat or defraud the government; rather, it seems to be due to the taxpayer's basic lack of concern for these types of matters. These taxpayers are artists and are totally committed to their work and doing whatever it takes to become a success. Preparation of their yearly tax returns is an*

*afterthought and the quality of the records they maintain to sup-
port their tax return often bears this out.*

The manual is interesting in that it advises the agent not to get too carried away auditing musicians, because the agent can spend a great deal of time
fixing "messy" books and then not come up with a deficiency (i.e., cash!).

The music industry guide is concerned with many of the same items
that we see in the entertainment guide, such as personal items being deducted
as business expenses. The guide discusses the musical entertainer's argument
that they must maintain a "look" for the benefit of their fans, and that it will
be on this basis that the musician attempts to deduct a variety of clothing and
other personal items. The guide warns that "while the taxpayer's argument is
not totally without merit and can even sound reasonable," the agent should
not allow the performer to deduct personal expenses.

A key focus for the auditor appears to be unreported income. The guide
mentions that while royalties will be reported (Form 1099-MISC), the musician might well have freelance income from performing that will go unreported. The guide also acknowledges the prevalence of trades and trading in
the music industry. The IRS considers trades as income too.

The guide tells the agent to review contracts to see if expenses were
reimbursed. If the agent is auditing a "star" who paid all the expenses of
the band and crew while on the road, it instructs the agent to selectively sample some returns from these folks, to see if they had double dipped and taken
travel expenses. The agent is informed that it may be necessary to cross-check
"related returns of taxpayers in the music industry due to the close working
relationships between taxpayers in the industry."

3. Artists and Art Galleries

In this guide the IRS is mainly concerned with actual galleries and gallery
owners rather than with visual artists, but it does contain some items of
interest. It tells the agent to be aware of the prevalence of trading between
artists and gallery owners. The agent is told that the trades are often not
even reported in the books of the gallery. Should the IRS audit a gallery
that has unreported income from trades with artists, you can be sure that
the next thing it is going to do is look at the artist's return to see whether
the trade was reported there. In general, the guide warns the auditor to
look out for unreported income. It mentions inventory as being an error-
prone item on the artist's return. The error arises because the visual artist
does not correctly account for framing and supplies that are left unsold at
year-end.

Audit Etiquette

Generally, the IRS agents I have dealt with are fair and reasonable people. This is not to say that you will not have arguments and subsequent appeals, but many issues can be settled at the agent's level. The formal appeals process is very time consuming and you want to avoid this if possible; always try to settle your audit at the agent level. Characteristically, IRS agents are classic bureaucrats: they want to process your audit and get it off their desks as soon as possible. That being said, I have had a number of audits recently where the agent seemed to enjoy learning about the taxpayer's profession. I had a Broadway producer showing an agent cast photos and playbills from her shows, and a musician showing the agent pictures of his many instruments and offering to play them for him if the agent wanted to come to his studio. These conversations helped create a sympathetic relationship with the agents that definitely helped in the audit process.

One thing that I cannot state too strongly: audits are *very* time-consuming. There is no way around that. I have not been involved in any audit that has not taken the taxpayer many hours of preparation.

Here are some other pointers:

1. Be fully prepared with details on *only* the item the agent requested, and no more. Do not bring anything extra to the audit. Answer questions as simply and honestly as you can, explaining the nature and the reason for the deduction with no unnecessary embellishment.

    In the long run, you will benefit if you give detailed and complete information and are forthcoming in your answers. Approaching the audit this way will often keep the agent from delving deeper into the return. I liken IRS agents to thieves looking for a car with the keys still in the ignition. If you give the agent the feeling right off the bat that you have your act together and are fully prepared, it can have the effect of taking the agent off his or her guard. While you do not want to be overly friendly, you do want to try and develop a certain warmth and openness with the agent.

    For instance, if one of the audit items is car mileage and you provide a neatly typed list outlining each trip, the miles driven, and the business purpose, the agent might not ask any specific questions, but simply take a copy of the list for his or her files. You would follow the same procedure for all the questioned items:

have a list of each deduction, including amounts and description, to give the agent. Receipts and proof of payment should accompany each list. From a voluminous list, the agent might just pick a few receipts to "audit" or review.

2.   An old canard suggests bringing in messy receipts and "letting them do the work." This is a fool's advice. You should appear neat and be as forthcoming as possible. Incidents have been reported of the agent being given less than complete records and receipts, but because the package was so neat and orderly, he or she assumed it was complete and didn't even review the package!

3.   Never cop an attitude or try to "snow" the agent in any way! I know quite a few IRS agents and believe me, they have seen and heard it all. Treat the experience as a task (however unpleasant) that has to be worked through. Treat the agent with respect and courtesy and make sure your tax professional does the same. Try to settle matters on the agent level. If you ultimately need to fight something, that's OK; just don't make it a first impulse.

4.   *Never* go to any audit without a tax professional. As a tax professional, I only have the taxpayer present if I feel the taxpayer is the best one to answer the larger questions relating to their business. A lot of responses to auditor questions do rely on some judicious "spin-doctoring" though. More play acting is in order here:

> *Agent: Ima, what about this meal with Joe the Plumber on October 15?*
>
> *Ima: Joe is casting a new film that has a part for a sultry lounge singer that I would be perfect for.*
>
> *Agent: So what did you do to try to get the part?*
>
> *Ima: I didn't want to directly discuss business during the lunch. I was just trying to get to know him a little and butter him up a bit. Right after the lunch I sent him a nice letter and copies of my résumé, a CD, and a DVD of my singing with The Blue Jazzbos so he would know that I could sing as well as act. I also sent him a link to my website where he can view some video clips.*
>
> *Agent: So what happened?*
>
> *Ima: Unfortunately I did not get the part.*

This is how she should have responded:

> *Agent: Ima, what about this meal with Joe the Plumber on October 15?*
>
> *Ima: Joe is casting a new film that has a part for a sultry lounge singer that I would be perfect for.*
>
> *Agent: So what did you do to try to get the part?*
>
> *Ima: While we had lunch, I pitched him the idea of doing the part and gave him copies of my résumé, CD, and a video of my singing with The Blue Jazzbos so he would know that I could sing as well as act.*
>
> *Agent: So what happened?*
>
> *Ima: Unfortunately I didn't get the part.*

Don't forget, there has to be business transacted at some point during the meal or the IRS is going to disallow it. Whether Ima got the part does not matter; the deduction will stand or fall on its own merits. It doesn't really matter if there is a specific part she is going after, she can be taking Joe out to let him know she is available for consideration for any parts he may have.

Is it possible for an actor to be allowed a deduction for over-the-counter makeup, or the musician to be allowed a write-off for a business lunch where no business was transacted? Definitely yes! Could the visual artist get audited and not be questioned about ending inventory or the writer not have the IRS agent even ask about his travel deduction? Yes again! There is always a chance that the agent will not ask about a particular deduction. You might have an inexperienced agent who accepts your justification for a deduction as valid. Conversely, you may have an agent unfamiliar with your business as an artist who makes you justify and argue everything.

I don't necessarily try to "make friends" with the agent. At its core, it is an adversarial relationship. A measure of cordial respectfulness is best. Without being bellicose, I always want the agent to know that we will fight if necessary, but we would rather not.

Develop a strategy with your tax professional before you even meet with the agent and assess your weaknesses and strengths. By going to an audit with a strategy, the process is less likely to get out of control. Your tax professional may see from the outset the course the audit might follow. A writer with 5 years of continuous losses would want to be ready to deal with the "hobby-loss" matter. A visual artist who has never listed an ending inventory would want to be ready to answer questions on that. A musician or film director with high travel and meals deductions would want to be ready to address those questions.

Record Keeping

We have discussed record keeping throughout the book without addressing how to actually do it. Our website at www.artstaxinfo.com has some very handy and easy-to-use Microsoft Excel downloadable worksheets for simple organization of income and expenses throughout the year. There are also several accounting programs for this purpose; I can recommend four that I like and list the websites where you can get some additional information on each one:

1.   Quicken: www.quicken.intuit.com

2.   Mint: www.mint.com. A cloud-based program, great for those who travel.

3.   QuickBooks: www.quickbooks.intuit.com. This is a good program for those needing more advanced accounting features. QuickBooks also has a great cloud-based service, QuickBooks Online: www.quickbooks.intuit.com.

4.   XERO: www.xero.com/us. One of the better cloud-based accounting systems.

There are a fast-growing number of apps for digital recordkeeping on your phone or tablet; Expensify is amazing for doing your own expense reports, OneReceipt is excellent for keeping and organizing receipts, and MileIQ and taxmileage do a great job of tracking business mileage.

Once these programs and apps are set up properly, they do a great job and are easy to operate. They will be an enormous help at year-end. Purchase an accordion file at an office supply store to keep your receipts in, buy a receipt scanner, or use an app to keep the information digitally (be sure to back up your data; you will have to print these receipts if you get audited— the agent is NOT going to sit and look at your device screen). Remember, I have great, free worksheets available on www.artstaxinfo.com as printable forms, as well as Excel downloadable worksheets. These spreadsheets are easy to customize and keep with you throughout the year to track your income and expenses.

Consider hiring a good bookkeeper if you are too busy in your professional life to do the record keeping. Bookkeeping help is relatively inexpensive and can save you a world of headaches.

One last note on record keeping (and I cannot stress this too firmly!): while *you* may live in the digital world, doing your accounting in the cloud on your iPad, recording your notes and keeping your schedule on your smartphone, and keeping and preparing your documents in the cloud, that is *not* the world of the Internal Revenue Service! As I tell my clients, when you are audited you are back in 1957—it is a paper, hard-copy world. Keep this in mind and print and/or back up often and safely so you have all notes and records for at least 3 years in case Uncle Sam comes calling.

Your Rights as a Taxpayer

Several years ago the IRS created a publication that explains your rights as a taxpayer. It includes an eight-part "Declaration of Taxpayer Rights," as well as a section on audits, appeals, collections, and refunds. Here is the text of Publication 1:

DECLARATION OF TAXPAYER RIGHTS

I. PROTECTION OF YOUR RIGHTS

IRS employees will explain and protect your rights as a taxpayer throughout your contact with us.

II. PRIVACY AND CONFIDENTIALITY

The IRS will not disclose to anyone the information you give us, except as authorized by law. You have the right to know why we are asking you for information, how we will use it, and what happens if you do not provide requested information.

III. PROFESSIONAL AND COURTEOUS SERVICE

If you believe that an IRS employee has not treated you in a professional, fair, and courteous manner, you should tell that employee's supervisor. If the supervisor's response is not satisfactory, you should write to the IRS director for your area or the center where you file your return.

IV. REPRESENTATION

You may either represent yourself or, with proper written authorization, have someone else represent you in your place. Your representative must be a person allowed to practice before the IRS, such as an attorney, certified public accountant, or enrolled agent. If you are in an interview and ask to consult such a person, then we must stop and reschedule the interview in most cases.

You can have someone accompany you at an interview. You may make sound recordings of any meetings with our examination, appeal, or collection personnel, provided you tell us in writing 10 days before the meeting.

V. PAYMENT OF ONLY THE CORRECT AMOUNT OF TAX

You are responsible for paying only the correct amount of tax due under the law—no more, no less. If you cannot pay all of your tax when it is due, you may be able to make monthly installment payments.

VI. HELP WITH UNRESOLVED TAX PROBLEMS

The Taxpayer Advocate Service can help you if you have tried unsuccessfully to resolve a problem with the IRS. Your local Taxpayer Advocate can offer you special help if you have a significant hardship as a result of a tax problem. For more information, call toll free 1-877-777-4778 (1-800-829-4059 for TTY/TDD) or write to the Taxpayer Advocate at the IRS office that last contacted you.

VII. APPEALS AND JUDICIAL REVIEW

If you disagree with us about the amount of your tax liability or certain collection actions, you have the right to ask the Appeals Office to review your case. You may ask a court to review your case.

VIII. RELIEF FROM CERTAIN PENALTIES AND INTEREST

The IRS will waive penalties when allowed by law if you can show you acted reasonably and in good faith or relied on the incorrect advice of an IRS employee. We will waive interest that is the result of certain errors or delays caused by an IRS employee.

EXAMINATIONS, APPEALS, COLLECTIONS, AND REFUNDS

EXAMINATIONS (AUDITS)

We accept most taxpayers' returns as valid. If we inquire about your return or select it for examination, it does not suggest that you are dishonest. The inquiry or examination may or may not result in more tax. We may close your case without change; or, you may receive a refund.

The process of selecting a return for examination usually begins in one of two ways. First, we use computer programs to identify returns that may have incorrect amounts. These programs may be based on information returns, such as Forms 1099 and W-2, on studies of past examinations, or on certain issues identified by compliance projects. Second, we use information from outside sources that indicates that a return may have incorrect amounts. These sources may include newspapers, public records, and individuals. If we determine that the information is accurate and reliable, we may use it to select a return for examination.

Publication 556, Examination of Returns, Appeal Rights, and Claims for Refund, explains the rules and procedures that we follow in examinations. The following sections give an overview of how we conduct examinations.

By Mail

We handle many examinations and inquiries by mail. We will send you a letter with either a request for more information or a reason why we believe a change to your return may be needed. You can respond by mail or you can request a personal interview with an examiner. If you mail us the requested information or provide an explanation, we may or may not agree with you, and we will explain the reasons for any changes. Please do not hesitate to write to us about anything you do not understand.

By Interview

If we notify you that we will conduct your examination through a personal interview, or you request such an interview, you have the right to ask that the examination take place at a reasonable time and place that is convenient for both you and the IRS. If our examiner proposes any changes to your return, he or she will explain the reasons for the changes. If you do not agree with these changes, you can meet with the examiner's supervisor.

Repeat Examinations

If we examined your return for the same items in either of the 2 previous years and proposed no change to your tax liability, please contact us as soon as possible so we can see if we should discontinue the examination.

APPEALS

If you do not agree with the examiner's proposed changes, you can appeal them to the Appeals Office of IRS. Most differences can be settled without expensive and time-consuming court trials. Your appeal rights are explained in detail in both Publication 5. Your Appeal Rights and How To Prepare a Protest If You Don't Agree, and Publication 556, Examination of Returns, Appeal Rights, and Claims for Refund.

If you do not wish to use the Appeals Office or disagree with its findings, you may be able to take your case to the U.S. Tax Court, U.S. Court of Federal Claims, or the U.S. District Court where you live. If you take your case to court, the IRS will have the burden of proving certain facts if you kept adequate records to show your tax liability, cooperated with the IRS, and meet certain other conditions. If the court agrees with you on most issues in your case and finds that our position was largely unjustified, you may be able to recover some of your administrative and litigation costs. You will not be eligible to recover these costs unless you tried to resolve your case administratively; including going through the appeals system, and you gave us the information necessary to resolve the case.

COLLECTIONS

Publication 594, The IRS Collection Process, explains your rights and responsibilities regarding payment of federal taxes. It describes:

- What to do when you owe taxes. It describes what to do if you get a tax bill and what to do if you think your bill is wrong. It also covers making installment payments, delaying collection action, and submitting an offer in compromise.

- IRS collection actions. It covers liens, releasing a lien, levies, releasing a levy, seizures and sales, and release of property.

Your collection appeal rights are explained in detail in Publication 1660, Collection Appeal Rights.

Innocent Spouse Relief

Generally, both you and your spouse are responsible, jointly and individually, for paying the full amount of any tax, interest, or penalties due on your joint return. However, if you qualify for innocent spouse relief, you may not have to pay the tax, interest, and penalties related to your spouse (or former spouse). For information on innocent spouse relief and two other ways to get relief, see Publication 971, Innocent Spouse Relief, and Form 8857, Request for Innocent Spouse Relief (And Separation of Liability and Equitable Relief).

REFUNDS

You may file a claim for refund if you think you paid too much tax. You must generally file the claim within 3 years from the date you filed your original return or 2 years from the date you paid the tax, whichever is later. The law generally provides for interest on your refund if it is not paid within 45 days of the date you filed your return or claim for refund. Publication 556, Examination of Returns, Appeal Rights, and Claims for Refund, has more information on refunds.

If you were due a refund but you did not file a return, you must file within 3 years from the date the return was originally due to get that refund.

10

Other States, Other Taxes, Other Countries, and the "Tax Home"

In this chapter I want to touch on three tax issues that I often get questions on: state, sales, and foreign taxes. We will also look at one of the sneakiest and worst audit challenges a performer can encounter: the "tax home." While the scope of my book precludes tackling any of these issues in great detail, I do want to address them in general terms.

State Taxes

Up to this point we have avoided the issue of state taxes. One of the reasons state taxes are rarely discussed is that most states accept some version of the current Internal Revenue Service code, so differences are, generally speaking, not significant. I would say 99% of all the expense deductions and income items we have discussed in this book would be identical on a vast majority of state income tax returns. The area where the artist will have to address more complex state taxes concerns the multistate environment. In general, if you work and earn money in a state other than the one you reside in, you may have to file taxes in that state. You create a "nexus" in most states by being physically present in that state, working and earning money.

Our actress, Ima Starr, worked in a play in Philly and received a W-2 from Pennsylvania, so she will have to file taxes in Pennsylvania, but she will not be double taxed. While this income will appear on both her New York and Pennsylvania returns, she will receive a tax credit in New York for the taxes that she paid to Pennsylvania on that income.

Why does the same income appear on both tax returns? Ima reports the income in Pennsylvania as a nonresident because it was earned in Pennsylvania. She reports it on her New York return because she is a resident of New York and all her income has to be reported on her New York resident tax return, but New York will give her a tax credit for the amount of taxes Pennsylvania charged her, so there is effectively no double taxation.

Does the fact that you have a W-2 reporting (say) $500 in income in Wisconsin and $19 in Wisconsin state taxes withheld mean that you *have* to file a tax return in Wisconsin? The answer is, not necessarily. When the amounts involved are minimal, the states typically do not demand a return be filed. You and your tax preparer will have to judge in which states to actually file. Your tax professional might run each return to see how the return looks. If the Wisconsin nonresident return for the $500 in W-2 income comes up with only $19 in tax liability, you may choose not to file it. In this example it is highly unlikely that the taxpayer would ever hear from the state of Wisconsin.

When an artist is self-employed and works in multiple states, they are really on the honor system because there will probably not be any third party tax document (1099) specifically alerting states to your tax presence. If you have Schedule C income that is split between several states, you will want the help of a tax professional as this can get complicated. You can either do a separate state Schedule C form or simply split the bottom line of the federal Schedule C based on the allocation of the gross income. For instance, if our bass player Sonny had a net Schedule C of $50,000 and the income was earned half in his home state of Maine and half in neighboring Massachusetts, then the tax return would allocate $25,000 of self-employment to his nonresident Massachusetts return. Maine would allow him a tax credit for the taxes paid in Massachusetts on the allocated $25,000 of income, so he would not be double taxed.

Sales Tax

For artists selling tangible products (CDs, merchandise, books, art work, DVDs, etc.), there is the matter of state sales taxes. If you are selling products in states that have a sales tax, you are required to register with the state taxing authorities, collect the appropriate tax on the goods that are taxable, and remit it to the state. People make more out of sales tax than it warrants. After all, you are simply adding the sales tax to the product you sell and then sending it to the state. Sales tax is what is termed a "fiduciary" tax: it is not an expense of your business, but a tax the seller collects on behalf of the state and then remits to the state. All that being said, it can be a record-keeping hassle for folks disinclined to keep records. There are many sources on the Internet to get info on sales taxes by state, but I suggest you avoid getting involved in sales tax for de minimis, casual, or haphazard sales. Many states don't require sales taxes on casual sales. However, I would advise a discussion with a good, common-sense tax person on the subject if you think you need to address it.

International Taxes

When a writer has a book sold overseas, a musician tours in Europe, or a performer is hired for a show in Spain, they encounter foreign taxes. If a band plays in France, the French government will require that taxes be withheld on the band's payment upfront, *before* the band gets its money. If a writer sells a book in Germany, the agent will be required to withhold German taxes on the advance. It's the same for any American artist or performer earning money in Europe. Luckily, international tax treaties allow you to avoid the withholding by acquiring a Form 6166 from the Internal Revenue Service. By giving Form 6166 to your agent, the payer is no longer required to withhold the foreign taxes on your payment.

To obtain Internal Revenue Service Form 6166, you must first file Form 8802: "Application for United State Residency Certification." On Form 8802 you identify yourself, the tax form you filed, and other information. Once the Internal Revenue Service certifies that you are up to date in your U.S. tax filings, they issue you the Form 6166. On the last page of Form 8802, you check off which countries you need the forms for and pay a user fee of $35 for each one. The Internal Revenue Service will send you the Form 6166 to provide to your agent and/or foreign payer.

Why do I want to go through all this hassle to avoid the foreign taxes withheld? After all, much like the states noted above, the Internal Revenue Service gives us a foreign tax credit for amounts paid on foreign-earned income. It is because the foreign tax rates are generally much higher than those the taxpayer is going to pay in the United States. And while we get a foreign tax credit for amounts paid overseas, due to the tax rate differential it never really equals out. So taxpayers are almost always better off not paying the foreign taxes and just dealing with their worldwide income on their U.S. tax return.

Ain't Got No Home—The "Tax-Home" Trap

"Ain't got no home," sang my friend, Clarence "Frogman" Henry, on his hit record back in 1956, and this brings us to one of the most dreaded Internal Revenue Service audit attacks. This is the claim that the musician or performer is traveling so extensively that they, in fact, have no "tax home." Why do we care? Because if the taxpayer has no tax home, then virtually *all* deductions for travel, travel meals, hotels, auto mileage, airline tickets, rental cars, temporary residences, mileage, etc., vaporize in an instant. Why do we lose our travel deductions? Because if the artist doesn't have a tax home, there's no home to travel *to or from*.

What is a tax home? One thing it is *not* is your primary residence. It can be, but not necessarily. The Internal Revenue Service concept of the tax home is your economic home base, a ring around your primary work location. Conversely, a principal residence is where you maintain your legal ties: driver's license, car and voter registration, etc. For the vast majority of us these two places are one and the same, but for the performer or artist who travels extensively they might not be. IRS Publication 463 explains the concept of tax home like this:

> If you do not have a regular or main place of business or work, use the following three factors to see if you have a tax home;
>
> 1. You perform part of your business in the area of your main home and use that home for lodging while doing business in the area.
> 2. You have living expenses at your main home that you duplicate because your business requires you to be away from that home.
> 3. You have not abandoned the area in which both your traditional place of lodging and your main home are located; you have a member or members of your family living at your main home; or you often use that home for lodging.
>
> If you satisfy all three factors, your tax home is the home where you regularly live, and you may be able to deduct travel expenses. If you satisfy only two factors, you may have a tax home depending on all the facts and circumstances. If you satisfy only one factor, you are a transient; your tax home is wherever you work and you cannot deduct travel expenses.

There are two essential ways to solidify your tax home:

1. It is your place of business; you work there. This is achieved by earning at least 25% of your income at this location.

2. You used to work there, you don't anymore, but you now maintain a residence at this location.

For the artist who is traveling a majority of the time, the touring musician, or the actor on location, this can be a huge issue. You need to pick a home location and have a stable address in an area that makes sense for your profession. For a touring musician who continues to use his or her parents' address in a state to which they have no economic connection, this is one of the biggest invitations to this line of attack. The performer is better off picking a logical address, New York City or Los Angeles perhaps, preferably someplace that you are looking for work, could work, or actually do work on occasion. Next, get a private mailbox (with mail forwarding) as well as a bank account in that area so that there is a consistent and logical tax home/residence. Of course, you will have to file a resident tax return in that state.

Whenever I have encountered this line of audit attack it has always taken the taxpayer completely by surprise. The whole concept of a "tax home" as opposed to your regular home seems weird, but from now on it should leap to your mind if you find you have extensive travel-related deductions.

None of these techniques can guarantee that the Internal Revenue Service won't level this attack, but they will certainly make it much less likely.

11

Choosing a Tax Advisor

There are two main characteristics you look for in a tax professional. I call them "the two Cs": competence and communication.

The accountant/client relationship is a symbiotic association. The accountant has the knowledge and is able to communicate the information that the client needs to take full advantage of that knowledge. There are two designations for tax professionals (other than attorneys) that might affect your choice.

The first is the CPA (certified public accountant). The CPA is an individual who has successfully completed the Uniform CPA Examination. This exam is a computer-based exam given at various testing centers around the country, and it consists of four sections: auditing and attestation; regulation; business environment and concepts; and financial accounting and reporting. The exam is not principally concerned with taxation; therefore, the CPA designation, while important, does not necessarily guarantee competence in tax matters. The CPA is required to meet stringent standards of state licensing, ethics, and educational requirements, and this should give the client some comfort that the CPA is honest and professional.

The second designation is that of the EA (enrolled agent) and is bestowed directly by the Internal Revenue Service. They explain it this way:

> An enrolled agent is a person who has earned the privilege of practicing, that is, representing taxpayers, before the Internal Revenue Service. Enrolled agents, like attorneys and certified public accountants (CPAs), are generally unrestricted as to which taxpayers they can represent, what types of tax matters they can handle, and which IRS offices they can practice before. In contrast, practice before the IRS is much more limited for other individuals such as unenrolled tax return preparers, family members, full time employees, partners, and corporate officers.

To become an EA, the individual must take a grueling three-part test that centers on taxation and ethics. The EA, like the CPA, has ethical and educational requirements to uphold.

Only CPAs, EAs, and attorneys are allowed to practice and fully represent clients before the Internal Revenue Service. In audit situations, the difference between these designations can be significant, as CPAs now have a limited attorney–client privilege that EAs do not enjoy.

The best place to start your search for a tax professional is with a referral from a colleague. Ask who your friends are using, if they like that person, and why. You can also check with your state society of CPAs or with professional organizations such as Actors' Equity; SAG; American Society of Composers, Authors and Publishers (ASCAP); The American Society of Journalists and Authors (ASJA); American Federation of Musicians (AFM), etc. They will often have referrals available. When you get the name of a few folks, decide who you want to talk to and make an appointment with each for a free consultation. I would not hire any professional who will not grant free consultation time. Try to interview several tax advisors before you decide.

You will probably ask first if the accountant has experience with, and clients in, your particular artistic endeavor. This is the most important question, and it will lead to a conversation that will let you know if this person "gets it." Feel free to ask for references. Bring along some specific questions about *your* return; this allows you to really kick the tires. If you bring along a copy of your past year's return, you can ask the accountant to quickly review it and see if he or she has anything of interest to say about it. This is a great way to see if the accountant spots missed deductions or comes up with tax planning ideas.

I hate the question "what can you do for me?" and I'm sure I'm not alone. It's better to ask specific questions, such as:

✓ "Reviewing my returns from last year, do you think I missed any deductions?"
✓ "Do my deductions from last year seem reasonable?"
✓ "Do you see any audit flags?"
✓ "Reviewing last year's return, do you have any ideas on how I could reduce my taxes this year?"
✓ "Do you consider tax planning a part of the preparation process?"
✓ "Are you available for questions during the year and do you charge extra for this service?"
✓ "Do you have a website?"
✓ "Can you do a video conference if I am away on business?"
✓ "Do you answer e-mails every day?"
✓ "Do you give out your cell phone number?"
✓ "Do you have a secure way for me to transfer files to you?"

✓ "How many client audits do you have every year? What percentage of your clients are audited?"

✓ "Do you have other clients in my profession and do you enjoy working with them?"

✓ "How do you bill, and when do you get paid?"

✓ "Approximately how much will it cost for you to prepare my tax return?"

✓ "I often have other states to file in. Are you familiar with tax returns from other states?"

✓ "How do you help clients who get audited?"

✓ "Have you ever read any of the IRS MSSP audit guides?"

✓ "Do you have checklists or other worksheets that will help me prepare my information for you?"

✓ "Will you be preparing my return personally?"

✓ "Do you make it a practice to sit with your clients and review the information before you prepare the return?"

✓ "How early should I make an appointment with you?"

✓ "How long does it usually take you to complete the return?"

✓ "Can I communicate with you directly via e-mail to make an appointment or to ask questions?"

When you finish an interview like this you will know if you have any rapport with the accountant (part of my second important "C"—communication). If you don't feel comfortable talking with your accountant, you won't be inclined to ask questions. When you do not ask questions, you will not get the best result on your tax return. It is through conversing with my clients that I have found we really ferret out all the deductions. Checklists are great but they only go so far.

A final reminder: even though you have someone else prepare your return, *you are the person ultimately responsible for the information on it.* There is a statement on your 1040 tax return printed over the place where you sign that reads: "Under penalties of perjury, I declare that I have examined this return, and accompanying schedules and statements, and to the best of my knowledge and belief they are true, correct and complete."

12

Tax Planning

Due to the changing nature of tax law, I am not going to mention many specifics of tax planning. I will be posting weekly tax tips on our website and daily updates on Twitter. Our website has a number of great "Life Cycle" brochures under our "Information Center," as well as the Online Advisor and other breaking news on the book's website (www .artstaxinfo.com) and my firm's website (www.cpa-services.com). Be sure to visit and research before deciding on any of the strategies discussed here. On www.cpa-services.com you can sign up for our monthly tax newsletters as well.

Tax planning should be a vital part of your work with your tax advisor and should accomplish two things:

1.   Lower your tax liability
2.   Remove any surprises from the tax liability you do have

By being proactive in developing tax strategies with your advisor, you will make changes in your business that will lower your tax liability. Your tax advisor will be able to estimate your liability so that you can plan your cash flow properly and not have any nasty surprises at year-end. Tax planning has two main goals:

1.   Delaying taxes
2.   Lowering taxes

While most tax planning concerns delaying the payment of income taxes, there are some schemes that actually lower the tax you pay. Some strategies do both. The very heart of this book has been essentially a tax planning exercise. By being aware of your income and expenses, you discover how to maximize your deductions and lower your taxes. When you understand your tax situation, you are much better prepared to strategize and be proactive with your finances.

Timing Your Deductions

The basic technique in tax planning concerns the timing of deductions. I have touched on this throughout the book, as when I talked about purchasing equipment or moving deductions into the current year by spending money (or charging expenses) in December. This accelerates the expense into the current year. If the current year is a low-income year and you expect higher income next year, you may prefer not to do this. In that case, it may be better for you to push the deduction forward into the following year and offset it against higher income and higher tax brackets. A decision such as this is an essential part of the important year-end meeting with your tax advisor. Work with your advisor to decide when major expenses should take place. You need to have a good grasp of your finances and expected income first.

If the expense is the purchase of a computer, digital camera, technology, a musical instrument, or some other asset, you have the option of using the Section 179 election—an election that allows you to write off the purchase in a lump sum in one year rather than prorate the deduction over a number of years. This can be a tremendous late-in-the-year tax-saving move, especially when you are surprised at year-end with more income than you were expecting. See our Taxes QuikGuide on www.artstaxinfo.com for the latest rates and information.

I always enjoy questions that begin with "Should I buy . . . ." Let's be clear: *never* buy anything, anytime, simply to save taxes. I respond to the above question, "Well, do you need (whatever the expense or asset is)?" When I discuss spending money in December, I am talking about an expense or purchase that was definitely going to be made within the first 2 or 3 months of the next year. We are just considering whether to move it into the current year.

Artists tend to overlook what I call "cross-over" expenses. They must not forget personal assets that have been used in the production of income. Frequently, expenses are not an "all or nothing" proposition. As we have already noted, deductions such as Internet service, home office, and cars are going to be allocated with some costs to your business, and the balance to personal use. You will see this work out in our sample returns.

Certain expenses are deductible only to the extent that they exceed set income "floors." You will recall that Form 2106, used to deduct employee business expenses, must exceed 2% of your adjusted gross income. For example, you will see on Guy Focal's 1040, the trip to New York City found on his 2106 was not enough to rise above the "phase out" amount on Line 27 of his Schedule A. If you find you are close to these income floors, try to bunch payment of as many expenses into one tax year as possible to secure your deduction.

Retirement Planning

You can set up a retirement plan if you are self-employed or have self-employment income, such as royalties or other non–W-2 contract income. These plans allow you to start building a tax-deferred retirement fund and help to reduce current taxes in the process. Any funds you put into the plan are fully tax deductible for federal purposes (and sometimes for state purposes) and the earnings within the plan are not taxed until the money is taken out.

Simplified Employee Pensions (SEPs)—The SEP is the most common retirement plan for self-employed individuals. The maximum deduction-allowed contribution to a SEP is 20% of net earnings. Compensation for the self-employed individual is calculated as the net Schedule C income less the self-employment tax deduction from page 1 of the 1040.

Keogh/Profit-Sharing Plans—Keogh/profit-sharing plans offer self-employed individuals an excellent way to set aside money for retirement. These plans must cover any eligible employees you may have. Contributions to the plan (within tax law limits) and any earnings on plan investments are not taxed until distributed from the plan. Keogh plans may be either defined contribution or defined benefit plans. Defined contribution plans provide for employer contributions to individual plan accounts for employees (and the self-employed owner). Defined benefit plans don't maintain individual accounts. Instead, the employer funds the plan based on projections of how much the plan will need to pay promised retirement benefits.

The above two retirement plans should be established by year-end, although tax-deductible contributions can be made any time up until the return is filed (with extensions, this can be delayed up to October 15th of the following year).

Note: If you're close to retirement age, you may be able to build a retirement fund more quickly with a defined benefit than with a defined contribution plan.

401(k) Plans—With a 401(k) plan, you contribute part of your pay to a plan account set up just for you through your W-2. The maximum amount that you can contribute to your 401(k) in 2016 is $18,000, with an additional "catch-up" of $6,000 for workers over 50. These contribution limits are adjusted annually for inflation—see our Taxes QuikGuide on www.artstaxinfo.com for the latest rates and information. You don't pay federal or state taxes on the amount you contribute or on the investment earnings in your plan account until you withdraw funds from the plan, usually when you retire. If your employer matches any of your contribution, this is an added tax-deferred benefit.

The IRS allows a 401(k) plan for sole proprietorships and small, family-owned corporations that is commonly called the "Solo" or "Single" 401(k). This 401(k) follows essentially the same 401(k) rules discussed above and has become the plan of choice for many sole proprietors and closely held corporations.

SIMPLE Retirement Plans—Self-employed individuals and small business owners have a newer type of plan available to them. A "saving incentive match plan for employees" or "SIMPLE" retirement plan may be structured either as an individual retirement account (IRA) for each employee or as a 401(k) salary deferral plan. Employers currently without a plan and employing one hundred or fewer employees earning at least $5,000 each in compensation during the previous year are eligible to adopt a SIMPLE retirement plan. In a SIMPLE IRA, employees (and self-employed persons) can elect to contribute up to $12,500 to the plan, with an extra $3,000 for those over 50 in 2016 (adjusted annually for inflation—see our Taxes QuikGuide on www.artstaxinfo.com for the latest rates and information). There is also an "employer match" of 3% of net compensation.

IRAs are always an option if you already have a retirement plan available but wish to put away some additional funds. You may contribute up to $5,500 annually to an IRA account in 2016, with an extra $1,000 to those over 50 year of age. The deductibility of your contribution is dependent on several factors: (1) your level of earned income, (2) whether you or your spouse is eligible for an employer-sponsored retirement plan, and (3) your adjusted gross income. If you and your spouse are not eligible for an employer's sponsored or self-employment-based plan, your entire allowable IRA contribution is deductible. If you and/or your spouse are able to participate in a plan, your deduction may be limited or eliminated altogether when your adjusted gross incomes exceed specific levels.

Many of you have no doubt read about Roth IRAs. The Roth IRA is an IRA account to which individuals may make nondeductible IRA contributions. Distributions from Roth IRAs are generally federal and state tax free, as long as they are made more than five tax years after the first tax year for which a contribution is made, and are made on or after the date on which the taxpayer turns 59 1/2.

This has been just a quick overview of some of the more common techniques and strategies employed in tax planning. You should always discuss any change with a qualified tax advisor who is familiar with your financial situation before making any decision. I would also caution you not to look at your work with your tax advisor as being a simple function of getting your tax return prepared at year-end. Make your work with him or her an ongoing process that balances planning and preparation.

13

In Closing

My goal in writing this book was to give you an understanding of the basic elements of your tax return, especially your professional income and deductions. It was never intended to be comprehensive and should not be taken as such. Federal and state taxation is complicated and very much subject to interpretation. Your personal circumstances, record keeping, and organization can play a large role in whether or not a particular expense is deductible.

In this new edition I have added representative tax returns for each of my four players. These returns will be updated each year on our website, www.artstaxinfo.com, so that you will be able to follow any changes year by year. There is also a wealth of tax help on both www.artstaxinfo.com and our firm's website, www.cpa-services.com. This information is updated constantly, so I hope you will avail yourself of this resource.

I hope that by reading this volume you walk away with enough of a feel for taxation that you will be ready to be proactive in organizing, planning, and discussing your personal situation intelligently with your tax professional. I also hope that you will get your record keeping in order and be ready for an audit, should it ever come about. Above all, I hope you will *never* forget any deductions and *never* pay a dollar more in taxes than you have to!

While we have covered much ground, some things are beyond our scope, such as the very complicated subject of foreign earnings, which changes depending on the country involved. I have only touched briefly on the matter of state taxation; many states follow federal law closely, but not all.

Tax laws, of course, are affected by the whimsy of our government, and because of this most of the issues I have discussed in this book are subject to change. I have tried to keep to the general matters that are unlikely to change a lot, but, inevitably, some things will. To help you keep current with changes between updates of the book, I will be posting information on the book's website, www.artstaxinfo.com.

I welcome your comments and questions concerning the book. Let me know what you would change, or would like to see added in subsequent editions. You may contact me through the book's website or directly via e-mail at peter@cpa-services.com. As my noble predecessor, R. Brendan Hanlon, said, I want to "keep this the best book of its kind on the market." With your help, I think I can.

Appendix A:
Web Resources

The Internet is a tremendous source of insformation—these are some of the sites I have found most useful. At www.artstaxinfo.com, you can find quick links to the sites listed here, as well as various checklists, worksheets, and updates on all the latest tax changes that affect you.

General Resources

ArtMorpheus: artmorpheus.org (Massachusetts-based nonprofit for local artists and arts communities)

Fact Checker for the Internet: www.refdesk.com

The Internal Revenue Service: www.irs.gov

TaxSites.com: www.taxsites.com

United States Copyright Office: www.copyright.gov

For Actors, Directors, Dancers, and Other Show Biz Folk

Academy of Motion Picture Arts and Sciences: www.oscars.org

Actors' Equity Association: www.actorsequity.org

AllMovie: www.allmovie.com

The American Film Institute: www.afi.com

The American Society of Composers, Authors and Publishers: www.ascap.com

Dance Magazine: dancemagazine.com

Directors Guild of America: www.dga.org

Dramatists Guild of America: www.dramatistsguild.com

The Hollywood Reporter: www.hollywoodreporter.com

The Independent Filmmaker Project: www.ifp.org

Indiewire: www.indiewire.com

The Internet Theater Magazine of Reviews, Features, and Annotated Listings: www.curtainup.com

Magic Magazine: www.magicmagazine.com

Manhattan Association of Cabarets & Clubs: macnyc.com

Motion Picture Association of America: www.mpaa.org

The National Academy of Television Arts & Sciences: www.emmyonline.org

Performing-arts organizations: www.dmoz.org/Arts/Performing_Arts
/Organizations

Performingbiz: Booking & Touring Success Strategies for Musicians &
Performing

Artists: www.performingbiz.com (Agent Jeri Goldstein's excellent site)

Playbill Magazine: www.playbill.com

Pointe Magazine: pointemagazine.com

Screen Actors Guild and the American Federation of Television and
Radio Artists: www.sagaftra.org

Show Business: www.showbusinessweekly.com

Stage Directions Magazine: stage-directions.com

Theater Resources Unlimited: truonline.org

TheatreBooks: www.theatrebooks.com

Variety Magazine: variety.com

Women's Project Theater: wptheater.org

For Musicians and Singers

AllMusic: www.allmusic.com

American Federation of Musicians: www.afm.org

American Songwriter Magazine: americansongwriter.com

American Society of Composers, Authors and Publishers: www.ascap.com

Audio Engineering Society: http://www.aes.org

Billboard Magazine: www.billboard.com

Broadcast Music, Inc.: www.bmi.com

CMJ: www.cmj.com

The Copyright Society of the USA: www.csusa.org

Film Music Magazine: www.filmmusicmag.com

Film Score Monthly: www.filmscoremonthly.com

Jennifer Truesdale Studios: www.jennifertruesdalestudios.com

Just Plain Folks Music Organization: www.jpfolks.com (Music community
networking resource)

Live Sound International: www.livesoundint.com

Music Business Solutions: www.mbsolutions.com

Musicians Contact Service: www.musicianscontact.com (Connecting musicians and singers to paying gigs)

Music Publishers Association of the United States: www.mpa.org

National Music Publishers' Association: nmpa.org

Performingbiz: Booking & Touring Success Strategies for Musicians & Performing Artists: www.performingbiz.com (Agent Jeri Goldstein's excellent site)

Pollstar: www.pollstar.com (Touring info on the Web)

Professional Sound Magazine: www.professional-sound.com

The Recording Industry Association of America: www.riaa.com

Recording Magazine: www.recordingmag.com

Songstuff: www.songstuff.com

Ultimate Band List: www.ubl.com

For Visual Artists

AbsoluteArts.com: www.absolutearts.com

Art Access: www.artaccess.com

ArtBusiness.com: www.artbusiness.com

Art Business News: artbusinessnews.com

The Artchive: www.artchive.com

Art History Resources: arthistoryresources.net/ARTHLinks.html

Art Museum Network: www.artmuseumnetwork.com

Art on the Net: www.art.net

ArtSource: www.ilpi.com/artsource

Art-Support: art-support.com

Dan Heller Photography: www.danheller.com/bizfaq.html (Info on the business of photography)

Graphics Artist Guild: www.graphicartistsguild.org

Ken Rockwell: www.kenrockwell.com (Reviews of photographic equipment, extensive articles, tips, and teaching)

iStockphoto: www.istockphoto.com

New York Foundation for the Arts: www.nyfa.org

Passion4Art: www.passion4art.com

Resource Library: www.tfaoi.com/newsmus.htm

For Writers

American Booksellers Association: www.bookweb.org

American Society of Composers, Authors and Publishers: www.ascap.com

American Society of Journalists and Authors: www.asja.org

The Authors Guild: www.authorsguild.org

Bookwire.com: www.bookwire.com

Dramatists Guild of America: www.dramatistsguild.com

Editorial Freelancers Association: www.the-efa.org

Forwriters.com: www.forwriters.com

International Association of Media Tie-in Writers: iamtw.org (For writers using existing movie, TV, book, game, and cartoon characters)

National Writers Union: nwu.org

National Writing Project: www.nwp.org

PEN America: pen.org

Poets & Writers: www.pw.org (The nation's largest nonprofit for creative writers; contests, grants, awards, job listings, etc.)

Poewar.com: www.poewar.com (A collection of articles about revising and editing your novel)

Publishing Law Center: www.publaw.com

Right-Writing.com: www.right-writing.com (Advice, links, articles compiled by agent/editor/writer W. T. Whalen)

Script Fly: www.scriptfly.com (Great resource for screenwriters)

Small Publishers, Artists, & Writers Network: spawn.org

Society of Professional Journalists: www.spj.org/index.asp

Writers Write Entertainment: www.writerswrite.com

Writer's Digest: www.writersdigest.com

Writers Guild of America: www.wga.org

Appendix B:
IRS Publications and Other Resources

IRS Publications

These are some of the publications that are available free from the IRS. You can call the IRS and order them or download them directly from the IRS website, www.irs.gov.

- Publication 17 — Your Federal Income Tax: For Individuals
- Publication 54 — Guide to US Citizens and Resident Aliens Abroad
- Publication 334 — Tax Guide for Small Business
- Publication 463 — Travel, Entertainment, Gift and Car Expenses
- Publication 501 — Exemptions and Standard Deductions
- Publication 505 — Tax Withholding and Estimated Tax
- Publication 514 — Foreign Tax Credit for Individuals
- Publication 521 — Moving Expenses
- Publication 525 — Taxable and Nontaxable Income
- Publication 526 — Charitable Contributions
- Publication 529 — Miscellaneous Deductions
- Publication 530 — Tax Information for Home Owners
- Publication 531 — Reporting Tip Income
- Publication 535 — Business Expenses
- Publication 547 — Casualties, Disasters and Thefts
- Publication 556 — Examination of Returns, Appeal Rights, and Claims for Refund
- Publication 560 — Retirement Plans for Small Business
- Publication 587 — Business Use of Your Home
- Publication 929 — Tax Rules for Children and Dependents
- Publication 936 — Home Mortgage Interest Deduction

- Publication 946   How To Depreciate Property
- Publication 970   Tax Benefits for Education

Other Tax Books

- *J.K. Lasser's Your Income Tax*, published annually by John Wiley & Sons, Inc. In my opinion the best overall, single-income tax guide available.
- *What the IRS Doesn't Want You to Know* by Martin S. Kaplan, CPA, published by John Wiley & Sons, Inc. A great commonsense book giving insight into the operations and quirks of the IRS. Essential reading if you are audited!
- *Tax Deductions A to Z for Writers, Artists, and Performers* by Anne Skalka, CPA, published by Boxed Books (sadly now out of print, but used copies still available on Amazon.com). Great, easy-to-use, super-comprehensive listing of tax deductions for artists.
- *422 Tax Deductions for Businesses & Self-Employed Individuals* by Bernard B. Kamoroff, CPA, published by Bell Springs Publishing. Mr. Kamoroff is the first person that I have run across who attempts an alphabetical encyclopedia of tax deductions. Excellent and amazingly easy to read. Mr. Kamoroff is also the author of the excellent *Small Time Operator, 13th Edition: How to Start Your Own Business, Keep Your Books, Pay Your Taxes, and Stay Out of Trouble.*
- *Taxation of the Entertainment Industry* by Schuyler M. Moore, Esq., published by CCH Inc. This is the most comprehensive and professional book on the market.
- *U.S. Master Tax Guide* published by CCH Inc. This is the bible of the tax preparation industry, published annually and used by tax professionals the world over. CCH also publishes the excellent *State Tax Guide* annually, which is a superb quick reference to taxation state by state. These are beyond the needs of most laypeople but may serve as an excellent reference to have on your shelf.

Best Tax Apps

- Bloomberg BNA "Quick Tax"—excellent resource for the latest tax rates, pension limits, exemptions, and mileage rates
- CCH Tax Rates—similar to the above Bloomberg "Quick Tax" but a bit more extensive

- CCH Mobile—the venerable "Master Tax Guide" on your smartphone or tablet
- IRS2Go—make payments to the Internal Revenue Service and check on your tax refund
- Per Diem for the Continental U.S.—the General Service Administration's fabulous per diem rate tool, find rates by city in an instant